Stein and Hemingway

Stein and Hemingway
The Story of a Turbulent Friendship

LYLE LARSEN

McFarland & Company, Inc., Publishers
Jefferson, North Carolina, and London

Also of interest: *As Others Saw Them: Observations of Eminent Literary Figures by Their Contemporaries*, edited by Lyle Larsen (McFarland, 1985).

Library of Congress Cataloguing-in-Publication Data

Larsen, Lyle.
    Stein and Hemingway : the story of a turbulent friendship / Lyle Larsen.
        p.   cm.
    Includes bibliographical references and index.

    ISBN 978-0-7864-6056-4
    softcover : 50# alkaline paper ∞

    1. Stein, Gertrude, 1874–1946 — Friends and associates. 2. Hemingway, Ernest, 1899–1961— Friends and associates. 3. Friendship — United States — History — 20th century. 4. Authors, American — 20th century — Biography.   I. Title.
    PS3537.T323 Z694   2011
    818'.5'209   2010050477

British Library cataloguing data are available

© 2011 Lyle Larsen. All rights reserved

No part of this book may be reproduced or transmitted in any form or by any means, electronic or mechanical, including photocopying or recording, or by any information storage and retrieval system, without permission in writing from the publisher.

On the cover: Ernest Hemingway, 1954; Gertrude Stein ca. 1943 (both from Photofest)

Manufactured in the United States of America

McFarland & Company, Inc., Publishers
    Box 611, Jefferson, North Carolina 28640
    www.mcfarlandpub.com

Table of Contents

Preface	1

Part I. Just Like Brothers

1. The Genius of Montparnasse	9
2. Shadowboxing Along the Seine	20
3. Crafting a Style and an Image	32
4. Making the Heavyweight Class	47
5. Composition as Explanation	62
6. Old Faces and New	71

Part II. Taking Patches of Skin Off

7. Poor Old Papa	87
8. Getting Even	99
9. Knowing the Vital Spots	115
10. To Be One Succeeding	131
11. In Time of War	145
12. Three-Cushion Shots	160
13. Broken Beyond Repair	175
Epilogue	185
Chapter Notes	187
Select Bibliography	199
Index	207

*There are a great many cases of
not continuing to be friends.*
— Gertrude Stein

*There is not much future in men being friends with great women
although it can be pleasant enough
before it gets better or worse.*
— Ernest Hemingway

Preface

Friendship between authors may not be any more turbulent as a general rule than friendship between other individuals. After all, Beaumont and Fletcher, Goethe and Schiller, Mark Twain and William Dean Howells maintained strong, amicable, and mutually supportive friendships for much of their lives. On the other hand, writers are said to possess certain characteristics that sometimes, when brought into contact with similar traits in other writers, produce stormy relations. Accounts of such friendships can be fascinating just from seeing what happens when two or more passionate, highly-creative, highly-competitive authors are put in the same room together. Such accounts can also be instructive. By examining the interaction between noted authors, we sometimes learn more about the personalities involved than if we looked at each writer separately. Further still, such accounts often provide insights into the creative process — how writers work and how they influence one another.

What follows is the story of Gertrude Stein and Ernest Hemingway's friendship, one of the most fascinating and instructive literary associations of the twentieth century. The broad outlines are fairly well known. What I have done is piece together the events and fill in the less familiar details. To that end, I have drawn upon the wealth of material available in published memoirs, biographies, letters, and so on; but I have also made use of previously unpublished sources found primarily in the Ernest Hemingway Collection at the John F. Kennedy Library in Boston and the Beinecke Rare Book and Manuscript Library at Yale University.

Two books have appeared on the relationship between Ernest Hemingway and F. Scott Fitzgerald. Both volumes show how the friendship rapidly grew and then slowly crumbled due chiefly to Hemingway's waning respect for what he considered Scott's weak character and his prostitution of a great talent. One book carries the subtitle "The Rise and Fall of a Literary Friendship."[1] By contrast, instead of simply rising and then falling, the friendship of Gertrude Stein and Ernest Hemingway fluctuated. Over the span of twenty-four years it fluctuated dramatically, passing several times through love, admiration, jealousy, resentment, mockery, and name-calling. This is the first book devoted exclusively to tracing the course of that turbulent friendship.

Although it ebbed and flowed over the years, the friendship never completely collapsed, for each held strongly ambivalent feelings about the other. Shaken by competitive rivalry, the clash of egos, and accusations of laziness, cowardice, and betrayal, the relationship maintained at its core a mutual respect and affection that neither party could destroy, or really wished to. For Gertrude Stein, no matter how strained relations with her younger colleague became, no matter how strong the rancor of the moment, she had to admit, "I have a weakness for Hemingway." And he had a weakness — a need, actually — for her.

When the two first met in Paris, Gertrude Stein was forty-eight years old. Confident, outgoing, and sometimes intimidating, she loved to talk. She loved to talk with just about everyone. She avoided, however, people like James Joyce and Ezra Pound, writers of her own generation, for she viewed them, not as friends and fellow artists, but as rivals. She nevertheless liked younger men, especially young male writers. They furnished her with an appreciative audience, and she loved few things better than to lecture, counsel, and shape the views of impressionable young men. She established close friendships with some of them, but she had difficulty maintaining those friendships over the long term. The main reason was Alice Toklas.

Toklas had been Stein's live-in companion since 1910. She worked tirelessly and efficiently to free Gertrude from the mundane cares of daily life. She saw her primary duty as making life easier for Stein so that she could think and write. Alice took care of things. She ran errands, wrote letters, supervised the domestic help, and often did the cleaning and cooking herself. She typed Gertrude's handwritten copy, being the only one who could decipher the nearly illegible scrawl. Gertrude Stein came to depend on Alice, and Alice worked hard to maintain that dependence. Besides freeing Gertrude from everyday chores, she kept a close eye on friends and casual visitors, and if she felt her territory invaded and her position threatened, she could be ruthless.

Virgil Thomson, who knew Gertrude Stein for twenty years, from 1926 until her death in 1946, and who knew Alice Toklas for twenty years after that, stated that to his knowledge, Alice engineered four major separations in Stein's life. The first was from her brother Leo. The siblings had been extremely close, moving to England in 1902 and then to Paris the following year. They took a flat together in the rue de Fleurus and began exploring the fascinating world of modernist art. But when Leo could not share his sister's enthusiasm for Picasso's cubist paintings, and when he began expressing contempt for Gertrude's experimental writing, Alice subtly drove the two further apart, eventually taking Leo's place as Gertrude's closest friend and confidant.

The next separation was from Mabel Dodge, a wealthy, eccentric heiress and later patron of the arts. She met Stein soon after Alice, displacing Leo, moved in to the rue de Fleurus. Dodge and Stein quickly became friends. Not long after, Gertrude and Alice visited Dodge at her home in Florence, Italy, where Stein began composing "Portrait of Mable Dodge." As Stein worked on the piece, "she seemed to grow warmer to me," recalled Dodge in her memoirs, "to which I responded in a sort of flirtatious way." One day at lunch, "Gertrude, sitting opposite me..., sent me such a strong look over the table that it seemed to cut across the air to me in a band of electrified steel." Alice noticed the look and hurriedly left the table, visibly upset. "From that time on," wrote Dodge, "Alice began to separate Gertrude and me —*poco-poco*."[2]

Virgil Thomson said the third separation Alice engineered was from the French poet Georges Hugnet, of which more later. And the fourth separation was from Ernest Hemingway. Alice orchestrated other separations, including from Thomson himself, but these were the major four according to Thomson.[3]

When Hemingway, at age twenty-two, first met Gertrude Stein, he was shy and uncertain about himself. His creative drive had not yet achieved focus and discipline, yet he possessed a strong determination to make himself into a great writer. Falling under Stein's tutelage was the perfect arrangement for both, as she had much to teach, and he had much to learn. The deference he paid to her opinions helped confirm her self-image as the preeminent authority on writing, while the care she took in teaching him to see and think like a writer helped him to fully develop his talent. In this way, each validated the other. In addition, both truly enjoyed the other's company. Like Stein, Hemingway possessed a warm smile and engaging personality, and he made friends easily. Also like Stein, he had trouble keeping them, especially if they were fellow writers. During his formative years, Hemingway acquired many literary friends. Besides Gertrude Stein, there were Sherwood Anderson, Ezra Pound, James Joyce, Robert McAlmon, Ford Madox Ford, Harold Loeb, F. Scott Fitzgerald, Ernest Walsh, Donald Ogden Stewart, Max Eastman, Morley Callaghan, John Dos Possos, Archibald MacLeish, and more. Yet by the end of the thirties, he had quarreled with most of them. He concluded they were either "pretentious faking bastards,"[4] had wronged him in some way, or were no longer useful to him. He eventually decided that writers were a pain and were best avoided altogether. Throughout the 1930s, he associated with actors, war buddies, fellow sportsmen, and assorted drinking companions — but seldom with writers.

The most important thing to him at this time was his work. "I've always thought that only one thing mattered," he said, "your own career, and like a general in a battle I would sacrifice anything to my work and I would not let my self [sic] be fond of anything I could not lose."[5] Early in the 1940s, however, he began to soften his attitude. He came to realize that he had been too hardnosed and sanctimonious in his dealings with other writers. He regretted having treated Anderson shabbily, for example, and he forgave Max Eastman for sharply criticizing one of his books. In 1943 he tried to make amends with Archibald MacLeish, inviting him to Cuba for a visit and promising not to be "self righteous, no-good and bastardly as in my great 37–38 epoch when [I] alienated all my friends (who I miss like hell) (not to mention my sonofabitching epoch of 1934 when was even worse)."[6] His last meeting with Gertrude Stein near the close of World War II was an effort to patch things up with her.

Given their respective temperaments, Stein and Hemingway could never have maintained a smooth, untroubled friendship. Both were assertive people who took strong stands on writing and on life. Their stands on writing grew more at odds as Hemingway's confidence increased and his talents matured. For one thing, he was predominately a story-teller. She was more a psychologist, more a grammarian and rhetorician. Yet her approach to psychology, grammar, and rhetoric was not academic. It was artistic and experimental. She focused on the relationship between units of composition — words, sentences, paragraphs, and punctuation — combining and restructuring those units in an effort to gain fresh insights, to create new effects, and to find solutions to compositional problems. She liked the sound of words and the look of words, and she liked to experiment with patterns the words made. "Successions of words are so agreeable," she wrote as the first sentence of "Arthur A Grammar."[7]

Hemingway was interested in these things only insomuch as they advanced his story line or enhanced the narrative effect he wished to achieve. Gertrude Stein did not care much about story lines. She took little interest in traditional narration. "A thing you all know," she told a group in America, "is that in the three novels written in this generation that are the important things written in this generation, there is, in none of them a story. There is none in Proust in The Making of Americans or in Ulysses."[8] What interested her was finding new ways of depicting existence — existence divorced from traditional narration. This she found intellectually and artistically challenging, and she felt that readers shared her interest. She wrote, "It is quite characteristic that in *The Making of Americans*, Proust, *Ulysses*, nothing much happens. People are interested in existence."[9]

Although Hemingway always acknowledged Stein's valuable insights into the use of language, especially her discoveries regarding rhythm and repetition, he grew increasingly disenchanted with her apparent lack of discipline as a writer. It seemed the more well-known she became, the lazier she got. She seldom revised what she first set down, and she never threw anything away. As time went on, she seemed to lose all critical judgment, and her pronouncements became progressively more bizarre.

Likewise, Gertrude Stein increasingly found much to criticize in Hemingway. She thought him too derivative and too conventional. He tried to incorporate into his writing modernist techniques — techniques he learned primarily from her, but also from Sherwood Anderson and others — without really understanding them. Worst of all, as she stated in *The Autobiography of Alice B. Toklas* (1933), he was yellow. As a writer he lacked courage. Stein saw Hemingway as a deeply sensitive individual whose sensitivity embarrassed him because it made him feel weak and vulnerable. To protect himself, he tried to hide behind a façade of toughness and masculine virility, which Stein thought only concealed his finer qualities as both writer and man. Stein was not the only one to sense these things. Robert McAlmon noticed that Hemingway seldom reacted to a situation directly. McAlmon wrote, "Some code belonging to simple, hard-boiled guys, gruffly modest about their sensibilities, informed him how to feel, think, and react.... In his stories his characters talked in clipped phrases, muscle-bound emotionally, to reveal the maimed psychology of their author. They too bravely withheld all emotions, wisecracked and joked to conceal any gentle or tender feelings, and seldom spoke more than three- or five-word phrases."[10] McAlmon also observed that Hemingway's "real nature is probably gentle or tender. He's afraid that might be discovered, so he acts as he writes: hard-boiled realism."[11]

Gertrude Stein, by publicly calling Hemingway yellow for hiding his real nature, further agitated a relationship already grown unsteady. Ernest by this time had become for Gertrude Stein a literary rival, while Stein had become for Hemingway one of the "pretentious faking bastards" he claimed to despise. Yet the public and private squabbling that ensued over the coming years was punctuated by occasional reconciliations, for, despite the increasing animosity, Gertrude Stein still had a weakness for Hemingway and he, on a more subconscious level, still sought her criticism and approval. And although the relationship continued turbulent as the pair drifted in and out of one another's lives for more than two decades, each was seldom far from the thoughts or influences of the other.

PART I
Just Like Brothers

— 1 —

The Genius of Montparnasse

Three men with drinks before them sat talking at a small round bistro table. The two younger men had lately come from America. They were part of the new generation of writers showing up in ever larger numbers now that the Great War was over. The oldest of the three, also an American, had lived in the city for many years. It was afternoon, the place the long outdoor terrace of the Café du Dôme, a brasserie in the Montparnasse section, the riotous center of artistic Paris.

One of the younger men, Wambly Bald, said to his friend Samuel Putnam, "Come on, let's go up and see Gertie." Gertrude Stein lived nearby in the rue de Fleurus.

Putnam hesitated. He was afraid of Stein. "What do you mean?" he said. "She'd throw us out." Though he had never met Stein, Putnam envisioned her as a distant, cloistered being who did not like to be disturbed, "one who could be approached only with genuflections and the odor of incense." She reminded him of Amy Lowell, the large, intimidating, cigar-smoking author he had known in America.

Bald also thought of Stein as massively formidable, like a Roman emperor. He had earlier named her "the Woman with a Face like Caesar's."

"What are you afraid of?" asked the third man, who happened to be Leo Stein, Gertrude's older brother. "My God, Sam, you have no idea how dumb she is! Why, when we were in school, I used to have to do all her home work for her." Putnam reflected on what he had heard of Gertrude

Stein's studies in brain anatomy and abnormal pathology at Johns Hopkins and Harvard Annex, and decided that Leo exaggerated.[1]

Leo and Gertrude Stein, since coming to Paris just after the turn of the century, had been strong advocates of the modernist art movement in Paris. They numbered among their acquaintances Henri Matisse, Georges Braque, and Pablo Picasso. The Steins had developed a keen taste for modernist art, especially Impressionism and Post-Impressionism. Now they were engaged in a sibling dispute over the merits of Cubism and whether Picasso's work had any importance or not. Gertrude liked what Picasso did. Leo thought it rubbish.

Putnam and Bald decided to call on Miss Stein, Bald agreeing to do the talking while Putnam remained in the background. At number 27 rue de Fleurus they were shown in through the large double doors by Gertrude Stein herself. Standing five feet two inches tall, Stein was dark-featured and heavyset. Everything about her conveyed a sense of mass and solidity. She usually wore loose blouses, heavy brown corduroy skirts that reached down to her ankles, and sturdy sandals over thick wool socks. Her abundant dark hair she brushed up in a bun on top of her head. Putnam later described the meeting in his memoirs, recalling that oil paintings and watercolors hung everywhere about the studio — striking works by Cézanne, Matisse, Renoir, Toulouse-Lautrec, and Gauguin. Bald commented on the large number of Picassos among them. "Yes," Miss Stein said, "Picasso has done eighty portraits of me. I sat for that one ninety-one times." She indicated a large canvas done in varying shades of brown and gray. Begun in 1905 and finished in 1906, the portrait showed her seated and leaning slightly forward. The face communicated determination, the body immovability.

Bald, being a newspaper man, and perhaps not wishing to let Stein seize the upper hand, immediately went on the offensive: "Your prose, Miss Stein, strikes me as being obscure, deliberately obscure."

"My prose is obscure only to the lazy-minded," Miss Stein replied in her strong clear voice. "It is a well, a deep well, well it is like a well and that is well."

"There are some people," said Bald, "who are inclined to believe that it is a bottomless well — or one with a false bottom."

Stein bristled slightly. "Naturally, I have my detractors. What genius does not?"

1. The Genius of Montparnasse

Gertrude Stein and Picasso's portrait of her (Beinecke Rare Book and Manuscript Library, Yale University).

"You *are* a genius then?" asked Putnam. It was the first time he had spoken. Stein looked at him he said afterward like he was a dot that had suddenly appeared on a map.

"There are three of us," she answered. "Myself, Picasso, and [Alfred North] Whitehead."

"You feel, then, Miss Stein, that your place in literature is secure?"

"My place in literature? Twentieth-century literature *is* Gertrude Stein. There was Henry James, of course — "

"Yes, there was Henry James — "

"He was my precursor, you might say; but everything really begins with my *Three Lives*."

Bald asked if she thought the English were jealous of Americans.

"They have a right to be," she said. "After all, America made the twentieth century just as England made the nineteenth. America has given Europe everything. America has given Europe Gertrude Stein — "

"What about the other great American writers?"

"There are the big four: Poe, Whitman, James, myself. The line of descent is clear. And James, Whitman, and Poe are dead. I am the last. But I am truly international. My reputation is growing all the time."

"Do you feel that your writing is really American writing?"

"Certainly. What has been the tendency of American writing?"

The two men paused and looked at one another, each expecting the other to answer.

"Toward abstraction, of course. But an abstraction without mysticism. That is the great contribution of Gertrude Stein. Her work is abstract without being mystical. There is no mysticism in my work."

"No mysticism?"

"None whatever. My work is perfectly natural. It is so natural that it is unnatural to those to whom the unnatural is natural. I reproduce things exactly as they are and that is all there is to it. The outer world becomes the inner world and the inner world becomes the outer, and the outward is no longer outward but inward and the inward is no longer inward but outward and it takes genius to do that and Gertrude Stein *is* a genius."[2]

Being a genius, of course, was not easy. It demanded patience and a great deal of time. Stein acknowledged that "you have to sit around so much doing nothing, really doing nothing."[3] It took a lot of time, first of all, just to recognize that you *were* a genius, but once Gertrude recognized it, her brother Leo saw it too, and it troubled him. "It is funny this thing of being a genius," she said, "there is no reason for it, there is no reason that it should be you and should not have been him, no reason at all that it should have been you, no no reason at all." But both saw that it *was* her and not him, and that awareness made them start drifting apart. "The only thing about it was that it was I who was the genius, there was no reason for it but I was, and he was not."[4]

She realized that being a genius required action, so for many years she followed a set writing schedule. Working at night when everything was still, she wrote slowly, four or five lines to a page, "letting it ooze up from deep inside her," recalled a friend, "down on to the paper with the least possible physical effort; she would cover a few pages so and leave them there and go to bed."[5] She could seldom write for more than half an hour at a time, but she observed that if you write for half an hour a day,

1. The Genius of Montparnasse

it adds up over the years.[6] She seldom revised what she first set down, and she never threw anything away.

The poet William Carlos Williams, a practicing physician, once remarked to her that if all the manuscripts piling up in her Spanish armoire were his, he would probably pick out what he thought best and toss the balance into the fire. "No, oh no, no, no, no, that isn't possible," said Stein. "You would not find a painter destroying any of his sketches. A writer's writing is too much of the writer's being; his flesh child. No, no, I never destroy a sentence or a word of what I write. You may, but of course, writing is not your métier, Doctor."

"But Doctor Stein," countered Williams, "are you sure that writing is your métier? I solve the economies of life through the profession of doctoring, but from the first my will was toward writing. I hope it pleases you, but things that children write have seemed to me so Gertrude Steinish in their repetitions."

Stein said later that she could not see Williams after that. She told her maid to say that she was out if he called again. "There is too much bombast in him."[7]

Many besides Williams considered Stein the writer, with her obscurities and repetitions, little better than a charlatan. Her work often excited ridicule and scorn. Others, however, mostly young writers seeking new techniques and fresh avenues of expression, thought her work artistically liberating. Said one approvingly, "Miss Stein has added enormously to the vagueness of the English language, and vagueness is a quality that belongs to the English language."[8] The poet E. E. Cummings found *Tender Buttons*, published in 1914, a triumph over realism, a "subordination of the meaning of words to the esthetic significance (i.e., beauty) inherent in the words themselves."[9]

What tradition-bound scoffers failed to see, or chose to ignore, was the conscious method that lay behind the apparently unconscious and meaningless writing. Having enjoyed the experimental nature of her psychological and scientific training in college, she brought the same zest for experimentation to her writing. Yet Stein rejected the notion that her work was in any way experimental. "Artists do not experiment," she said. "Experiment is what scientists do; they initiate an operation of unknown factors in order to be instructed by its results. An artist puts down what he knows and at every moment it is what he knows at that moment."[10]

William James, her favorite professor at Harvard, was her greatest early influence. James, who lectured in psychology, focused on the workings of the subconscious mind, and it became the representation in words of *internal* reality, as distinguished from conventional representations of *external* reality, that most intrigued Stein. William James's brother, Henry James, had explored this matter in some of his novels, and so it was that Stein regarded him as her precursor. Poe and Whitman, the other two American writers she considered great, had also probed internal states of perception and awareness.

William James had taught that knowledge is what we know, and what we know is what we experience now, at the present moment. Stein, subsequently in her writing, became interested primarily in the immediacy of experience, in life's ever-present *now*. If her writings appeared at times to have no meaning, part of the reason was that immediate experience has none either. It is only afterward, as we begin to quantify, arrange, compare, and analyze based on past events, that experience takes on meaning for us. Stein tried to get as close to the source of experience as possible, to capture in words the effect of the immediate, ever-present, ever-moving now of existence.

Once Gertrude Stein arrived in France, some of the lessons she had learned from William James became reinforced by her exposure to the works of Impressionist and Cubist painters. Stein carefully examined how they addressed in paint certain problems she confronted in words. Her chief interest remained immediacy, capturing the continuous present, for "moving is existing" she maintained.[11] "The business of Art is to live in the actual present, that is the complete actual present, and to express that complete actual present."[12]

About 1906 she began "The Making of Americans." This was an experimental novel based on types of personalities she observed. While engaged in the long, ambitious work over the next several years, she slowly came to realize what she felt were two important truths: that knowledge is gained through memory, but that when you really know something, memory plays no part. In writing about what you really know, "You have the sense of the immediate." After discovering these truths, she tried, she said, "in every possible way to get the sense of immediacy, and practically all the work I have done [since] has been in that direction."[13]

1. The Genius of Montparnasse

One technique she devised to establish immediacy, or a sense of the "continuous present," depended largely on present participles, italicized for emphasis in this passage from *Three Lives*, written in 1905 but not published until 1909:

> Jeff sat there this evening in his chair and was silent a long time, *warming* himself with the pleasant fire. He did not look at Melanctha who was *watching*. He sat there and just looked at the fire. At first his dark, open face was *smiling*, and he was *rubbing* the back of his black-brown hand over his mouth to help him in his *smiling*. Then he was *thinking*, and he frowned and rubbed his head hard, to help him in his *thinking*. Then he smiled again, but now his *smiling* was not very pleasant. His smile was now *wavering* on the edge of *scorning*.[14]

Also evident in this passage is Stein's conscious effort to limit and simplify her vocabulary. She did not want to use words rich in connotations, words fraught with associations she did not intend. She wanted her writing to be exact, "as exact as mathematics," she explained; "that is to say, for example, if one and one make two, I wanted to get words to have as much exactness as that."[15]

Pleased though not entirely satisfied with the innovative quality of her work so far, Gertrude Stein continued to grapple with ways of expressing in words the complete actual present. "Funnily enough," she said, "the cinema has offered a solution of this thing. By a continuously moving picture of any one there is no memory of any other thing and there is that thing existing."[16] The repetition of words and phrases, she discovered, created much the same effect attained by motion pictures, "So we have now, a movement lively enough to be a thing in itself moving."[17]

But Stein did not like to call what she did repetition. "There is only repetition when there are descriptions being given of these things not when the things themselves are actually existing."[18] She preferred to call what she did *insistence*—"insistence that in its emphasis can never be repeating, because insistence is always alive and if it is alive it is never saying anything in the same way because emphasis can never be the same."[19] As an example, by her own reckoning, her famous phrase "a rose is a rose is a rose is a rose," is not repetition. It is an insistence on the rose existing from moment to moment, not on a rose as something remembered. It is also an insistence that a rose is, after all, a rose, and not a worn-out literary word made stale by thousands of poems written over the centuries about roses.[20]

16   I. Just Like Brothers

This phase of Stein's writing (call it repetition or insistence) can be seen in a passage from her 1912 "Portrait of Picasso":

> One whom some were certainly following was one who was completely charming. One whom some were certainly following was one who was charming. One whom some were following was one who was completely charming. One whom some were following was one who was certainly completely charming. Some were certainly following and were certain that the one they were then following was one working and was one bringing out of himself then something. Some were certainly following and were certain that the one they were then following was one bringing out of himself then something that was coming to be a heavy thing, a solid thing and a complete thing.[21]

Of particular significance to her at this stage were the paintings of Paul Cézanne. His pictures provided insights into the relationship of various parts of a composition. "Up to that time," she said, "composition had consisted of a central idea, to which everything else was an accompaniment and separate but was not an end in itself, and Cézanne conceived the idea that in composition one thing was as important as another thing. Each part is as important as the whole, and that impressed me enormously."[22]

Picasso further taught her about nonrepresentational art, the disassociation of geometrical forms (in her case words) from meaning. Her writing became more abstract, corresponding to a similar development in Cubism. The following comes from her 1914 volume *Tender Buttons*, the book that so impressed E. E. Cummings:

> A PIECE OF COFFEE.
>   More of double.
>   A place in no new table.
>   A single image is not splendor. Dirty is yellow. A sign of more is not mentioned. A piece of coffee is not a detainer. The resemblance to yellow is dirtier and distinctor. The clean mixture is whiter and not coal color, never more coal color than altogether.
>   The sight of a reason, the same sight slighter, the sight of a simpler negative answer, the same sore sounder, the intention to wishing, the same splendor, the same furniture.[23]

If the public did not understand this sort of thing, it was entirely their fault. "People are lazy," said Gertrude Stein. "That's why they don't understand me. My work is simple but unfamiliar."[24] Yet she confessed that when she read her things years after writing them, they often did not make much sense to her either. Her writing was clear as mud, she admitted, but mud eventually settles and streams run clear.[25] She later explained that *Tender Buttons* was her first conscious struggle with the process of elimination, "with the problem of correlating sight, sound and sense, and eliminating rhythm; some of the solutions in it seem to me still alright, now I am trying grammar and eliminating sight and sound."[26] She would eventually try eliminating punctuation as she had already eliminated meaning.

Although she admitted to sometimes being obscure, she argued that clarity had little to do with good writing anyway. Nobody fully understands a writer's meaning no matter how clearly the writer expresses it. More desirable than clarity are force, inner vitality, and truly knowing yourself what you mean. "Clarity is of no importance," she said,

> because nobody listens and nobody knows what you mean no matter what you mean, nor how clearly you mean what you mean. But if you have vitality enough of knowing enough of what you mean, somebody and sometime and sometimes a great many will have to realise that you know what you mean and so they will agree that you mean what you know, what you know you mean, which is as near as anybody can come to understanding any one.[27]

She felt, furthermore, that the artist bore no responsibility to the reader, only to the problem of creation. Stein claimed not to be interested in what people thought when they read one of her pieces: "I was entirely taken up with my problem and if it did not tell my story it would tell some story. They [her readers] might have another conception which would be their affair." The matter simply did not concern her. "In a created thing it means more to the writer than it means to the reader. It can only mean something to one person and that person the one who wrote it."[28]

This attitude naturally placed Stein in a difficult position. She desperately wished to have everything she wrote published and appreciated whether anyone understood it or not. Yet if she felt no responsibility toward ordinary readers, why should ordinary readers take any interest in her? Asked in an interview why she published works that actually were written only for herself, she replied, "There is the eternal vanity of the mind. One wants to see one's children in the world and have them admired like any fond parent.... Anything you create you want to exist, and its means of existence is in being printed."[29]

Increasingly more young writers became excited by the sheer audacity of Stein's work. They found it stimulating and liberating. It swept clear the literary circus floor, said one of them, for future performances.[30]

William Carlos Williams acknowledged that it was not only modernist painters who helped writers break free from the worn-out conceptions of the late nineteenth century: "Gertrude Stein found the key with her conception of the objective use of words."[31]

Others remained skeptical and unimpressed. They continued to think Stein little better than a charlatan. "Gertrude does not know what words mean," claimed her brother Leo. "She hasn't much intuition but thickly she has sensations, and of course her mania, herself. Her idea of herself as a genius."[32]

One of Gertrude Stein's admirers was Sherwood Anderson. Only two years younger than Stein and nearly two decades older than the new postwar generation of writers, Anderson was among Stein's earliest and most enthusiastic devotees.

Anderson had got a late start in literature. He published his first novel, *Windy McPherson's Son*, in 1916, at the age of forty, followed in 1919 by his masterpiece, *Winesburg, Ohio*, a book that clearly showed Stein's influence. Anderson had read Stein's "portraits" of Matisse and Picasso in 1912, but he took special notice when in 1914 a brother introduced him to *Tender Buttons*. "It excited me," he said, "as one might grow excited in going in a new and wonderful country where everything is strange." He realized that *Tender Buttons* "was something purely experimental and dealing in words separated from sense — in the ordinary meaning of the word sense," but the freshness and originality jolted him into a new state of awareness. It was then, he said, that he really fell in love with words. After finishing the volume, he went around for days with a notebook "making new and strange combinations of words." He found, as a result, "a new familiarity with the words of my own vocabulary."[33] When he tried to learn something about the author of *Tender Buttons,* all he heard were strange stories. The main impression he got is that Gertrude Stein "was a fat woman, very languid lying on a couch, people came into the room and she stared at them with strange cold eyes."[34]

On a trip to Paris in 1921, Anderson noticed a copy of his *Winesburg, Ohio* in the shop window of Shakespeare and Company, an English language bookstore in the rue de l'Odéon. He stepped in and introduced himself to the owner, Sylvia Beach, who, after a brief conversation, offered to take him to the rue de Fleurus to meet Gertrude Stein.

1. The Genius of Montparnasse

Stein and her live-in companion of twelve years, Alice Toklas, liked Anderson immediately. He seemed modest, soft-spoken, and polite. There was something sweet in his nature, a quality the two women thought lacking in most young men of the up-and-coming generation. Not the least of his attributes was an unreserved enthusiasm for Stein's works, this at a time when Stein still had few admirers. Anderson, for his part, found Stein outgoing and friendly, not at all strange like he had heard. The two remained close for the rest of their lives. Anderson often acknowledged his debt to Stein's pioneering efforts and maintained, "I think that Stein is a genius."[35]

2

Shadowboxing Along the Seine

Half a dozen outdoor cafés stand bunched together near where the Boulevard du Montparnasse intersects the Boulevard Raspail. In late winter and early spring of 1922, a patron at one of these Left Bank establishments might occasionally see a large, dark-haired young man coming down the street, feinting this way and that, throwing powerful hooks and quick jabs, his lips moving as he taunts an imaginary opponent. Ernest Hemingway had recently arrived in Paris, intent on becoming a writer.

One of his early Paris comrades, Robert McAlmon, recalled that he approached a café with a small-boy, tough-guy swagger. "At times," said McAlmon, "he was deliberately hard-boiled and case-hardened; again he appeared deliberately innocent, sentimental, the hurt, soft, but fairly sensitive boy trying to conceal hurt, wanting to be brave, not bitter or cynical but being somewhat both, and somehow on the defensive."[1] McAlmon was perhaps the first to recognize this fundamental dichotomy in Hemingway's character.

Hemingway lived with his wife of nearly six months, the former Hadley Richardson, in a two-room flat on the fourth floor of an apartment house in the rue du Cardinal Lemoine. The apartment lacked hot water, electricity, and an inside toilet. The bed was a mattress and springs on the floor. But these inconveniences mattered little, for the couple was young and in love, and it was Paris.

Hemingway had been in the city once before, during the war. It had been a brief stay, not much more than a stopover on his way to Italy where

2. Shadowboxing Along the Seine

he served as a volunteer ambulance driver with a unit of the American Red Cross. On the lower Piave River at Fossalta, less than two weeks before his nineteenth birthday, a shell from an Austrian trench mortar exploded just yards away, nearly killing him. It killed an Italian soldier standing close by and took off both legs of another. Hemingway spent three months in the American Red Cross Hospital in Milan recuperating from shrapnel wounds to his legs and a machine gun bullet taken in the right knee.

After a total of seven months in Europe, he returned home to Oak Park, Illinois, in January 1919 walking with a limp and using a cane. A hometown friend said that Ernest returned "figuratively as well as literally shot to pieces." But he also came back with a great urge to write. "He seemed to have a tremendous need to express the things that he had felt and seen."[2]

After all he experienced in Europe, he also had a tremendous need to escape the oppressive conditions of his mid–Western upbringing, especially the boredom of his orthodox family and the smothering influence of his mother. Ernest felt reluctant, despite constant prodding, to talk to his family about what he had been through in the war. He had not yet had time to sort it all out. His emotions still lay too close to the surface. He said he had nothing to talk about anyway since he had spent all his time in hospitals. "I was having a pretty bad time," he remarked later, "and my mother started eating me out for drinking and not taking things seriously etc. and I told her that I had had a sort of bad time some of the time in the war and that if she would leave me alone I would work out of it okay." He had worked through difficult problems before. He just needed time.

"I don't know what you can mean saying you had a bad time," his mother told him. "By your own admission you spent all your time in hospitals."[3]

Grace Hall Hemingway, a heavyset, ambitious, and domineering woman, always seemed to be "eating out" her oldest son over something or other. Ernest eventually grew to loath her as the embodiment of conventional middle class values and emasculating womanhood. His early story "A Soldier's Home," written in 1924, captures the stifling ordeal of returning to his parents' home and having to deal with his mother following his brief but eventful time in Europe.

Before going to the war, Ernest had worked for seven months as a cub reporter for the Kansas City *Star*. He covered mostly the local police station and the city hospital's receiving ward. After returning from the war, he spent months lying around the house, uncertain what to do with his life and trying to assimilate all that had happened to him in Italy. He poured over historical accounts and analyses of the war, attempting to place his personal experience within the context of the overall conflict.

When not idling away his days reading, writing, or entertaining neighborhood girls with war stories, he stayed with friends for extended periods of time. He had to get away from home occasionally, get away from his solicitous father, overbearing mother, four sisters, and five-year-old brother. With the passing weeks and months, his father grew increasingly more concerned, his mother more irritable. Grace Hall, approaching fifty and dealing with emotional pressures brought on by menopausal changes, her large family, and her moody older son, increasingly censured Ernest for his laziness. He, in turn, would lose his temper and speak rudely to his mother. He once accused her of reading nothing but moron literature and asked sarcastically if she read the *Atlantic Monthly* just so someone would see her doing it.[4]

Ernest's parents were eager for their twenty-one-year-old son to attend college or at least get a job. They felt he simply could not go on in this shamefully idle fashion. After eighteen months, his mother finally lost all patience. During one of his times away from home, she wrote him a letter scolding him for being a loafer and pleasure seeker, for "borrowing with no thought of returning." She accused him of grafting a living off everybody, squandering his money on luxuries for himself, trading on his handsome face to impress little girls, "and neglecting your duties to God and Your Savior Jesus Christ." She said that until he grew up and became a man, "there is nothing before you but bankruptcy. *You have overdrawn.*" She made it clear that he was no longer welcome in her home. "Do not come back," she wrote, "until your tongue has learned not to insult and shame your mother."[5]

The family squabble eventually got patched up by year's end — at least to all appearances. But Ernest knew that it could never be the same. He always remembered that his mother had thrown him out, and though he had done much to inflame the situation, he would never completely forgive Grace Hall for what she had done.

Ernest eventually got work as a feature writer for the Toronto *Star*

2. Shadowboxing Along the Seine

Weekly and then for the Chicago *Co-Operative Commonwealth*. Years later the feature editor of the *Star Weekly* remembered Hemingway as having been a hard worker and eager to learn. He also recalled the young man's disturbing habit of shadowboxing while he conversed or while others around him talked. The editor thought it denoted a lack of confidence.[6]

While in Chicago in January of 1921, Ernest met Sherwood Anderson. The two became friends and saw much of each other before Anderson left for Paris in April. Hemingway showed Anderson some stories he was working on. Anderson critiqued them, discussed his theories of writing, and advised Ernest on authors and specific books he should read. The two also discussed sports, Anderson recommending shadowboxing as a good means of exercise. Hemingway listened intently to all that Anderson had to say and benefited from the instruction.

In Chicago Hemingway also met and fell in love with Hadley Richardson. The two married in September. The couple planned to go to Italy at the end of the year and visit places Ernest had been during the war, but Anderson, on his return from France in November, told Hemingway that if he really wanted to be a serious writer, he should go to Paris instead. That is where a new writer of talent had the greatest opportunity to learn his craft and where he stood the best chance of getting noticed. Anderson explained that Paris was the home of modernism and in modernism lay the future. He spoke of the little magazines that offered exposure to new talent. He talked of Gertrude Stein, Ezra Pound, James Joyce, Pablo Picasso, and others who were doing new and exciting things in literature and art. Ernest became convinced that he had better go to Paris.

Anderson furnished him with letters of introduction to some of his newfound Paris acquaintances, among them Stein, Pound, and Sylvia Beach. Anderson addressed his letter to Stein as follows:

Dear Miss Stein:

I am writing this note to make you acquainted with my friend Ernest Hemingway, who with Mrs. Hemingway is going to Paris to live, and will ask him to drop it in the mails when he arrives there.

Mr. Hemingway is an American writer instinctively in touch with everything worthwhile going on here and I know you will find Mr. and Mrs. Hemingway delightful people to know.

They will be at 74 Rue du Cardinal Lemoine.

Sincerely,
Sherwood Anderson[7]

I. Just Like Brothers

The Hemingways arrived in Paris in December of 1921. Ernest officially held the job of roving freelance correspondent for the Toronto *Star*. He sent back twice-weekly feature articles and sometimes covered news events of particular interest to Canadian readers. Although the pay was meager, the job allowed him some leisure to work on his fiction. He lost little time finding his way to Shakespeare and Company. "I was very shy when I first went into the bookshop," he later wrote, but Sylvia Beach quickly made him feel at ease. A small woman with finely chiseled features and wavy hair, "she had brown eyes that were as alive as a small animal's and as gay as a young girl's," said Hemingway. "She had pretty legs and she was kind, cheerful and interested, and loved to make jokes and gossip. No one that I ever knew was nicer to me."[8]

He also introduced himself to Ezra Pound, a humorous, highly idiosyncratic man who, despite his irascibility, always seemed to be helping others. Hemingway later described Pound as the most generous writer he had ever known. "He helped poets, painters, sculptors and prose writers that he believed in and he would help anyone whether he believed in them or not if they were in trouble."[9]

Hemingway delayed for three months sending Anderson's letter to Gertrude Stein. He may have been intimidated, like other young American writers in Paris, by stories of the forbidding and unapproachable "Sumerian monument" as Robert McAlmon termed her. Even Anderson had spoken of her as "a strong woman with legs like stone pillars sitting in a room hung thick with Picassos."[10]

But in March Ernest got Hadley to write Gertrude Stein a short cover letter to accompany Anderson's letter of introduction. The return post brought an invitation for Hemingway and his wife to come to tea at 27 rue de Fleurus on Wednesday. "I do like Anderson so much," wrote Stein, "and I would like to meet his friends."[11]

Hadley wrote back, "Mr. Hemingway and I are delighted at hearing from you so soon and will come in to tea with you tomorrow with pleasure. Sherwood has told us so many nice things that we are glad to come right away to see you."[12]

The Hemingways showed up at Gertrude Stein's large studio apartment about five o'clock the following afternoon. They found Stein and her companion gracious and friendly, and they loved the big room with all the magnificent paintings on the walls. "It was like one of the best rooms in the finest museum," Hemingway recalled, "except there was a big fireplace and it was warm and comfortable and they gave you good things to eat and tea and natural distilled liqueurs made from purple plums, yellow plums or wild raspberries."

Despite the magnificent pictures, the most fascinating object in the room was Gertrude Stein. Hemingway noted that she was "very big but not tall and was heavily built like a peasant woman." He was struck by her beautiful eyes and strong German-Jewish face. She reminded him of a "northern Italian peasant woman with her clothes, her mobile face and her lovely, thick, alive immigrant hair which she wore put up in the same way she had probably worn it in college. She talked all the time and at first it was about people and places."[13]

Ernest Hemingway, 1922 (Beinecke Rare Book and Manuscript Library, Yale University).

Hemingway made an equally strong impression on Stein. "I remember very well the impression I had of Hemingway that first afternoon," she later wrote. "He was an extraordinarily good-looking young man, twenty-three years old." He appeared somewhat foreign looking "with passionately interested, rather than interesting eyes." While she talked, he sat "and listened and looked."[14]

Gertrude Stein and Alice Toklas evidently liked the young couple. The two women treated them, said Ernest, like bright, well-mannered children. While Gertrude Stein talked and Hemingway listened, Miss Toklas served refreshments and kept Hadley occupied in another part of the room. The Hemingways learned afterward that Miss Stein did not like to be bothered by wives. She did not like to chitchat with them. That was Miss Toklas's job. Miss Toklas had the dual responsibilities of serving refreshments and keeping wives out of the way while Gertrude Stein talked to the husbands.

Miss Toklas, an English visitor to the studio recalled, looked like a Spanish gypsy and spoke like a Bostonian.[15] Actually she came from San Francisco, had never been to Boston, and spoke with what most considered a pleasant voice. At least two inches shorter than Stein, slightly built, and very dark, she had a hooked nose and a faint dark moustache on her upper lip. In contrast to Gertrude Stein's openness and volubility, Alice Toklas seemed reserved. She gave the impression of being furtive and mysterious. Her dark, critically observant eyes hinted at a will far stronger than her diminutive size and self-effacing manner otherwise suggested. "But we liked Miss Stein and her friend," Hemingway later wrote of this first meeting, "although her friend was frightening."[16] Just before leaving, Hadley invited the two women to tea, and they accepted.

Gertrude Stein and Miss Toklas seemed to like the Hemingways even more at the second meeting, but perhaps, thought Ernest, four people crowded into a small flat only made it appear that way. Stein sat on the bed on the floor and read the things Hemingway had written up to that time. There were poems, the beginnings of a novel, and some stories. She liked the poems; "they were direct, Kiplingesque," she said. But she did not care for the novel. "There is a great deal of description in this," she told Hemingway, "and not particularly good description. Begin over again and concentrate."[17]

She liked all the stories except one called "Up in Michigan." Begun in Chicago in the summer of 1921, it was a stark, explicit account of a young woman's blossoming sexuality and her subsequent seduction by the town blacksmith, a man named Jim. Told from the young woman's point of view, the story owed much of its treatment to Anderson, yet recent revisions showed that Hemingway had already begun to learn something from Stein. The second paragraph imitated Stein's technique of repetition as the main character, Liz, thinks about Jim the blacksmith:

> She liked it the way he walked over from the shop and often went to the kitchen door to watch for him to start down the road. She liked it about his

mustache. She liked it about how white his teeth were when he smiled. She liked it very much that he didn't look like a blacksmith. She liked it how much D. J. Smith and Mrs. Smith [Liz' employers] liked Jim. One day she found that she liked it the way the hair was black on his arms and how white they were above the tanned line when he washed up in the washbasin outside the house. Liking that made her feel funny.

Six repetitions of "she liked it," each repetition gathering nuance and meaning, increases the reader's awareness of Liz' subconscious erotic desires. Less successful, perhaps, is Hemingway's use of "liking" in the concluding sentence. It comes off as simply an aping of Stein's method, for Hemingway brandishes the present participle without seeming to understand the purpose behind its use, which for Stein was to establish a sense of the "continuous present."

Nevertheless, despite the slightly awkward compliment to her unique modernist style, Miss Stein disapproved of the story overall. It was good, she said. That wasn't the question. But it was *inaccrochable*, an invented term indicating a picture that cannot be displayed — one, furthermore, that nobody will buy because it cannot be shown. "You mustn't write anything that is *inaccrochable*," she said. "There is no point in it. It's wrong and it's silly."[18] Stein was getting her first glimpse of something that would trouble her increasingly as time went on. This was an obsession in Hemingway's writing, as she saw it, with sex, brutality, and death.

Stein said that she wanted to be published in the *Atlantic Monthly* and would be. She told Hemingway that he was not good enough to be published in the *Atlantic Monthly*. Still, he might be some new kind of writer in his own way. She talked about buying pictures and how one needed to sacrifice purchasing clothes to have enough money to buy pictures. When Miss Stein and Miss Toklas left, the Hemingways were still popular, Ernest thought, "and we were asked to come again to 27 rue de Fleurus."[19]

Some days afterward, Hemingway encountered Stein while walking in the Luxembourg Gardens. She invited him to drop by her studio after five o'clock in the afternoon whenever he liked. He got into the habit of doing so, for he found the paintings, the refreshments, and the conversation a welcome relief after a day's work.

Gertrude Stein genuinely liked her young guest. She found him gentle, sensitive, emotional, and extremely shy. He was also a good listener. The two conversed on many subjects, Stein taking up the education of Ernest Hemingway where Sherwood Anderson had left off. "She talked, mostly," said Ernest, "and she told me about modern pictures and about painters." She encouraged him to study the modernists, especially Cézanne, for Cézanne's pictures revealed many things useful for a writer to know. She praised Spanish bullfights and showed him photographs of bullfights and bullfighters. One photograph, taken during a summer trip to Spain, showed Alice and Gertrude Stein sitting in the front row of the bull ring at Valencia.

Gertrude Stein often talked about her own work and expounded on her theories of writing. She said that writing, like painting, was most exciting when nothing was happening. Excitement came from a thing simply existing. The twentieth century had grown tired of events. It had experienced too many dramatic events for too long a time. The excitement the nineteenth century got from events was over. For contemporary artists events were no longer important. What excited people now was existence. Three soldiers standing on a street corner doing nothing was more exciting than soldiers going out of a foxhole and into battle.[20]

To capture the excitement of existence, writing must be exact. The more exactly the words fit the thing or the emotion being written about, the more beautiful the words. But the focus must always be on the thing existing in the present moment, not on a thing or emotion remembered. This was a point she often repeated to others — that writing is not remembering; it is creating from what you know. If you "try to remember what you are about to write," she once cautioned, "you will see immediately how lifeless the writing becomes that is why expository writing is so dull because it is all remembered, that is why illustration is so dull because you remember what somebody looked like and you make your illustration look like it. The minute your memory functions while you are doing anything it may be very popular but actually it is dull."[21]

She specifically told Hemingway, "Write, and bring me back whatever you wrote. And write exactly what you see, just as you see it. Don't tell whether you like it or don't like it, how you feel. Just write what you see." She also urged him to be concise. "Cut out words. Cut everything out, except what you saw, what happened."[22]

Gertrude Stein often discussed with Hemingway the importance of sentences and paragraphs as discrete units, and she talked about the arrangement of words and patterns within those units. Hemingway noted that she had "discovered many truths about rhythms and the uses of words in repetition that were valid and valuable and she talked well about them."[23] She nevertheless expressed disappointment that so many of her things continued piling up in her armoire with no one interested in publishing them. Her novel "The Making of Americans" had so far failed to entice any publishers. They were put off by the work's tremendous length, its unusual content, and its peculiar style. It started out being the history of a family recently arrived in America. Then it changed, Stein said, to being "a history of everybody the family knew and then it became the history of every kind and every individual human being."[24] She regarded it as her masterpiece, but there it lay in the armoire, a large bound manuscript, with the rest of her unpublished writings.

Gertrude Stein advised Hemingway to give up journalism as soon as he could. "If you keep on doing newspaper work," she told him, "you will never see things, you will only see words and that will not do, that is of course if you intend to be a writer." If he really intended being a writer, he was better off running a laundry instead of working as a journalist. Earning a living and writing should be kept separate.[25]

One cold afternoon Gertrude Stein began lecturing Hemingway about sex. "By that time," he said, "we liked each other very much and I had already learned that everything I did not understand probably had something to it." Stein thought his attitudes about sex provincial; he knew too little about the subject, and he admitted that he held certain prejudices against homosexuality. He claimed to have seen its more primitive aspects in Kansas City and Chicago, and also during the war.

Stein agreed that male homosexuality was ugly and repugnant. "In women it is the opposite," she said. "They do nothing that they are disgusted by and nothing that is repulsive and afterwards they are happy and they can lead happy lives together." She spoke for three hours defending lesbianism and explaining the mechanics of it. Ernest felt uncomfortable but said that he understood. He was glad when the conversation finally moved on to something else.[26]

Miss Stein liked very much to talk about people, and she talked occasionally about other writers and their works. Hemingway noticed that except for F. Scott Fitzgerald and Ronald Firbank, she never spoke well of any contemporary writer who had not written approvingly of her work or done something to further her career. When Hemingway mentioned that he had been reading Aldous Huxley and D. H. Lawrence, she wanted to know why he read such trash. "Huxley is a dead man," she exclaimed. "Why do you want to read a dead man? Can't you see he's dead?" As for Lawrence, he was impossible. "He's pathetic and preposterous. He writes like a sick man."[27]

She sometimes spoke of Sherwood Anderson, but as a person rather than a writer. He was so charming and so kind, she remarked. "What about his novels?" asked Hemingway. But Miss Stein did not wish to discuss his novels. She mentioned his great, beautiful, warm Italian eyes. "I did not care about his great beautiful warm Italian eyes," Hemingway said later, "but I liked some of his short stories very much." But Anderson's stories were too good for Miss Stein to enjoy talking about them.[28]

She nevertheless praised Anderson's genius for writing sentences that conveyed direct emotions. No one else in America, she insisted, could write a clear, passionate sentence like Anderson. Hemingway disagreed and said that he did not like Anderson's taste. "Taste has nothing to do with sentences," she told him. She added that Scott Fitzgerald was the only one among the younger writers who wrote naturally in sentences.[29]

Hemingway found these afternoon talks useful and stimulating. He also thought that it did his mind good to get away from Paris and from writing altogether now and then. Ernest and Hadley, during their first twelve months in Europe, visited and hiked through various parts of Spain, Switzerland, Italy, and Germany. Hemingway particularly loved being in the mountains, but "Gertrude Stein was always telling me how dull the mountains are and asking when I would grow up and not enjoy them. Hills, of course," she would say, "are pleasanter than mountains." She also did not understand his love for the sea. "Maybe you should grow up and not like the sea," she told him.[30]

To keep fit when in Paris, Hemingway liked to play tennis and box. Standing six feet tall and weighing almost two hundred pounds, he was awkward on the tennis court, but in the ring he was a formidable opponent, a hard puncher, and proud of his pugilistic skills. He sparred at a local gym with anyone he could get to climb into the ring with him. He even tried to teach Ezra Pound to box but with no success. Pound was short-winded and clumsy, and he could not give Hemingway much of a work out. "I have to shadow box between rounds to get up a sweat," Ernest complained.[31]

Robert McAlmon commented that Ernest shadowboxed a lot that first year in Paris. Walking down the street, "he would prance about, sparring at shadows."[32] The following year, after seeing his first bullfight, Hemingway substituted shadow-bullfighting for shadowboxing. "The amount of imaginary cape work and sword thrusts he made in those days was formidable," said McAlmon. "He has a boy's need to be a tough guy, a swell boxer, a strong man."[33]

3

Crafting a Style and an Image

Sherwood Anderson was special, Gertrude Stein told him in a letter. She was about to publish, through a vanity press, a collection of her short pieces, the book to be called *Geography and Plays*. Anderson had written an introduction for it, and she was pleased with him for that. "Besides," she said, "there are the Hemingways you sent and they are charming. He is a delightful fellow and I like his talk."[1]

Hemingway wrote to Anderson about the same time saying that he and Stein were "just like brothers." He and Hadley saw a lot of her. "We love Gertrude Stein." Ezra Pound was also a terrific guy with a "fine bitter tongue onto him."[2] Pound was trying to make Hemingway into a writer, reading his stories, marking them up with a blue pencil, crossing out most of the adjectives, and appending critical comments. But Hemingway thought his criticisms often unsound. Hemingway later told a friend, "Ezra was right half the time, and when he was wrong, he was so wrong you were never in any doubt about it. Gertrude Stein was always right."[3] Gertrude Stein never offered specific criticisms but confined herself to general principles and observations.

Nearly everyone who assisted Hemingway or worked with him during these apprenticeship years found him a pleasant companion and an eager pupil. The Canadian writer Morley Callaghan stated in his memoir *That Summer in Paris* that "Hemingway in his prime, the man I knew in Paris, ... was perhaps the nicest man I had ever met."[4]

Max Eastman, a fellow journalist, about sixteen years older than

Ernest, thought the young Hemingway quiet and exceptionally friendly; he was "a modest and princely-mannered boy," deferential and youthfully attentive to everything going on around him.⁵ He learned quickly and worked hard, believing that concentration and severe discipline were essential to mastering his craft, whether journalism or fiction.

His self-discipline and commitment to work set him apart from the majority of hopeful young writers in the city. Sylvia Beach's roommate and business associate, Adrienne Monnier, told a group of young writers, "Hemingway will be the best known of you all." When asked why she thought so, she replied, "He cares for his craft."⁶ He visited the Musée du Luxembourg almost every day to look at the Monets and Manets and to study the Cézannes. He also reportedly went to a print shop in the evenings and personally set his day's work in type so that he could see exactly how it would look on the printed page.

Ezra Pound (Beinecke Rare Book and Manuscript Library, Yale University).

Near the end of 1922 he finished "My Old Man," a racetrack story that owed much of its theme and style to Anderson. It was the best piece of fiction he had yet written, but it still was not what he wanted. For one thing, it dealt with a subject he knew little about from direct experience. Secondly, the style was loose and discursive like Anderson's. It lacked the tautness he had come to value in journalistic work.

Hemingway realized from what Gertrude Stein had been telling him that he needed to write about things he knew firsthand, not things he had only read or heard about. He hoped to write one story about each thing he knew, writing in simple, clean, declarative sentences without scrollwork or ornamentation of any kind. This type of prose he had cultivated in his feature articles and newspaper reports. To achieve this focused, compact style in his fiction, he knew he must learn to write over again, and this time concentrate, just as Gertrude Stein said. He must begin with one true sentence. It must be the truest sentence he knew. From there he could go on to the next sentence, and then the next.

He had to keep in mind other details as well. Gertrude Stein talked to him endlessly about paragraphs, sentences, words, grammar, and punctuation. And she discussed how all these things related to the composition as a whole. She had pondered such matters carefully and for a long time, and she was constantly formulating theories regarding them. Cézanne's paintings had first caused her to look at a composition in relation to its individual parts.

After much deliberation, she discovered that sentences are not emotional and paragraphs are. This was not to say that sentences and paragraphs were incompatible, only that they bore distinct characteristics a writer must keep in mind. Nouns she did not like. Nouns contributed nothing to movement, so she eliminated as many nouns from her writing as she could. Adjectives, too, she did not like. They were not interesting. Verbs and adverbs were more interesting than nouns and adjectives, but what she liked best were articles and prepositions. She held equally strong views about marks of punctuation. The comma, for instance, she had little use for. It was mostly an irritation and a nuisance. "If you think of a thing as a whole," she said, "and the comma keeps sticking out, it gets on your nerves; because, after all, it destroys the reality of the whole."[7]

Trying to keep in mind everything he had learned, Hemingway began a series of prose sketches, some not more than a brief paragraph. In these sketches he tried to combine his own ideas about writing true, simple, declarative sentences with all that Gertrude Stein had taught him. One sketch dealt with six cabinet ministers brought into the rain-drenched courtyard of a shuttered hospital, there to be executed. One is so ill with typhoid he cannot stand against the hospital wall with the others. Finally, in the driving rain and among the wet dead leaves, he is shot hunched over in a pool of water. The sketch is taught, tense, and concentrated. It consists of only 130 words in eleven sentences and contains no commas. Hemingway repeats the phrase "against the wall" three times, underscoring the feeling of hopelessness and the finality of death. The stark images of rain, the shuttered hospital, the minister ill with typhoid, and the wet dead leaves further heighten the effects.

A later sketch focused on a matador named Maera who has just been gored. As he lies bleeding face down on the ground, his head on his arms, he feels the bull's head bump him; he then feels a horn go all the way through his body and into the sand. The flat, understated prose enhances the scene's horror. A subsequent sentence captures the movement of events as they unfold in the present moment: "Some men picked Maera up and started to run with him toward the barriers through the gate out the passageway around under the grandstand to the infirmary." Irony and more understatement follow as the doctor rushing to attend Maera must stop to wash his hands, having just come from sewing up picador horses. "Maera felt everything getting larger and larger and then smaller and smaller. Then it got larger and larger and larger and then smaller and smaller. Then everything commenced to run faster and faster as when they speed up a cinematograph film. Then he was dead."

This was more like what he hoped to bring to his stories — words and sentences that were simple, crisp, clear, and dramatic. Several years later he explained to Gertrude Stein that in his writing he gradually turned down his flame more and more until there was a great explosion. "If there were nothing but explosions," he said, "my work would be so exciting nobody could bear it."[8] But for now he was striving to master just words and sentences. He had much yet to learn, more than Anderson or Stein or Pound or the Impressionists could teach him. It now required time, experience, and more hard work. Looking back he said, "I was learning something from the painting of Cézanne that made writing simple true sentences far from enough to make the stories have the dimensions that I was trying to put in them."[9]

Gertrude Stein, meanwhile, continued to write in her peculiar fashion, a style marked by word-play and repetition, by specificity of detail and vagueness (even absence) of meaning. She had always liked to look at oil paintings, and she liked to look at them *as* oil paintings. They did not have to represent objects or scenes as they appear in actual life. The paintings might employ objects, shapes, and designs from actual life in their composition, but oil paintings were to be looked at and enjoyed simply as oil paintings. A written work of hers was to be looked at in the same way, not as a representation necessarily of actual life, but an artistic creation to be read and enjoyed as a thing contained within itself. Then, too, with her scientific training as a student in brain anatomy and psychology, she was interested in looking inside of things — inside herself, inside others, inside words, sentences, paragraphs, objects — and expressing accurately and specifically, yet artistically, what she found there. She recognized, of course, that everything has an outside as well as an inside, but she was interested mostly in knowing everything inside. She had an interest, also, in the relation of one thing to another thing — the relation of one type person to another type person, of one sound to another sound, one rhythmic pattern to another, the relation of words to sentences to paragraphs, and so on. She was interested, as well, in the relation between the inside of any one thing and the outside. She had formulated principles along these lines that guided what she wrote, and she believed that by working within herself, she produced writing that was original and important. It also produced writing not subject to after-thought and labored revision. As she told one of her young male protégés,

> I have never understood how people could labor over a manuscript, write and re-write it many times, for to me, if you have something to say, the words are always there. And they are the exact words and the words that should be used. If the story does not come whole, *tant pis*, it has been spoiled, and that is the most difficult thing in writing, to be true enough to yourself, and to know yourself enough so that there is no obstacle to the story's coming through complete.[10]

Gertrude Stein had so far subsidized most of her published works herself. Commercial publishers would not take a chance on the bizarre things she wrote. The vanity press publisher who printed *Three Lives* in 1909 told her frankly that she had written "a very peculiar book and it will be a hard thing to make people take it seriously."[11] One editor of a commercial house in London returned her "portraits" of Matisse and Picasso along with a letter explaining his reasons for rejecting the works:

> Dear Madam,
>
> I am only one, only one, only one. Only one being, one at the same time. Not two, not three, only one. Only one life to live, only sixty minutes in one hour. Only one pair of eyes. Only one brain. Only one being. Being only one, having only one pair of eyes, having only one time, having only one life, I cannot read your M.S. three or four times. Not even one time. Only one

look, only one look is enough. Hardly one copy would sell here. Hardly one. Hardly one. Many thanks. I am returning the M.S. by registered post. Only one M.S. by one post.[12]

Yet despite constant ridicule and rejections, Gertrude Stein persevered, confident of her genius and of her modernist approach to literature. One of her compositions in 1922 was a short play called "Objects Lie On a Table." It is a highly abstract and obscure piece containing a passage that may reflect her early talks on writing with Hemingway. Although the play contains no dialogue in the ordinary sense, the passage appears to be an exchange between a mentor and a pupil. "He says he invents nothing," the passage begins. The mentor tells the pupil to invent a table cloth, "do not let the table table that you invented stay. And he says I am very willing but I have had to invent something to fill in." The mentor cautions that he "had better really have it and he said I am not able to get it and I say to him I am sorry I have not one to lend you." The pupil responds, "you will be of great assistance to me and as for the result that is still in question."[13]

Whether or not this records an actual conversation between the two, their talks continued, Hemingway often calling on Gertrude Stein in the afternoons. Stein told him that he was welcome, even if she and Miss Toklas were out. The maid would let him in and serve him whatever he liked. She told him that he had the run of house.[14]

Contrary to usual practice, he showed up one morning around ten o'clock, "and he stayed," said Gertrude Stein, "he stayed for lunch, he stayed all afternoon, he stayed for dinner and he stayed until about ten o'clock at night." Obviously something troubled him though he would not say what it was. Finally, toward the end of the evening, he announced with much bitterness that his wife was pregnant. Stein thought it hilarious, but Hemingway despaired, saying, "I am too young to be a father." And what about his career? This might ruin everything. After nearly a year of hard work in Paris, his first book would soon be out, *Three Stories & Ten Poems*, to be published by Robert McAlmon in his Contact Editions. It was a modest start, but things were beginning to click. "My Old Man" had been accepted for inclusion in *The Best Stories of 1923*, and his head was full of ideas for more stories he wanted to write. "We consoled him as best we could," said Stein, "and sent him on his way."[15]

The Hemingways, after talking the matter over between themselves, decided to leave Europe. They wanted their child born on the other side of the Atlantic. Another consideration was that the Toronto *Star* organization had offered Ernest a full time job, and he needed the money. Ernest decided that he would work for a year and then, with what he and Hadley could save, together with the little they already had, he would give up newspaper work and they would return with the baby to Paris where Ernest could resume his writing career. They would put off their departure for Toronto, however, for as long as possible. It was now January and the baby was due sometime in October. This allowed Hemingway a little more time to write. It also allowed him to accept Bob McAlmon's offer to bankroll a quick trip to Madrid where both of them could see their first bullfights.

As their train pulled in for a brief stop on its way to Madrid, Hemingway and McAlmon noticed, lying on a flatcar sitting on a neighboring track, the maggot-eaten corpse of a dog. McAlmon, feeling a bit queasy anyway (probably from too much drink), looked away. Hemingway noticed the reaction and immediately launched into a discourse on facing reality. He told McAlmon of seeing the bodies of men piled up and maggot-eaten in a similar way during the war. "He advised a detached and scientific attitude toward the corpse of the dog," McAlmon recalled. "He tenderly explained that we of our generation must inure ourselves to the sight of grim reality."

"Hell, Mac," Ernest said, "you write like a realist. Are you going to go romantic on us?" With the sun shining on the rotting corpse of the dog, Hemingway remarked that such tokens of reality were actually beautiful.

"Christ," said McAlmon. "What posturing!" and he adjourned to the dining car for a whisky.[16]

Once in Madrid, the two men were joined by William Bird. He ran the Three Mountains Press in conjunction with McAlmon's Contact Publishing Company. Years afterward, Bird recalled how Hemingway had taken advantage of McAlmon on the trip. Robert had paid for everything, yet when it came time to choose seats at the bullfight, Hemingway had to have the best seat closest to the action "because he was 'studying the art of it,' while Bob and I, not knowing anything, I suppose, about art in any shape or form, could just as well sit in the bleachers as long as Hem would explain it all to us anyway after the dust had cleared." Bird further recalled that while in Spain, Hemingway had to have his Johnnie Walker, or some other expensive scotch, and he expected McAlmon to pay for it.[17]

As it turned out, McAlmon did not like the bullfights, especially what happened to the picador horses, but Hemingway found the whole thing exhilarating. McAlmon decided that Ernest's enthusiasm resulted from Gertrude Stein having praised the spectacle earlier. This enthusiasm, McAlmon felt, and the attitude about the dead dog, were all part of what Ezra Pound called Hemingway's "self-hardening process," his attempt to a be realist, not a romantic, and to face calmly those grim realities of life. Soon others began to notice the sharp contrasts in Hemingway's character — the shifting moods and poses, the need to be pampered and pitied, yet the urge to appear tough and robust. They observed the outward signs of some inner struggle, a struggle between the shy, sensitive boy Gertrude Stein first saw and the hard, rugged individual Hemingway so much wanted to be.

Robert McAlmon (Beinecke Rare Book and Manuscript Library, Yale University).

Despite his size and strength, his clumsiness predisposed him to injury. He also suffered from psychosomatic disorders. The novelist John Dos Passos, who knew him well during this period, said that Hemingway "was horribly prone to accidents. I've never known a man who did so much damage to his own carcass." If Ernest was not recovering from some accident, he was down with a sore throat. "He was like one of those professional athletes who, although strong as an ox, is always nursing some ailment." Dos Passos noted too that Ernest was "a moody kind of fellow even then.

sorry for himself." It was usually during his self-pitying spells that he came down with an illness and took to his bed for days at a time. "I never knew an athletic vigorous man who spent so much time in bed as Ernest did," said Dos Passos.[18]

A woman acquaintance described Hemingway at this time as generous, soft-hearted, and simple — "so different from his legend." She thought his animal prototype would be a rabbit — "white and pink face, soft brown eyes that look at you without blinking. As for his love for boxing and bullfighting — all that is thrashing up the ground with his hind legs."[19]

Hemingway's growing tendency to thrash up the ground, to bully others occasionally, and to play the hardened veteran of life, all seemed to be symptomatic of a man trying to conceal the sensitive, vulnerable side of his nature. James Joyce told Sylvia Beach that it was a mistake for Hemingway to think he was such a tough fellow and for McAlmon to try passing himself off as the sensitive type. It was really the other way around.[20]

Shortly after arriving back in Paris, Ernest set off again for Spain, this time with Hadley on the first of their annual visits to Pamplona and the uproarious week-long Festival of San Firmín. They returned to Paris about mid–July and prepared to leave for Canada. There Hemingway would take up his duties with the Toronto *Star* and Hadley would prepare for the birth of her child. A little less than two weeks before their departure, Hemingway enjoyed seeing his *Three Stories & Ten Poems* in print. Besides the poems, the volume contained "Up in Michigan," "My Old Man," and his latest story, "Out of Season."

Hemingway continued to work on his short prose sketches. With the aid of Pound's slashing blue pencil, he ended up with eighteen of them. Pound helped arrange for them to be published in the coming months, when Hemingway would be in Canada, by Bill Bird at the Three Mountains Press under the title *in our time*. Just before the Hemingways' departure, Gertrude Stein gave Ernest a brief composition, something she described to Sherwood Anderson in a letter as "a little skit I presented to him on going away."[21] It was one of her "portraits," titled "He and They, Hemingway," in which she combined her usual cryptic references with plays upon his name: "On their way and to head away. A head any way. What is a head. A head is what every one not in the north of Australia returns for that. In English we know. And is it to their credit that they have nearly finished and claimed...."

If Hemingway understood what this "portrait" meant, he did not record the fact.[22]

Ernest and Hadley finally left Paris on August 16, 1923, arriving in Canada on September 4. They had not been in Toronto long when Ernest received galley proofs of *in our time,* his second published book. This was just before Christmas, three months after beginning work for the *Star* and two months following his son's birth. John Hadley Nicanor Hemingway, later nicknamed Bumby, arrived on the tenth of October. Ernest wrote Miss Stein and Miss Toklas telling them the particulars and saying that he was getting very fond of the child. He thought it was a bad decision to come back, however. He and Hadley had become very homesick for Paris. He wanted Miss Stein to know that he would probably soon chuck journalism for good. "You ruined me as a journalist last winter," he said. "Have been no good since."[23]

Although Ernest had planned to work in Toronto for a year, after only two months on the *Star,* he was fed up. He hated his job, hated his boss, hated Canada, and hated the time wasted that should have been spent writing fiction. He and his wife decided that when the baby turned three months old and was strong enough to travel, Ernest would quit his job and they would return to Paris.

They arrived in January 1924, only five months after having left. "Hemingway is just back," Gertrude Stein wrote to Sherwood Anderson. "He seems very much not to have liked Canada. It's nice having him back."[24] Once the couple settled into their new apartment above a sawmill in the rue Notre Dame de Champs, Hemingway turned his attention to writing and to advancing his career. Now that he was a published author with two slim volumes to his credit, he started on some new stories with greater confidence than ever.

Ezra Pound, meanwhile, anticipating Hemingway's return, had made plans to get him a job on the *transatlantic review*. This was a new literary magazine edited by the English novelist Ford Madox Ford and financed chiefly by the wealthy American John Quinn. Pound brought Ford to his studio in the rue Notre Dame de Champs, not far from Ernest's apartment, to meet Hemingway. In the large, dimly-lit studio, Ford saw a sturdy young man "dancing on his toe points" and "threatening with his fist" a silk hanging depicting a fat Buddhist monk.

"That young man," said Ford to Pound, "appears to have sinophobia."

Pound explained that he was only shadowboxing to work off excess energy. "You ought to have him for your sub-editor," said Pound. "He's an experienced journalist. He writes very good verse and he's the finest prose stylist in the world." As Ford was lax in his business dealings, Pound added, "He's disciplined too." Ford agreed that the young man looked disciplined in a Herculean way, and he agreed to take Hemingway on as sub-editor. His primary duty would be to read manuscripts.

Every Thursday Ford held a tea in the offices of Bill Bird's Three Mountains Press, which also served as the offices of the *transatlantic review*. "On most Thursdays," said Ford, "Mr. Hemingway shadow boxed at Mr. Bird's press, at the files of unsold reviews, and at my nose."[25]

From the start, Hemingway did not like the way Ford operated. He was careless about finances and he ran the *transatlantic* as a compromise, publishing the same old things the slick magazines ran, along with occasional Dadaist trash in French. Hemingway thought he should print the best of the moderns — Joyce, Pound, Stein, himself. There were no advertisers for him to please so why not shoot for the moon? Trying to convince Ford of that became a constant struggle, and working with him proved frustrating. Ernest suggested to Pound that the only thing to do with Ford was to kill him. But Pound mustn't misunderstand: "I am fond of Ford. This aint personal. It's literary."[26]

Hemingway showed up at Gertrude Stein's apartment one day very excited. Ford had finally agreed, at Hemingway's urging, to publish something of Stein's in the next issue of the *transatlantic*. Hemingway wanted to run "The Making of Americans" serially, and he needed the first fifty pages right away. Gertrude Stein described herself as quite overcome with excitement by the idea, having tried unsuccessfully for thirteen years to get the work published, but all she had was the original bound manuscript. That was all right; Hemingway and Miss Toklas would copy what was needed.

Hemingway soon sent Gertrude Stein a note saying that Ford was delighted with her stuff. Ernest advised her to be haughty in negotiating with Ford on a price — but not too haughty. Ford was under the impression, he said, that she got big money when she consented to publish. She should get thirty francs a printed page, more than her writing had fetched prior to this. In a playful dig at her vanity, something he could hazard considering his efforts on her behalf, Hemingway wrote, "I made it clear it was a remarkable scoop for his magazine obtained only through my obtaining genius."[27]

The first installment of "The Making of Americans" appeared in the April number of the *transatlantic review*. The same issue included Hemingway's story "Indian Camp" and a selection from Joyce's still-untitled *Finnegans Wake*. From that time on, Gertrude Stein expressed gratitude for Hemingway's efforts in getting a portion of her novel published. Alice Toklas, on the other hand, suspected Hemingway of acting from self-interest. She could not put her finger on it, but she thought there was more to the story than simply generosity. Gertrude Stein had long depended on Toklas for the things Hemingway was now doing — praising her work, typing her manuscripts, proofreading copy, and searching out literary markets. The closer Gertrude Stein drew to Hemingway and the more she depended on him, the more Alice resented it.

Alice saw that Gertrude and Ernest were mutually attracted to one another and that the attraction went beyond literary camaraderie or teacher and pupil affection. She saw how they interacted and noted the possible euphemism in Stein's repeated statement that she had a weakness for Hemingway. As far-fetched as it looks now, Toklas became fearful that Gertrude and Ernest would enter into a liaison that might eventually lead to marriage. This notion reveals more about Alice's neurotic jealousy than it does about Stein and Hemingway's real relationship, though Alice did, in fact, correctly notice something libidinous in Hemingway's conduct.

Most men at one time or another encounter a woman who, though not conventionally attractive, possesses some quality — something in the manner, the voice, the personality — that makes her sexually appealing. Alice saw that Hemingway entertained fantasies about Gertrude. What she probably did not know was that Hemingway had bluntly told friends at the time exactly what he would like to do with Stein.[28]

Henceforth Alice disliked Hemingway and did what she could to poison Stein against him. She insisted that Hemingway was crude and insincere. He used four-letter words and fabricated stories to make himself appear more virile.[29] But Stein would not be swayed. She still admitted to having a weakness for Hemingway. For what he had done with "The

Making of Americans" in particular, she thought him wonderful. "Hemingway did it all," she said. "He copied the manuscript and corrected the proof." Correcting proofs was like dusting, she claimed. You really got to know the value of a thing when you dusted it for a while. "In correcting these proofs Hemingway learned a great deal and he admired all that he learned."[30]

As Hemingway corrected proofs of Gertrude Stein's novel, he wrote to her, saying, "I think it gets better and better. It is the best stuff I have ever read."[31] Perhaps as a result of all that he learned, his own writing changed. The stories he produced during the spring of 1924 completely broke free of Sherwood Anderson's influence, and now some of them showed the exclusive impress of Gertrude Stein. Her *Geography and Plays*, published two years earlier, contained a poem titled "Accents in Alsace." The poem included a line, "In the photograph the Rhine hardly showed." This line reappeared, only slightly altered, in Hemingway's story "A Soldier's Home," written in April of 1924. The second paragraph of the story reads, "There is a picture which shows him [Harold Krebs] on the Rhine with two German girls and another corporal. Krebs and the corporal look too big for their uniforms. The German girls are not beautiful. The Rhine does not show in the picture."[32]

The story "Mr. and Mrs. Elliot," finished the same day as "A Soldier's Home," so closely imitates Gertrude Stein's mode of cryptic references and ironic repetitions that it seems Hemingway had a copy of Stein's work at his elbow as he composed. At least it was her voice that sounded in his head as he wrote. Those who recognized the similarities in the two styles noted also that, unlike Stein, Hemingway actually had something to write about.

With so much happening in his professional life, Hemingway had neglected a certain family matter that he now felt needed attention. Bumby was already five months old and still not baptized. Hemingway asked Gertrude Stein and Miss Toklas to stand as godmothers, and he got Chink Dorman-Smith, an old war buddy, to be godfather. "We were all born of different religions," recalled Gertrude Stein, "and most of us were not practising any, so it was rather difficult to know in what church the baby could be baptized."[33] After much deliberation they decided to hold the service in the Episcopalian chapel.

3. Crafting a Style and an Image

As a baptismal present for Goddy (short for "godchild," the nickname Miss Stein and Miss Toklas gave to Bumby), Alice Toklas embroidered a small chair cushion and knitted him a brightly colored garment. On his sixth month birthday, she brought him some rubber animals and a silver christening cup. Miss Toklas took her responsibilities as godmother seriously.

Ernest, meanwhile, continued writing stories at what for him was a remarkable pace. In May he informed Pound that he had ten new ones done. He sent out feelers to friends to see if they knew of a publisher who might be interested in bringing out a book he had in mind. It would contain the material from *Three Stories & Ten Poems* plus ten or twelve new stories, each story separated by a sketch from *in our time*. Hemingway also tried to get the Paris agent for the New York firm of Boni and Liveright to buy the rights to Gertrude Stein's "The Making of Americans." Things looked promising for a time, but finally they came to nothing. Stein was naturally disappointed, but Hemingway remained upbeat and willing to do what he could for her: "I thought, I will do my best to serve her and see she gets justice for the good work she had done as long as I can."[34]

In May, Hemingway began his most ambitious story yet, one in which nothing much seemed to happen, one that focused ostensibly on existence in the present moment. It was a tale about a young man named Nick who hikes into the backwoods of Michigan to fish. He sets up camp on a river bank, cooks his meals, smokes cigarettes, tends to his gear, and fishes for trout. At one point he looks into the river and sees trout in the clear, brown water "keeping themselves steady in the current." He watches them a long time "holding themselves with their noses into the current." Later he hooks a large fish that puts up a tremendous fight before snapping the line and swimming away. The excitement has almost been too much for Nick. He has to sit down and rest. "He didn't want to rush his sensations any."

Nearby stands a swampy pool, dark and overgrown with big cedars, that Nick is afraid to fish. That is where the biggest trout would be, but "Nick did not want to go in there now. He felt a reaction against deep wading with the water deepening up under his armpits, to hook big trout in places impossible to land them...; in the fast deep water, in the half light, the fishing would be tragic. In the swamp fishing was a tragic adventure. Nick did not want it."

The long story, eventually called "Big Two-Hearted River," is deceptively simple. Nick is the only character, the narrative focusing on his heightened sensations and on specific sensory details. Yet beneath the surface of commonplace activities lies genuine drama. Although never mentioned, the Great War forms the backdrop to the entire story. The experience of war has shattered Nick emotionally. He strives to hold on to his sanity; he struggles to hold himself steady in the current. This trip, with the meticulous, even ritualistic, way Nick goes about setting up camp, cooking his meals, and caring for his equipment, has been a necessary stage in his recovery. It has been important to ease himself gradually back into the current of life, to reacquaint himself with the familiar and pleasurable activities of earlier times. He cannot yet rush his sensations; it would be dangerous to do so. Still he knows, "There were plenty of days coming when he could fish the swamp."

The story is a subtle, masterful performance overall. It was the best indication so far that young Ernest Hemingway, in combining experiences he really knew firsthand with all that Gertrude Stein had taught him, had found his own fictional voice and material. An important truth he had picked up from his talks with Stein, a truth that distinguishes this story and his best writing going forward, involves the process of elimination. "If you leave out important things or events that you know about," he later explained, "the story is strengthened. If you leave or skip something because you do not know it, the story is worthless. The test of any story is how very good the stuff is that you, not your editors, omit." The best thing he omitted from "Big Two-Hearted River" was the war. It underscores and gives meaning to everything. "So the war," he said, "all mention of the war, anything about the war, is omitted." He also left out the Indians. "[T]here were many Indians in the story, just as the war was in the story, and none of the Indians nor the war appeared."[35]

But he gave these explanations much later. While still at work on the piece, he wrote Gertrude Stein that he was trying to do the country like Cézanne "and having a hell of a time and sometimes getting it a little bit." He had written about 100 manuscript pages at the time "and nothing happens and the country is swell." He saw it all in his head and sometimes it came out right; "but isn't writing a hard job though? It used to be easy before I met you."[36]

4

Making the Heavyweight Class

The 1924 festival of San Firmín began as always on July 6. The Hemingways arrived in Pamplona by train, their second visit promising to be even more fun and exciting than the first. Among those joining them were Chink Dorman-Smith, John Dos Passos, and Donald Ogden Stewart. Bob McAlmon, along with Bill Bird and his wife, would show up later.

During the festival's week-long run, Ernest seized the opportunity to study carefully the ritual of bullfighting, what he was calling the greatest art and the beautiful dance involving death. He had tickets for each day's *corrida,* and he got up early to watch the 7:00 A.M. *encierro, or running of* the bulls, that were to fight that afternoon in the *plaza de toros.* He even got a few of his male companions to join him in the ring where, along with other amateurs, they tested their matadorial skills and courage against a heifer or young steer. Bill Bird and Dos Passos stayed out of it, but Don Stewart and Ernest entered into the spirit of things. During one amateur fight, a charging steer knocked Stewart down, breaking two of his ribs. Ernest grabbed the animal by the horns and tried unsuccessfully to wrestle it to the ground.

It was a fun celebration all around, but finally, after a week of summer heat, rich food, red wine and pernod, daily bullfights, incessant bustle and noise, fireworks, late hours, and lack of sleep, everyone felt exhausted and ready for it all to end. To help wind down, the gang decided to spend a couple of days just fishing and relaxing in Burguete, a village further up in the Pyrenees, about an hour's bus ride from Pamplona.

One evening the group took an after-dinner stroll to nearby Roncesvalles, Ernest and Hadley walking together, engaged in serious conversation. Suddenly Ernest picked up a rock, began knocking it against his head and exclaiming, "I'll kill myself, I'll kill myself. We can't have any fun anymore if we're just going on having babies." Hadley had missed her period and thought she might be pregnant again. Ernest protested that he was too young for a second child, and he told Hadley she wouldn't be a good playmate any longer. "He was tragic about it," recalled McAlmon later, "and Hadley, too, became upset."

Sally Bird finally told Ernest to stop acting like a damn fool and a crybaby. "You're responsible too," she told him. "Either you do something about not having it, or you have it." Hadley, perhaps at her husband's urging, began a regimen of quinine and hot baths hoping to induce a miscarriage, and either the regimen worked or she hadn't been pregnant to begin with, for soon everyone returned to Paris and life returned to normal.[1]

For Ernest, a normal life at this time meant working on his fiction, mailing out stories to stateside magazines only to have them rejected, and helping Ford Madox Ford with the *transatlantic review*. The journal had never been on a strong financial footing, but soon news arrived that John Quinn, principal backer of the magazine, had died in New York of cancer. Ford tried to keep things afloat by trimming expenses and finding new owners, but nothing could save it. The journal expired quietly with the January 1925 issue. In its one year existence, it had published three of Hemingway's stories and nine consecutive installments of Gertrude Stein's novel, which represented only a small portion of the complete text.

McAlmon, under Hemingway's prodding and based on what he had read in the *transatlantic*, considered bringing out the entire work in his Contact Editions. The press' stated aim was to publish works of quality not likely to be printed elsewhere for commercial reasons or due to censorship restrictions in America and England. When Gertrude Stein learned of McAlmon's interest, she invited the publisher to afternoon tea. There she argued that he should publish her work in six volumes over a two-year period. McAlmon thought it over and decided, "All or not at all. It's a unity."[2] Not that McAlmon felt enthusiastic about the venture. He considered it more a philanthropic enterprise than a money-making scheme. He had earlier written Gertrude Stein a letter in which he said, "I take your work — how shall I say, seriously, or at least with a potential or suspended respect. I don't get it, and believing that you have conviction to go on in your manner, simply have a waiting frame of mind."[3]

McAlmon did not much care for Stein personally. He said that the first time he met her at her studio in the rue de Fleurus, "she did monologue, and pontificate, and reiterate, and stammer." He reported her saying on one occasion, "No, nobody has done anything to develop the English language since Shakespeare, except myself, and Henry James perhaps a little."[4] McAlmon concluded that Gertrude Stein should be added to the world's list of megalomaniacs. Still, there was something engaging about her, and at their first private interview he was surprised to find her almost shy. During their conversation they discovered a mutual passion for Trollope's novels — also for documentary writing, and for biographies and autobiographies. She was more human, McAlmon decided, and a better specimen, than Amy Lowell, whom Stein was thought to resemble in physique and temperament. "I left thinking that one could become fond of Gertrude Stein if she would quit being the oracle and pontificating" — if she would get down off that throne chair of hers. "Our rapport never resulted in friendship, however. Miss Stein is apparently interested only in people who sit before her and listen. That does not mean she will not strike a blow at their solar plexuses at some future time, however."[5]

Robert McAlmon had early established himself as a gifted young writer and influential publisher. In 1919 six of his poems appeared in Harriet Monroe's *Poetry Magazine*, which had recently printed works by William Butler Yeats and T. S. Eliot. During 1920 and 1921, McAlmon, while living in Greenwich Village, joined William Carlos Williams in founding and publishing the literary magazine *Contact*. Although it lasted for only five issues, the magazine printed works by such writers as Ezra Pound and Marianne Moore.

After the magazine folded, McAlmon moved to Paris, where he published a collection of his own short stories, followed in 1923 by another collection of stories and a novel. The last two volumes appeared under the imprint of Contact Editions. Not wanting Contact Editions to be regarded as a vanity press, he also printed out-of-the-mainstream works by others, including Hilda Doolittle, Mina Loy, William Carlos Williams, Ford Madox Ford, Hemingway, and soon Gertrude Stein.

In 1924 McAlmon self-published his most highly-regarded book, *Village: As It Happened Through a Fifteen Year Period*, and in the following year his colleague Bill Bird at Three Mountains Press brought out his novel *Distinguished Air: Grim Fairy Tales*. By mid-decade, despite problems with heavy drinking, bouts of depression, and increasingly erratic behavior, Robert McAlmon had the reputation in Paris of being a significant young writer. Hemingway thought his prose style atrocious, "but the stuff," he told Ezra Pound, "is damn important. It is god damn important." McAlmon in his stories, said Hemingway, jumped around a lot, threw syntax and grammar overboard, and philosophized too much, "but three of the stories are among the best short stories ever wrote."[6]

Yet Hemingway would not go so far as his friend Ernest Walsh, who, earlier in a review, compared McAlmon favorably to Mark Twain. Hemingway wrote to Walsh acknowledging that McAlmon's work was underrated. It never got a fair hearing because McAlmon had made so many enemies, "usually while drunk and vomitty," and certainly Mark Twain wrote "vast quantities of Hog Wash." But Walsh should reread *Huckleberry Finn* as Hemingway had done recently, "and if you really believe, honest to ourselves believe that McAlmon has ever written anything or everything together that deserves to be mentioned in the same room, house, city, continent or magazine with Huckleberry Finn I will stop writing because there will be no damn use to write if such a state of things can be."[7]

Although Hemingway by mid-decade had published two slim books in Paris and an assortment of poems, reviews, and stories in various European journals, he still wanted to get his work before an American audience. Friends in New York carried the manuscript of his newly-revamped collection of stories and prose sketches to the publisher George Doran. After examining the manuscript, Doran rejected it. He did not think a volume of short stories by a new author would be profitable, but he said he would be interested in looking at a novel. Novels could usually pay their way, but short stories were a drug on the market.[8]

Hemingway's friends then approached Horace Liveright of Boni and Liveright publishers. Liveright initially had the same reservations as Doran, but strong support for the book came from an unsuspected and unsolicited quarter. Sherwood Anderson had recently moved from Huebsch to Liveright, and he spoke so favorably of the young writer that Horace Liveright decided to take a chance. He cabled Hemingway that he accepted his manuscript, a written contract to follow by post. Hemingway then wrote to Anderson thanking him for having placed his book with Liveright.[9]

Unknown to Ernest, Scott Fitzgerald was telling his own editor, Maxwell Perkins at Scribner's, "about a young man named Ernest Hemmingway [sic] who lives in Paris." His collection of short pieces, *in our time*, was "remarkable & I'd look him up right away. He's the real thing."[10] Perkins wrote to Hemingway asking to see his work, but by the time Ernest received the letter, he had already signed with Liveright. The contract called for an option on Hemingway's next three books. If Liveright did not exercise this option within sixty days of receipt of a second book-length manuscript, the option lapsed, and the contract became void. Hemingway explained all this to Perkins. He thanked the editor for his interest and assured him that if in the future he was ever able to send him anything, he would certainly do so.

Feeling ever more confident as a writer, ever more buoyant and self-assured overall, Hemingway made plans to return with his wife to Pamplona and the festival of San Firmín. This would be their third trip in as many years. Yet it proved less enjoyable than the previous two, partly because Pamplona had been "discovered" and was now overrun with tourists; but the main problem had to do with the people they were with. Joining the Hemingways in Pamplona were Lady Duff Twysden, her lover Pat Guthrie, the writer Harold Loeb, Ernest's boyhood friend Bill Smith, and Donald Ogden Stewart. Before arriving in Pamplona, Lady Duff and Loeb had slipped off to St. Jean-de-Luz for a week-long affair; Guthrie learned of it and was now sulky, furious, and jealous. Hemingway, who found Lady Duff attractive and Loeb insufferable, also grew jealous and angry. After several days of drinking and little sleep, everyone began to grow testy and nerves started to ravel. Tempers flared, and Hemingway and Loeb nearly came to blows.

Once the festival ended and Ernest was back in Paris, he began setting down a sketch intended to mock Harold Loeb. Hemingway had a propensity to lampoon in writing those who irritated him, and Loeb had irritated him plenty. He did not yet know where he was going with the piece, but venting his irritation through biting humor made him feel better. This is how he had come to write "Mr. and Mrs. Elliot." The story had originally been called "Mr. and Mrs. Smith" and was meant to ridicule the rumored sexual problems of the poet Chard Powers Smith and his wife, Olive. When

Smith read the story, he wrote to Hemingway, objecting to "this silly fiasco which you attempted to perpetrate" and accusing Hemingway of indulging in petty malice. "My reaction is less anger for anything you have done," said Smith, "than contempt for you as a worm who attempted a cad's trick and failed to pull it off."[11]

Hemingway wrote back saying it would be a pleasure to see Smith in Paris again and something of a pleasure to knock him down a few times "or perhaps once, depending on your talent for getting up." He closed by expressing a profound contempt for Smith personally, as well as for his past, present, and future. It was probably fortunate for Smith that the meeting did not take place.[12]

As for the present Loeb piece, Hemingway soon realized that he had something more serious in the making than a satiric sketch or a short story. The thing was quickly taking on the proportions of a novel, one based closely on the incidents and characters of the just-concluded summer in Pamplona. Hemingway considered many titles for the work, among them "Fiesta," "River to the Sea," and "Two Lie Together." Another title he considered was a phrase he picked up from Gertrude Stein. Ultimately he chose something else, yet her phrase helped clarify the novel's focus and was eventually adopted as the name for the American expatriate movement of the 1920s.

During one of their regular talks, Stein told Hemingway of having taken her Model T Ford to a garage to have the ignition repaired. The young mechanic who did the work bungled it in some way, and his *patron* scolded him for his incompetence. The young man had served in the war, and the *patron* said to him in exasperation, "You are all a *génération perdue*."

"That's what you are," Gertrude Stein assured Hemingway. "That's what you all are. All of you young people who served in the war. You are a lost generation."

Ernest began to object. "Don't argue with me, Hemingway," Stein said. "It does no good at all. You're all a lost generation, exactly as the garage keeper said."[13]

Hemingway thought briefly of calling his novel "The Lost Generation" but chose instead a phrase from a passage in Ecclesiastes: "One generation passeth away, and another generation cometh; but the earth abideth forever.... The sun also ariseth, and the sun goeth down, and hasteth to the place where he arose." He placed Gertrude Stein's remark "You are all a lost generation" as an epigram at the front of the book, above the passage from Ecclesiastes, leading readers to assume that "the lost generation" described the characters in the novel. Hemingway later said that he used the phrase only as a contrast to the biblical passage, that from the beginning he saw no validity in Gertrude Stein's remark. He recalled that while walking home the night of their conversation, "I thought of Miss Stein and Sherwood Anderson and egotism and mental laziness versus discipline and I thought who is calling who a lost generation?"[14]

In October 1925, *The Making of Americans*—all 925 pages in small type—finally appeared in McAlmon's Contact Editions. The book did not win the critical approval Gertrude Stein had hoped. One critic claimed the author had accomplished a perfect imitation of the Tower of Babel: "She has exhibited the most complete befuddlement of the human mind."

Another critic complained that the work "must be among the seven longest books in the world." In an attempt to give readers a taste of the style in which it was written, he said, "There is serious thinking and nice picturing of being living, but certainly we were sometimes feeling that anyone might be writing like this if they were abandoning their being to it."

Edmund Wilson, in the *New Republic*, admitted that he had not read the entire book:

> I do not know whether it is possible to do so.... With sentences so regularly rhythmical, so needlessly prolix, so many times repeated and ending so often with present participles, the reader is too soon in a state, not to follow the slow becoming of life, but simply to fall asleep.[15]

After two months, only seventy-four copies of the standard paper-bound edition had been sold, plus twenty-eight copies specially bound in leather.

By this time Hemingway's own attitude toward the novel had changed. "The book began magnificently," he said of it years afterward, "went on very well for a long way with great stretches of great brilliance and then went on endlessly in repetitions that a more conscientious and less lazy writer would have put in the waste basket."[16] Gertrude Stein remembered Hemingway coming up to her at a party shortly after the book appeared. He started to explain why he could not review it, but just then Ford Madox Ford interrupted by laying a hand on Hemingway's shoulder, saying that it was *he* who wished to speak to Gertrude Stein, and sending Hemingway away.

Alice Toklas recalled the incident a little differently. "Ford was talking to Gertrude," she wrote, "when Hemingway came up to speak to her. Ford wafted him away saying, Go away young man, it is I who am speaking to Miss Stein, do not interrupt me."[17] Whichever way it happened, Hemingway did not get to tell Stein why he could not review her novel, and he left no record of what he had intended to say. It is clear, however, that he had lost enthusiasm for the work just as he was losing faith in Stein as a writer. Whether he would have told her these things to her face remains open to question.

He felt especially sure of himself about this time, even a bit cocky. The same month that *The Making of Americans* appeared, Liveright published the New York edition of *In Our Time*. Hemingway presented a copy to Gertrude Stein, who told him not to expect a review from her as she thought it would be wiser to wait for his novel. In a momentary rage, Ernest wrote to Pound, "What a lot of safe playing kikes. Why not write a review of one book at a time? She is afraid that I might fall on my nose in a novel and if so how terrible it would have been to have said anything about this book no matter how good it may be."[18] It is not clear who refused to review the other's book first, Stein or Hemingway, but conflicting ambitions and competitive jealousies had already started to roil the waters of their friendship.

Just three weeks before publication of *In Our Time*, Hemingway finished the first draft of his Pamplona novel, and when the juices were flowing and he was working well, he felt especially combative. During these periods he tended to view writing as a competitive sport. It was something like prizefighting. At this point in his career he sometimes thought of himself as the challenger attempting to knock out more experienced writers. Later, as an experienced writer himself, he felt it necessary to defend his title against upcoming contenders. His greatest adversaries were writers already dead, but it was their reputations that he wanted to beat.

In a letter written at the peak of his career in 1949 he made a humorous yet revealing assertion, claiming to be a man without ambition "except to be champion of the world." He had first taken on Mr. Turgenev, he said, and didn't find it too difficult. He took on Mr. Maupassant next and

4. Making the Heavyweight Class

finally beat him with four of his best stories. He wouldn't fight Dr. Tolstoy in a twenty-round bout because he knew he would get his ears knocked off, but he would take him on in a six-rounder and Tolstoy would never touch him. Henry James he would thumb in a clinch "and then hit him once where he had no balls and ask the referee to stop it." He would be glad at any time, if in training, to go twenty rounds with Mr. Cervantes, but there were some guys nobody could ever beat "like Mr. Shakespeare."[19] Here in Paris in 1925, however, he was still the young, inexperienced challenger, anxious to step into the ring and win a title from somebody. He finally decided to take on Sherwood Anderson. He liked Anderson. He liked some of his writing. He owed him a debt of gratitude for convincing Liveright to publish his first American title. Yet none of that mattered. Boxing was nothing personal.

Anderson had recently published *Dark Laughter*, a novel Hemingway thought an inferior performance, just like his two previous books, *Many Marriages* and *A Story Teller's Story*. Annoyed by what he considered Anderson's sloppy work, Hemingway felt that it was time to call the older writer to account, so he sat down and in little more than a week wrote "The Torrents of Spring," subtitled "A Romantic Novel in Honor of the Passing of a Great Race." The short work specifically burlesqued the style, characters, and situations typically found in Anderson's novels, especially *Dark Laughter*. In addition, Hemingway saw "Torrents" as a satire on contemporary American literature in general.

In a letter to Ezra Pound, combining youthful exuberance, braggadocio, and humor, Hemingway said he had written the book "to destroy Sherwood and various others." "Torrents" was a regular novel, he claimed, "only it shows up all the fakes of Anderson, Gertrude, [Sinclair] Lewis, [Willa] Cather, Hergo [Joseph Hergesheimer] and all the rest of the pretentious faking bastards." He said that he felt the urge to be an American Henry Fielding; that whenever "one of the bastards" comes out with a book they all think is a masterpiece and isn't, he is going to write a *Joseph Andrews* to expose it. "Torrents" was the first. "Jesus Christ it is funny," he told Pound. "I don't see how Sherwood will ever be able to write again. Stuff like Gertrude isn't worth the bother to show up. It's easier simply to quote from it."[20]

Besides showing up all the fakes, specifically Anderson, Hemingway had other, more self-serving reasons for writing "Torrents." Had he wished only to censure Anderson for his sloppy work, he could have done so privately. By attacking Anderson publicly, Hemingway was making a statement for the world to hear. He was declaring his literary independence. For some time now critics had made him uncomfortable by pointing out his indebtedness to Anderson and Stein. "There is something of Sherwood Anderson, of his fine bare effects and values coined from simplest words, in Hemingway's clear medium," wrote one. "There are obvious traces of Sherwood Anderson in Mr. Hemingway and there are subtler traces of Gertrude Stein," said another.[21] In writing "Big Two-Hearted River" and his Pamplona novel, Hemingway had truly discovered his own voice. He was now eager to distance himself from his two primary mentors.

He could not attack Stein head-on. She would not have stood for it. He did get in a couple of light jabs though, one by calling Part Four of his parody "The Passing of a Great Race and the Making and Marring of Americans." In this section he wrote that in Paris there was a street named after Huysmans. "Right around the corner from where Gertrude Stein lived. Ah, there was a woman! Where were her experiments in words leading her? What was at the bottom of it? All that in Paris. Ah, Paris. How far it was to Paris now. Paris in the morning. Paris in the evening. Paris at night. Paris in the morning again. Paris at noon, perhaps. Why not?"[22]

Still, Gertrude Stein was too formidable to engage at close quarters. By attacking her dearest Sherwood, however, he would be declaring his independence from Anderson, and simultaneously severing literary ties with her. Anderson definitely was the easier prey and the logical target. He had a softer, less assertive nature than Stein, and fortunately he lived far off in Chicago.

Writing "Torrents" was also a business decision. Scott Fitzgerald, whom Ernest met toward the end of April 1925 and who was already a well-established author by his early twenties, encouraged Hemingway to switch publishers and come over to Scribner's. Hemingway was tempted, for he had heard disturbing news that Horace Liveright was in financial straights. He had lost $50,000 in a failed theatrical venture that forced him to sell half his business, including the popular Modern Library.[23] Scribner's, on the other hand, was expanding. The firm was actively seeking new talent and was in a position to do a lot toward promoting the work of a young writer. Hemingway wanted to make the move, and he saw

4. Making the Heavyweight Class

"Torrents" as a way to break his Liveright contract. He figured that Liveright would not publish a book that attacked one of its principal authors.

In the first week of December, Hemingway mailed Horace Liveright the manuscript of his parody, and as expected, Liveright turned it down. This left Hemingway free to approach Max Perkins with an offer of the Pamplona novel if Scribner's would publish "Torrents" first. Perkins agreed. Hemingway signed the Scribner's contract, and *The Torrents of Spring* appeared in May.

Anderson had no hint of what was coming. A month earlier, in a letter to Stein, he mentioned seeing Hemingway's story

Sherwood Anderson (© 2010 Georgia O'Keeffe Museum/Artists Rights Society [ARS], New York).

"The Undefeated" in the Paris little magazine *This Quarter*. "It was a beautiful story," Anderson wrote, "beautifully done. Lordy but that man can write."[24] Now, a month later, just on the eve of *Torrents* appearing, Hemingway wrote Anderson trying to explain the intent of his forthcoming book. Anderson thought the communiqué "the most completely patronizing letter I had ever received." He recalled Hemingway stating that the book was something he hated doing because of his personal regard for Anderson,

> but that he had done it in the interest of literature. Literature, I was to understand, was bigger than both of us.
> There was something in the letter that was gigantic. It was a kind of funeral oration delivered over my grave. It was so raw, so pretentious, so patronizing, that it was amusing but I was filled with wonder. Just what I said to him, in return, I don't remember. It was something to the effect that I thought it foolish that, while there was so much to be done in writing, we writers should devote our time to the attempt to kill each other off. In the letter he had used a prize fighting term, speaking of the knockout blow he

had given me, and in my answer I think I did say that I had always thought of myself as a pretty good middle weight and that I doubted his ever being able to make the heavy weight class.

However I can't be sure. I kept no copy of my letter.[25]

Anderson's memory was indeed faulty. He conflated several letters exchanged over a period of months. Hemingway dated his first letter May 21, 1926, from Madrid, where he and Hadley were vacationing. In it Hemingway did not say that he had written *Torrents* in the interest of literature, nor did he claim then to have given Anderson a knockout blow. Anderson was correct, however, in characterizing the letter's tone. It was one of breezy familiarity through which ran a strain of condescension and pugnacity. The letter was particularly striking in tone considering that it was written by a relative upstart of twenty-five to an established author of forty-nine.

Hemingway began his letter by reaffirming his low opinion of *Many Marriages* and *A Story Teller's Story*. He then added, "All I think about the Dark Laughter is in this Torrents book." He wished to emphasize that *Torrents* "is a joke and it isn't meant to be mean, but it is absolutely sincere."

"You see," he said, "I feel that if among ourselves we have to pull our punches, if when a man like yourself who can write very great things writes something that seems to me ... rotten, I ought to tell you so. Because if we have to pull our punches and if when somebody starts to slop they just go on slopping from then on with nothing but encouragement from their contemporaries," nothing comes of it but phony Great American Writers.

Hemingway admitted that his letter was snooty and that his book would seem snooty as well, but that wasn't the way he had meant them to be. "Though I didn't care so much about the book because the book isn't personal and the tougher it is the better." He knew the entire incident could make him look bad "because you had always been swell to me and helped like the devil on the In our time;" now it would appear "I felt an irresistable [sic] need to push you in the face with true writer's gratitude." He assured Anderson that "1 Because you are my friend I would not want to hurt you," but "2 Because you are my friend has nothing to do with writing." He concluded, "Anyway I think you'll think the book is funny — and that's what it is intended to be."[26]

4. Making the Heavyweight Class 59

Anderson was stunned. "I had taken it for granted that we were friends when he went off to Paris," he wrote in his memoirs. "I am told, he attributed what happened to the influence of Scott Fitzgerald, and there is even a story, born in the brain of Hemmy, that, wanting to leave the firm of Boni and Liveright" he had written the parody "figuring that they would not stand for an attack upon me, I being a special little pet of that firm, etc." Anderson doubted that his status with Liveright had anything to do with rejection of Hemingway's manuscript. "If I had ever been a special pet of the Liveright firm I wish someone had let me know of it. I might have got more money from them."[27]

Anderson, of course, did not find *The Torrents of Spring* funny at all. The unwarranted attack staggered him; he felt like he had been suckerpunched. He wrote Hemingway that his book and all his letters for the past two or three years conveyed a similar attitude of condescension: "Damn it man you are so final—so patronizing. You always do speak to me like a master to a pupil. It must be Paris—the literary life. You didn't sound like that when I knew you." Hemingway in his letter had spoken "so fully, tenderly, of giving me a punch. You sound like Uncle Ezra. Come out of it man. I pack a little wallup [sic] myself. I've been middle weight champion. You seem to forget that."[28]

Ernest wrote back in the same jaunty yet pugnacious tone as before. He conceded Anderson the point about having written snooty letters. He wouldn't even try to duck that one, he said, but would take it square on the nose. He still wanted Anderson to know that he had a grand time writing *Torrents* because it was funny and he got five hundred dollars for it. It was also grand that Anderson was the middleweight champion and didn't have a glass jaw, and that he, Ernest, didn't have a glass jaw either, but, he repeated, having made five hundred dollars on *Torrents,* he felt great. Although his previous letter must have sounded especially snooty, all he had meant to say was that he had admired Anderson's work for a long time "and I am now about to attempt to sock you on the jaw and here are my reasons." He signed off in the spirit of a fighter embracing his opponent after a good bout: "Anyway so long and good luck.... Hadley sends you and your wife her best. Best to you always, Ernest Hemingway."[29]

Appalled by Hemingway's manner and his sudden betrayal of friendship, Anderson still checked any urge to retaliate. "I don't have to hit him back," he said privately, "Ernest is such a shut-in, fathead sort of writer that he's going to end up burlesquing himself. And he'll do it a lot better than I could."[30]

Like Anderson, Gertrude Stein did not find *The Torrents of Spring* at all funny. Instead, according to Hemingway, she was "very angry. I had attacked someone that was part of her apparatus." He had criticized "one of her most loyal supporters."[31] That Anderson had also been one of Hemingway's most loyal supporters did not matter. To Stein, loyal support meant a great deal. She expected loyalty between friends. She also believed that the writer and what he creates are indivisible. To lack faith in one is to lack faith in the other. Once that faith, once that loyal support, is broken or violated, the friendship ends.

Stein's initial reaction to Hemingway's burlesque was to defend Anderson's work, but it was only after Anderson "had cracked up as a writer," claimed Ernest, that she began praising him so. It had become much easier for her to defend his failures than it had been to endure his successes.

The quarrel put a sudden strain on Hemingway and Stein's friendship. This strain reached the breaking point when Hemingway showed up unexpectedly one evening at Stein's apartment and created an unpleasant scene in front of guests. Someone who claimed to have been present, remembered years afterward that Hemingway barged in with two strangers, all three of them drunk. "Hi, Gertie," he reportedly exclaimed. "Ran into a couple of your fans at the Dome who wouldn't believe I was a friend of yours so I brought them over to prove it."

"I'm not at home to anyone in your condition," Stein replied, "and don't call me Gertie. Now get out and what's more, stay out!" The three stole off without further trouble.[32] Hemingway and Stein both avoided talking about the incident later, but it resulted in Stein deciding, at the insistence of Alice Toklas, that Hemingway no longer be admitted to 27 rue de Fleurus.

Unaware of the friction that had developed between her husband and Gertrude Stein, Hadley one day stopped by the apartment with her baby for a few minutes' chat as was her custom. "Alice came to the door and she said, 'I'm very sorry. Gertrude can't see you today.' It was just a complete dismissal. And I know of no explanation." Hadley met Stein several times afterward, and she tried to discuss the matter with her husband, but both were "as silent as the grave." Perhaps, she thought, Stein was only jealous of Ernest's growing success. "But I really don't know. I *do* know that everything was fine, our son was her god-son, and all of a sudden something happened. And of course Ernest kept things to himself and I don't know what it was."[33]

Alice felt gratified by the quick turn of events. She had helped run off her most dangerous rival for Gertrude Stein's attention. This had preserved her own position and prevented Gertrude from possibly doing something foolish.[34]

Ernest would normally have been outraged at the brush-off, but he understood all the complicated jealousies and resentments involved. Besides, he had greater problems to deal with just then. His marriage to Hadley seemed to be coming apart. The reason was that he had fallen in love with another woman, Pauline Pfeiffer, a fashion assistant and model for the Paris division of *Vogue* magazine. He fancied himself in love with both women and was in a quandary what to do. Stein's rebuff might have angered him more, too, except for the realization that Gertrude had nothing more to teach him. His novel, published by Scribner's in October 1926, quickly became a best-seller. Although a few critics complained that nothing happened in the book and that the characters were vapid and shallow, the novel received generally favorable reviews. It sold eleven thousand copies within three months of publication and by then was in its fourth printing.

Despite Anderson's doubts some months earlier, Hemingway, at age twenty-six, had made the heavyweight class. From now on he did not need any more tutoring. He did not need Sherwood Anderson or Gertrude Stein. *The Sun Also Rises* placed him ahead in the literary rankings and proved that he could whip either one of them any day of the week.

5

Composition as Explanation

Although her books did not sell, and though she received little money or serious critical attention, Gertrude Stein nevertheless enjoyed a growing international reputation, if only as a literary curiosity. Those who had no intention of reading *Geography and Plays* or *The Making of Americans* still had heard of Gertrude Stein and could repeat "a rose is a rose is a rose is a rose." Interest in the eccentric "mama of dada," as some critics mistakenly dubbed her,[1] grew to such a degree that the English poet and critic Edith Sitwell invited her to lecture at Cambridge University in the spring of 1926. Stein at first demurred. She had never spoken before a large audience, the thought of which terrified her. But at last she accepted, and she and Alice Toklas sailed for England in May.

Harold Acton of Oxford University, learning from Sitwell that Stein was to speak at Cambridge, invited Stein to address the "Ordinary Society" at Oxford, and Stein accepted that invitation also. The lecture at Cambridge went off tolerably well, though Stein suffered initially from stagefright. At Oxford three days later she felt much more relaxed and things went better. Edith Sitwell, looking like some rare, pale, and exotic longnecked bird, and Gertrude Stein, resembling, according to Harold Acton, "a squat Aztec figure in obsidian," were joined on the platform at Oxford by Sitwell's two large brothers, Osbert and Sacheverell, and Alice Toklas, "the gipsy acolyte."

Stein read her lecture, *Composition as Explanation*, "in a friendly American voice that made everybody feel at home." She lulled some in the audi-

5. Composition as Explanation

ence into a near trance with her flat, cadenced sentences and her many repetitions. Not that Stein, with her deep, rich voice and gentle inflections, came across as boring. It was just that hearing her read from her own work was like listening to an incantation; it was like being lowered into a warm bath of words. She began her lecture,

> There is singularly nothing that makes a difference a difference in beginning and in the middle and in ending except that each generation has something different at which they are all looking. By this I mean so simply that anybody knows it that composition is the difference which makes each and all of them then different from other generations and this is what makes everything different otherwise they are all alike and everybody knows it because everybody says it.

She went on to observe:

> The only thing that is different from one time to another is what is seen and what is seen depends upon how everybody is doing everything. This makes the thing we are looking at very different and this makes what those who describe it make of it, it makes a composition, it confuses, it shows, it is, it looks, it likes it as it is, and this makes what is seen as it is seen. Nothing changes from generation to generation except the thing seen and that makes a composition.

Following remarks of a similar nature, Stein became more personal. She spoke of writing in 1905 *Three Lives*, the book in which she created the continuous present:

> After that I did a book called *The Making of Americans* it is a long book about a thousand pages.
> Here again it was all so natural to me and more and more complicatedly a continuous present. A continuous present is a continuous present. I made almost a thousand pages of continuous present.
> Continuous present is one thing and beginning again and again is another thing. These are both things.

The act of composition, she stressed, was a continual beginning again, and eventually she began writing portraits:

> In the meantime to naturally begin I commenced making portraits of anybody and anything. In making these portraits I naturally made a continuous present an including everything and a beginning again and again within a very small thing. That started me into composing anything into one thing. So then naturally it was natural that one thing an enormously long thing was not everything an enormously short thing was also not everything nor was it all of it a continuous present thing nor was it always beginning again. Naturally

> I would then begin again. I would begin again I would naturally begin. I did naturally begin.

A few in the audience took notes, most sat still and listened politely, but an increasing number grew impatient. Following her prepared talk, Gertrude Stein read several of her portraits including one titled "Sitwell Edith Sitwell":

> Introduces have and had introduces have and had and heard.
> Miss Edith Sitwell have and had and heard.

Harold Acton observed Edith Sitwell, seated close to Stein, "trying not to look as embarrassed as she felt."

> Left and right.
> Part two of Part one.
> If she had a ball at all, if she had a ball at all too.

"Sachie looked as if he were swallowing a plum," Acton noted, "and Osbert shifted on his insufficient chair with a vague nervousness in his eyes."[2]

Stein concluded the event by taking questions, some of which, according to Acton, "were burning with indignation." But with her deep, infectious laugh "she answered each question in reassuring motherly tones, patting and soothing the obstreperous with gusty sallies, and everybody joined in her laughter."

All seemed to feel that the trip to England, the Oxford lecture in particular, had been a great success.[3]

Leonard and Virginia Woolf at The Hogarth Press in London soon published *Composition as Explanation*. It formed part of their series "The Hogarth Essays." Ernest Hemingway in November, following his break with Stein, picked up a copy at Shakespeare and Company. After reading the small, thin volume, he felt justified in his belief that Stein had gone to seed as a writer. He set down his thoughts in a parody of Stein's manner:

> It was happy and it was something and we all liked it. There were never any changes made and as it came out was the way it was and people saw that it was a happy living and there was no explaining except simple explaining and the explaining was intelligent and it was something and we all liked it.... It was done best where it was done and afterward it was copied on the typewriter and we all liked it. There were portraits and we were all in them.

5. Composition as Explanation

Then Stein changed. Possibly it was hormonal — the menopause Hemingway came to think. Whatever the reason, she had grown lazy. She was finished as a writer just as their relationship was finished.

> And now it is all over about a very great writer who had stopped writing because she was too lazy to write for other people because writing for other people is very hard because the other people know when the things do not come out right and are failures, at least always some of them do, and that is unpleasant when you are a great writer and brings discomfort and one is not satisfied, but one can eliminate the need for it to mean anything and simply write and sometimes it will mean something and sometimes it will not. Sometimes it will not.

Combining his anger of rejection with the empty feeling of something gone that had once been important, Hemingway concluded his parody with a poem:

> A mean poem. A poem written by a man with a grudge. A poem written by a boy who is envious. A poem written by someone who used to come to dinner. Not a nice poem. A poem that does not mention the Sitwells....
>
> Gertrude Stein was never crazy.
> Gertrude Stein was very lazy.
>
> Now that it is all over perhaps it made a great difference if it was something you cared about.[4]

Hemingway did not publish these remarks. They remained among his private papers during his lifetime. He wrote something else, however, that he sent to Max Perkins, asking the editor to find a market for it. Perkins sent it to the *New Yorker*, a new publication, where it appeared in the 12 February 1927 edition under the title "My Own Life." The short piece, occupying about a page of the magazine, was a broad parody of Frank Harris's recently published *My Life and Loves*. Hemingway did not write parodies simply for the fun of doing so. They served as vehicles to express some personal bitterness or to convey a hostile message. They were Hemingway's own method of composition as explanation. He evidently wrote this piece, like *The Torrents of Spring*, as a public announcement of independence. It was to inform critics and readers that Ernest Hemingway was no longer affiliated in any way with Gertrude Stein.

He divided "My Own Life" into three short parts. The first, titled "How I Broke With John Wilkes Booth," purports to be an interview with Booth following the assassination of President Lincoln. The narrator, supposedly Hemingway, asks Booth why he killed the President since he had paid for his seat. Booth replies that it was a matter of principle and, besides, he did not have time to consider the monetary aspect of the situation. "Still, I think it was a mistake," the narrator tells him.

The last part, titled "How I Broke With My Children" is equally thin. The narrator says that he came home several nights and could not find his children. After several months he received a cablegram from Australia that read, "IT IS USELESS TO TRY AND LOCATE ME YOU OLD STIFF SIGNED YOUR SON JOHN HADLEY NICANOR." Another cablegram arrived from New South Wales stating, "YOU ARE ONLY WASTING TIME LOOKING FOR ME FATHER SIGNED YOUR DAUGHTER PILAR CÉZANNE HEMINGWAY."

Sandwiched between these two sections is the heart of the piece, the segment titled "The True Story of My Break With Gertrude Stein":

> The real story of my break with Gertrude Stein may be interesting. For a long time I had noticed that when I would come to the door of Gertrude Stein's house and ring the bell nobody would answer. Sometimes a window would open and someone would look out and then the window would shut again.

Occasionally a maid answers the door to say that Miss Stein is not in. "I felt, though, that Miss Stein liked me and wanted to see me. So I took to dropping in informally." The fictional Hemingway sometimes drops in for dinner and stays for dessert. At other times he comes for tea.

> "Hemingway, why do you always come here drunk?" she asked me one afternoon.
> "I don't know, Miss Stein," I answered. "Unless it's to see you."
> Another time Miss Stein said, "Hemingway, why do you come here at all?"
> I was at a loss for an answer.
> I tried to talk about literature to Miss Stein. "I am trying to form my style on yours, Miss Stein," I said one rainy afternoon. "I want to write like you, like Henry James, like the Old Testament and —" I added, "like that great Irishman, James Joyce."
> "All you young men are alike," Miss Stein said. Frankly, I was hurt.

The next time the fictional Hemingway tries to visit Miss Stein's apartment, the maid hits him with a bicycle pump.

He returns several more times only to find the door locked. On his last visit it is nailed shut. A snarling bloodhound guards the entrance, and a large sign, written by Miss Stein herself, reads "Keep Out — This Means You!"

> It was then that I broke with Miss Stein. I have never ceased to feel that I did her a great injustice and, needless to say, I have never ceased to regret it.[5]

5. Composition as Explanation

If the *New Yorker* squib was not a masterpiece, at least it got the message out. It could have been much better, but Hemingway had weightier matters to deal with toward the end of 1926. For one thing, there were the growing numbers of people, "demented characters out of my books," who were angry and talking revenge for the manner in which Hemingway depicted them in his fiction, particularly *The Sun Also Rises*. Harold Loeb was supposed to have threatened to shoot Ernest the next time he saw him. Hemingway sent out word that he could be found at a certain brasserie between the hours of two and four on a particular Saturday and Sunday, "and everybody who wished to shoot me," he wrote Fitzgerald, "was to come and do it then or else for Christ sake stop talking about it. No bullets whistled."[6]

Besides being harried by these demented characters out of his books, Hemingway felt more troubled by his break with Gertrude Stein than he cared to admit. He had truly loved her in a way. He had depended on her. She had been his surrogate mother—giving advice and encouragement when he needed it, alternately scolding and praising him. Although it had been necessary to cut her leading strings and make his own way in the literary world, it still hurt to have been turned away from her door. Knowing that Stein had broken off with other friends, often at Alice's insistence, did not help any.

Another thing tormenting him was his impending divorce from Hadley. The two now lived apart, and he felt remorse for the breakup. He could not justify his shabby treatment of his wife, taking up with the more chic, sophisticated, and affluent Pauline, and shouldering Hadley aside in the process. Friends could hardly believe the two were separating. Ernest and Hadley had seemed like such an ideal couple. Bill Bird asked Hemingway why he and Hadley were divorcing and Ernest replied emphatically "because I am a son of a bitch."[7]

Fending off suicidal thoughts during the traumatic ordeal of ending one marriage and beginning another, Hemingway attempted to ease his conscience by signing over to Hadley all present and future royalties from *The Sun Also Rises*. By December things looked brighter. He could write Fitzgerald that he was watching his diet and getting plenty of sleep so he could use his head again. He was through with the suicide stuff. "Have refrained from any half turnings on of the gas or slitting the wrists with sterilized safety razor blades," he told Scott. "Am continuing my life in original role of son of a bitch sans peur et sans rapproche."[8]

Yet he had not completely left all worries behind as 1926 drew to a close, for he learned just before Christmas that Sherwood Anderson had arrived in Paris.

Anderson, during his brief stay in the French capital, called several times on Gertrude Stein, the two enjoying each other's company as much as ever. Gertrude and Alice arranged a special Christmas party for Sherwood's benefit. During his visits, Anderson talked with Stein about many things. They discovered a mutual admiration for Ulysses S. Grant and spoke of collaborating on a life of the Civil War general and president. Neither cared much about Lincoln.

One day Anderson showed up at the apartment and noticed something different about the way Gertrude looked. Gone was the mass of thick dark hair pushed up on top of her head. The night before, she had Alice start clipping off her hair until it got down to about half an inch long all over. With some trepidation, Alice asked Anderson what he thought. "I like it," he said; "it makes her look like a monk."[9]

During one of these afternoon get-togethers, the subject of Hemingway arose. Stein and Anderson joked about what a good pupil he had been, how much both had taught him, and how quickly he had learned. Anderson still felt puzzled by Hemingway's change of character, how in Chicago he had been so pleasant and even deferential only to turn belligerent for no good reason that Anderson could see. Stein explained that Hemingway could not stand the thought of Anderson having written "I'm a Fool" and "I Want to Know Why," two successful sports stories. "She suggested," said Anderson, "that he had, in his own mind, staked out the whole field of sports for himself. He could not bear, she said, having any one else write of sports."[10]

Hemingway avoided Anderson as long as he could. Yet it would have appeared cowardly to dodge him altogether, so Ernest finally stopped by his hotel on Christmas Eve, shortly before Anderson was to leave for the States. Both spent two pleasant afternoons together Ernest informed Max Perkins with evident relief. Anderson was not angry about *Torrents* and they both had a good time.[11]

Anderson, in his *Memoirs*, recounted their final meeting differently. Hemingway, according to him, avoided any contact until Anderson's last day in Paris. As Anderson sat in his room, having finished packing, there

5. Composition as Explanation

came a loud knock at the door. It was Ernest. "How about a drink?" he asked.

Anderson followed him downstairs and across the street to a small bar.

"What will you have?"

"Beer," Anderson replied. "And you?"

"Beer."

The beers arrived and Hemingway said, "Well, here's how."

"Here's how."

After downing his beer, Hemingway put down his glass, turned, and quickly walked off. "It was the sum of what happened between us after our having known each other well in Chicago, after what I had thought of as an old friendship, and, in fancy, I can still see the man, after the 'here's how' and after the beer had been gulped, as he hurried away."[12]

Which story is more accurate, Hemingway's or Anderson's, is difficult to say. Both men excelled in shaping true incidents to fit artistic intentions. Hemingway's version may claim the advantage for no other reason than it was set down shortly after the meeting took place. Anderson's account reads more like the dramatic denouement of a story, the final scene in which a young man turns his back on one to whom he owes much, walking out of the person's life without a single expression of gratitude or word of friendship.

Several factors contributed to the breach between Gertrude Stein and Hemingway. One was Alice Toklas's personal jealousy. She maintained a close proprietary watchfulness over Stein, becoming distrustful and antagonistic toward those who gained too much of Gertrude's affections. When she saw Gertrude and Hemingway getting too chummy, "Alice moved skillfully, catlike, to separate them," an acquaintance observed.[13]

Another factor was Hemingway's intense competitiveness and a growing tendency as he got more successful to distance himself from those who had helped him. This became one of his most noticeable and least attractive features. Donald Ogden Stewart, on whom most of the character Bill Gorton in *The Sun Also Rises* was based, recalled that once Hemingway began to love you, "or the minute he began to have some sort of an obligation to you of love or friendship or something, then is when he had to kill you. Then you were too close to something that he was protecting. He, one-by-one, knocked off the best friendships he ever had. He did it with Scott; he did it with Dos Passos — with everybody. I think it was a psychological fear he had that you might ask something from him. He didn't want to be overdrawn at your bank."[14] Except for Ezra Pound, Hemingway eventually quarreled with all his principal literary friends.

With Stein he felt particularly vulnerable. Her quick eye and sharp tongue allowed him little room to posture. Harold Acton, after leaving Oxford and coming to Paris in the winter of 1926, sometimes visited Stein at her studio and there observed other visitors. "Hemingway called now and then in clumsy homage," Acton reported, "but he was afraid of her. Her eye saw through his matador poses."[15]

Finally, contributing to the break, was Gertrude Stein's sense of betrayal, the feeling that Hemingway had violated her friendship and that of Anderson. A thread of professional jealousy ran around the edge of this sense of betrayal. The master seldom rejoices at heart to be overtaken and surpassed by the pupil, especially when the master remains convinced of her own superior genius. But as she and Picasso sometimes lamented, those who derive get noticed before those who originate. This is why Stein felt Hemingway probably would not last as a writer — he was too derivative and conventional — "he looks like a modern," she told Anderson, "and he smells of the museums."[16]

— 6 —

Old Faces and New

"Alice Toklas," said Gertrude Stein, "always liked a poem that used to go, Give me new faces new faces new faces I have seen the old ones and just then well there did not seem any reason why one should see the old ones any more."[1] Consequently, Alice set out to get rid of nearly all the young men (about half a dozen at the time) who frequented the studio. One of them, Bravig Imbs, a young writer, received a surprise phone call one day from Miss Toklas. Miss Gertrude Stein, she said, had asked her to inform Imbs that a plan he announced the previous evening of vacationing with his wife and baby in the region near Belley, where Stein and Toklas liked to spend their summers, was a colossal impertinence. Neither she nor Miss Stein ever wished to see Imbs and his wife again.

Imbs tried to explain that there must be some misunderstanding; he and his wife were not attempting to impose on the two women in their summer retreat. But Alice would hear none of it. "There's no use arguing or apologizing," she told Imbs; "your pretension is unpardonable. You must not come to the house or write, for neither visit nor letter will be accepted. We want never to see you again." And she hung up.

Imbs felt convinced that this was entirely Alice's doing and that Gertrude had simply gone along with it. Alice "was tired of all the young men who came to the studio," Imbs said later; "she wanted new faces, and above all she wanted Gertrude to give up living in Paris and spend more time in the country. Alice would gladly have lived in the country all year round."[2]

One of the few old faces allowed to remain was that of young Virgil Thomson, the twenty-nine-year-old American composer of modern music, then residing in Paris. He attended the Christmas party gotten up primarily in honor of Sherwood Anderson where there was a Christmas tree, the singing of carols, and a big cake decorated with ribbon and candles. Like most of the young men entering Gertrude Stein's apartment for the first time, Thomson felt apprehensive: "I saw the two old ladies sitting by the fire; they were waiting, and I couldn't help thinking of the line: 'Will you come into my parlour?' said the spider to the fly."[3]

Thomson had long been captivated by Stein's writing. While a student at Harvard, he became addicted, he said, to *Tender Buttons* and *Geography and Plays*. He hoped now, by setting some of Stein's text to music, "to break, crack open, and solve for all time," everything related to "English musical declamation." Stein's work seemed ideally suited to his purpose. "With meanings already abstracted, or absent, or so multiplied that choice among them was impossible, there was no temptation toward tonal illustration, say, of birdie babbling by the brook or heavy heavy hangs my heart. You could make a setting for sound and syntax only, then add, if needed, an accompaniment equally functional."[4]

His first venture was a score for Stein's "Susie Asado," set for voice and piano, which he carried to the rue de Fleurus on New Year's Day, 1927. Told that Miss Stein and Miss Toklas were out (actually they were exhausted from the week's holiday festivities and were denying themselves to everyone), Thomson left his score and departed. He soon received a note from Stein saying that she liked the looks of his piece and thought of framing it. Stein had never cultivated a taste for music and really did not much care for it. Alice, on the other hand, who had studied music in college, saw things in Thomson's work that intrigued her. She wanted to hear it played, but hearing it was not essential for Gertrude. She told Thomson, "I am completely satisfied with its looks."[5]

Stein was nevertheless flattered by Thomson's gesture, and the young composer quickly became a frequent guest at the apartment. Thomson set other short Stein pieces to music, and soon he began urging her to write him the libretto for an opera. The idea appealed to her. Thomson suggested the theme of the artist's working life, the life both were living. He also proposed that since all good things come in pairs — Joyce and Stein, Picasso and Braque, Protestants and Catholics, Christians and Jews, Harvard and Yale, Gimbel's and Macy's — the opera should project a dualistic view. This would allow him to have male and female leads around whom he could work up second leads and choruses. Thomson wanted to follow the structure of classical Italian opera, using recitatives, arias, and set pieces, and he further wished to observe the eighteenth century *opera seria* convention of dealing with a serious mythological subject leading to a tragic conclusion.

Gertrude Stein liked American history and considered doing something on George Washington, but Thomson thought that impractical — eighteenth century costumes made everyone look alike. Stein then considered saints. She had always liked saints, especially Spanish and Italian ones. "I think it should be late eighteenth-century or early nineteenth-century saints," she wrote Thomson. "Four saints in three acts. And others. Make it pastoral. In hills and gardens. All four and then additions. We must invent them."[6]

Gertrude Stein and Virgil Thomson, 1932 (Beinecke Rare Book and Manuscript Library, Yale University).

She finally chose two Spanish saints, Therese and Ignatius, as her principal characters, the theme of her text being the religious life, "peace between the sexes, community of faith, the production of miracles."[7] Gertrude Stein later said that she wrote the opera, not as a story, but as a Spanish landscape that is meant to be sung. She added, "I also wanted it to have the movement of nuns very busy and in continuous movement but placid as a landscape has to be because after all the life in a convent is the life of a landscape."[8] When Stein finished work in mid–July, she had more than twenty saints in four acts, though she retained the title *Four Saints in Three Acts*.

Thomson began composing in November, not altering, deleting, or adding to, a word of Stein's text. Even her stage directions he set to music. After completing the first act, he thought the piece showed great vitality in both words and music. He wondered though how people would respond to something so steeped in Anglican chant, "running from Gilbert and Sullivan to Morning Prayer and back."[9]

With the entire score finished by the summer of 1928, all that remained was finding someone to put up money to stage the piece; but based on past experience, with manuscripts piling up in her armoire, Stein held out no great hopes. At any rate, finding a producer and obtaining financial backing were Thomson's responsibilities.

During the period that Stein and Thomson collaborated on their opera, Ernest Hemingway moved ahead in his own life and career, further distancing himself from his former mentors. Ezra Pound spoke of being "somewhat contented to see," in looking at his recent work, "that Gertie Stein is losing her hold on what we used a few years ago to call 'the younger generation.'"[10] Pound also remarked, after reading an Anderson short story in the *American Mercury*, "that you *haven't* done him any good, or 'destroyed' anything. Not unless that tale was writ. before The Torrents."[11]

Based on the success of Hemingway's first novel and his collection of stories, various magazine and book publishers besieged the twenty-seven-year-old author for articles, essays, stories — anything, in fact, he cared to submit. The *Atlantic Monthly*, the magazine Gertrude Stein once told him he was not good enough to be published in, accepted his story "Fifty Grand." *Harper's* offered to serialize his next novel. Oxford University Press asked for a collection of essays. Virgil Thomson wrote him in March requesting a story for *Larus the Celestial Visitor*. This was a small literary magazine, published in Lynn, Massachusetts, and edited, said Thomson in his letter, by "a young poet of my acquaintance, devoted admirer of your stories."[12] But as the young editor could pay only thirty-three cents for every one hundred words, Hemingway felt the proposition not worth considering.

More enticing was an offer from *Vanity Fair* of two hundred dollars for an article on Spain. Hemingway felt that he could knock that off without much trouble, yet once he started writing, he found that he really had little to say. The more he wrote, the more he got bogged down in the shallow, flippant humor that characterized his piece in the *New Yorker* several months earlier. In a passage where he mentioned Spanish painters, he got in a dig at Gertrude Stein. He wrote that Juan Gris and Pablo Picasso were both capable and intelligent fellows who would go a long way in the painting game if they stuck to it. "Juan Gris is sad and Pablo Picasso is glad. Gris is full of dark thoughts. Juan Gris is a gris is a gris is a gris. Is a Gris? I learned to write this way about painters from Gertrude Stein."[13] But finally he abandoned the whole thing. The piece was just too flimsy. He wisely put it aside and forgot about it.

His divorce from Hadley became final on April 14, 1927. Hadley was to receive all royalties from *The Sun Also Rises* as previously arranged, and she was to get custody of their child. Once these matters were settled, Hemingway married Pauline Pfeiffer in a Catholic ceremony in a chapel of St. Honoré d'Eylau on May 10, the couple moving into a pleasant apartment at 6 rue Férou, just up from the Luxembourg Gardens and a short distance from the rue de Fleurus.

In September Ernest began work on a novel about the adventures of a professional revolutionist and his young boy. It explored the relationship between father and son and highlighted the boy's initiation into the difficult realities of life. Hemingway also finished putting together a collection of new stories, a volume Scribner's published in October under the title *Men Without Women*. The stories sold well, but the novel gave Hemingway more trouble the further he got into it.

Despite the good feeling he got when the writing went well, these days he often felt stale, restless, and out of sorts. It showed in his writing. He sent Pound the draft of a new story to look at, and Pound did not like what he saw. "I don't think it wd. be any kindness," Pound wrote him, "if one wuz trainin a man for a race to fake the time on him and tell him he wuz doing 100 yds. in 9 flat, when his time wuz 11½. Wd. merely lead to his thinkin' he cd. win easy." Pound had to be honest. After all, he said, the job of an editor is to edit — in other words, keep a man from rushing into a royal audience with his fly unbuttoned. "I think you are more intelligent than this mss," Pound said. "As you know, I think you are intelligent some times, and a damn fool others (not therein differing from man, woman, or any other animal.) Anyhow. IF you can improve this, DO. Goddamn it, DO improve it."[14]

Attending six-day bicycle races in Berlin and the annual festival in

Pamplona did little to rally Hemingway's spirits. Paris itself had lost its savor now that he was well-known and relatively prosperous. He avoided the old haunts, not only due to their associations with Hadley and their former life together, but also because the places themselves had changed. Post-war prosperity now attracted waves of mostly American tourists, who filled the Left Bank cafés where he used to sit alone and write or sometimes drink with friends. Sprinkled among these tourists were gossip columnists looking to catch sight of a Joyce or a Picasso or a Hemingway. Besides, the people he used to associate with — aside from those still angry with him for putting them in his books — were off doing other things: Ol' Ez had moved to Italy; Fitz was in the States whoring for movie studios in Hollywood; McAlmon was often drunk and usually unpleasant; and Stein was loading her armoire with more works that went unpublished.

Hemingway confided to Max Perkins that he should have returned to America two years earlier. He was through with Europe then and had planned to go, but he had stuck around. He felt guilty at not using the past two years more profitably, and he thanked Perkins for not pressuring him to write. He explained that he had busted up his life badly and wasted much time. He had gone through a rough period and messed up his head, and it took a long time to recover. Still, no matter how messed up you got, he told Perkins, you "must never let anyone know even that you were away or let the pack know you were wounded."[15]

Toward the end of February 1928, Gertrude Stein sent Hemingway a note informing him that an old friend of hers, Mildred Aldrich, a woman Hemingway knew and liked, had died the previous week. Letting Ernest know was a considerate gesture on Gertrude's part. Pauline acknowledged receipt of the message on February 27, and, in a return show of good-will, invited Miss Stein and Miss Toklas to lunch on the 29th. The two women accepted just as they had accepted the first Mrs. Hemingway's invitation nearly six years earlier.

The meeting proved cordial, if not affectionate. Hemingway did not like Stein's new close-cropped appearance. Now she really did look like a Roman emperor as people said, "and that was fine," thought Hemingway, "if you liked your women to look like Roman emperors." He certainly did not. Still there was Picasso's portrait showing her abundant dark hair, "and I could remember her when she looked like a woman from Friuli."

Stein cutting her hair took on symbolic meaning for Hemingway, who had something of a fetish for women's hair. It went beyond thinking Italian peasant women more sexually appealing than Roman emperors. The act, Hemingway thought, marked a major turning point in Stein's life. It coincided with the menopause and showed a complete abandonment of anything female. It seemed an unambiguous statement of her sexual alignment. It further corresponded to a change in her approach to writing. She had grown more careless and lazy than ever. Finally, Hemingway decided, it heralded a change in her attitude toward friends. She now seemingly went out of her way to pick quarrels, suddenly dropping those she quarreled with, offering them no explanations. But Hemingway also knew that Alice Toklas had a lot to do with that.

Yet for now he and Gertrude were again on speaking terms. And it was just as well. He was tired of the bitterness and the recriminations, tired of quarreling with people in general. He later wrote that he made friends again with Stein so as not to be stuffy or righteous: "But I could never make friends again truly, neither in my heart nor in my head. When you cannot make friends any more in your head is the worst. But it was more complicated than that."[16]

Hemingway finally gave up on his revolutionist novel. It simply was not going anywhere. It lacked focus, and he realized that he did not know enough about a revolutionist's activities to make what he wrote convincing. Almost immediately he began another novel, this one dealing with the war. The subject allowed him to draw upon people and places he knew and provided him the opportunity to incorporate some of his own war experiences. He grew eager to return to the States and really get down to work. He needed someplace where he did not have so many distractions. Pauline was pregnant, the child due sometime in June, and that was another reason to return home. They planned to settle for a time in Key West, Florida, where he would have the seclusion he needed to write and the opportunity to try deep sea fishing, a new experience for him.

The couple sailed for Havana on the 17th of March, arriving in Key West early in April. The next eight months, however, did not turn out to be a time of peace and solitude as he had expected. Instead it became a period of heightened activity — fishing for tarpon in the Gulf Stream and seeing Pauline through the difficult birth of their son Patrick by caesarian section; visiting his wife's family in Arkansas and his own family in Illinois; running up to New York City to confer with Max Perkins and pick up Bumby for a prolonged visit; racing back to Illinois on news that his father had committed suicide by shooting himself in the head; driving out to Wyoming for a month of hunting; and finally returning to Key West in time for Christmas. Yet in the midst of this commotion, Ernest managed to set aside a portion of nearly every day to write, so that by January he had completed the first draft of his novel, all except the ending, which he could not get right. Max Perkins came down to Key West for a visit in February and carried the typescript of the novel back to New York with him.

Having the bulk of the novel off his hands, and with his conscience lighter as a result, Ernest and his wife, with his sons Bumby and Patrick, returned to Europe early in May 1929. They had not given up their apartment at 6 rue Férou, but it seemed more exposed to distractions than before. The Fitzgeralds had returned to Paris in April and taken a flat just two blocks away. Hemingway avoided Scott as much as possible, for he soon had proofs of his book to correct and the conclusion to rewrite, and he could not afford to be disturbed. Besides, he wanted enough time to attend the annual festival in Pamplona and to get in some fishing.

Once Perkins had the corrected proofs and the revised ending, he quickly got the book on the market. Scribner's published *A Farewell to Arms* on September 27, Hemingway receiving a copy October 3. Two weeks later it went on display in the window of Shakespeare and Company.

By mid-October, three weeks after publication, *A Farewell to Arms* had sold 28,000 copies and was clearly a best-seller. Gertrude Stein and Alice Toklas were then in Bilignin getting ready to return to Paris for the winter months. Before leaving, Stein wrote a letter to a friend in which she mentioned Hemingway's new novel, asking for a copy, and comparing herself to the author. "I am the very highest thing in highbrow but not solemn," she said. "Now Hemingway is it he is solemn powerful and successful. I neither look nor am solemn."[17]

After getting situated once again in her Paris apartment, Stein resumed her evening walks around the city. She loved to stroll about Paris, going up one street and down another, stopping to talk with people when she got the chance. She now had a large white French poodle named Basket that accompanied her. People often stopped to look at the dog and remark that it was so white it looked like a lamb. Gertrude would talk to these people, questioning them about their work and hearing about their families. "I seem always to be doing the talking when I am anywhere," she said, "but in spite of that I do listen. I always listen. I always have listened. I always have listened to the way everybody has to tell what they have to say."[18] In walking around the city, talking with people, and listening to what they had to say, Paris was always fascinating, always different. "I never get used to it and I like to wander with Basket all about it."[19] Gertrude and the dog would go out every evening and be gone for several hours.

"Don't you come home with Hemingway on your arm," Alice would say as the two were leaving. She had learned that Hemingway was in town, and she knew how much Gertrude always enjoyed talking with him. As luck would have it, her apprehensions came true. "Sure enough one day she did come back bringing him with her."[20] The two had met on the street by chance, exchanged pleasantries, and found themselves getting on well. Hemingway was feeling unusually placid and non-confrontational. After finishing a big book, he usually entered a postpartum phase in which he felt emotionally drained.

Back at Stein's apartment, with the Picassos and Matisses on the walls, it almost seemed like old times. The two talked about Fitzgerald being in town. Stein said that of all the writers of the post-war generation, Scott possessed the most talent, and she would like to see him again. She had not yet read Ernest's new book, but still she scolded him for being conventional. "Hemingway," she said, "after all you are ninety percent Rotarian."

"Can't you make it eighty percent?" he asked.

"No," she replied, "I can't."

Alice was not pleased with the reconciliation. Jealous that Gertrude still found Ernest wonderful and his company engaging, she argued in private that Hemingway was a fake. His great display of virility was nothing but a show to cover up an insecure and duplicitous nature. Yet no matter what she said, Gertrude replied, "yes I know but I have a weakness for Hemingway."[21]

Within several days of their chance meeting, Gertrude Stein sent

Hemingway a note inviting him to her apartment on Wednesday evening about nine and asking him to bring Fitzgerald. Ernest felt apprehensive about facing Stein with only Scott present, so he telephoned Allen Tate, a young poet and critic whom he had recently met and who occasionally turned up at Stein's soirées. He asked Tate to meet him right away at the café Deux Magots where they could talk. When Tate arrived a few minutes late, Hemingway was already there, seated outside on the terrace keeping warm over a brazier. He seemed unusually taciturn. Handing Tate a copy of the *Paris Herald* and pointing to a picture on the front page showing President Hoover seated in a boat fishing, Hemingway said, "This fellow will never do anything for the likes of you and me." After a long silence he further remarked, "Don't make too much love while you're young; save up some for middle age." Tate wondered if this was all Hemingway had called him down to say or if he was just having trouble getting to the point. Finally Ernest said, "Gertrude has taken me back into favor. I'm taking Pauline to rue de Fleurus this evening, and I want other people to be there. You and Caroline [Tate's wife], along with the Fitzgeralds and the [John Peale] Bishops; they've all agreed to come."[22]

That night, the Tates, the Fitzgeralds, Bishop (without his wife), and the Hemingways walked over to Stein's together. When they arrived, Alice Toklas steered the women off to another part of the room for some chocolate cake and domestic chitchat, while Stein, from her low overstuffed armchair, addressed the men, all seated before her in a half circle. Also included in the small assembly were Ford Madox Ford and Stein's longtime friend Bernard Faÿ. Tate recalled that Hemingway sat as far back in the group as possible. Stein began to lecture on American literature. She claimed that America's true genius lay in abstraction. Emerson was a forerunner, followed, in the abstract design of his work, by Henry James, and culminating, as one might expect, in herself.

The entire evening seemed awkward and tense — even bizarre. Gertrude Stein pressed hard to maintain her position of literary authority over those present, some of them former protégés who had become peers. Scott was not so much the challenge. A groveling insecurity rendered him more pathetic than intimidating. But Hemingway projected an aura of superiority made all the more palpable by a half-hearted attempt to conceal it. At the evening's close, as the Hemingway entourage walked back toward the Luxembourg Gardens, Scott exclaimed, "I have seen Shelley plain."[23]

6. Old Faces and New

He thought Stein absolutely wonderful, but Tate was less impressed. He really couldn't stand her. Hemingway apparently kept his thoughts to himself. And it was only then that Tate, walking down the rue de Fleurus, wet from recent rain, suddenly realized that Gertrude Stein and Hemingway had not exchanged a single word the entire evening.

Stein, not long afterward, wrote a short cryptic piece titled "Evidence" in which the first two parts record her reactions to the Wednesday evening meeting and to Hemingway in particular. Although the entire work is difficult to understand, one picks up words and phrases that seem connected to the evening's events:

> Herman [Fitzgerald] and Ernest were sitting where they were willing to be sitting. As they were waiting they met with a disappointment all of a sudden. Their wives had been women. If their wives had been women they would not have been a disappointment or anything.[24]

Alice Toklas, in her book *What is Remembered*, records what appears to be a subsequent meeting, a more relaxed gathering, in which the only guests were Hemingway and Fitzgerald. By the time of this second meeting, both Gertrude and Alice had read *A Farewell to Arms*, and Ernest was eager to hear what Stein thought of it. She explained to him that some parts were less successful than others — the parts where he relied on memory instead of invention. She again praised Fitzgerald's work, and when Scott came up to join them, she remarked that Scott had a blazing furnace of talent whereas Ernest had a small flame — meaning that Hemingway had to work harder to achieve his effects. Noticing that Hemingway appeared quiet and subdued, Stein chided him for having no vitality.

Fitzgerald talked with Alice Toklas and asked her what she thought of Hemingway's book. When she grudgingly admitted to liking parts of it, Scott urged her to tell Ernest. She protested, "Oh no, I don't want to. I'll speak to him about it when I'm alone with him."

"Well you go on and tell him," Scott insisted; "he'll be pleased." He then called out, "Hem, come here and listen to what she has to say about your book."

When Hemingway came over, Alice said, "I think the retreat from Caporetto is *excellent*: it's *real*, it's *true*, it's *lively*. And I like that."[25]

The following day, Scott, who frequently construed compliments as backhanded criticisms, sent Hemingway a note. In it he fretted about what he took to be Gertrude Stein's slighting remarks the night before in comparing his works to Ernest's. He also thought Hemingway might feel hurt at Gertrude scolding him for having no vitality, and he cautioned Ernest not to worry about it.

Hemingway wrote back to assure Fitzgerald that Stein's remarks about Scott's writing had been sincere compliments, not negative criticisms. She had actually been praising him profusely when Scott came up. And she hadn't been comparing their writings. She was simply pointing out that their respective talents were of different types. Then to keep from praising Scott to his face and disparaging Ernest, she said their creative flames were of different qualities. "If you would have pressed her she would have told you to a direct question that she believes yours a better quality than mine."

It was all nonsense anyway, said Ernest. He liked for Gertrude to chew him out because it kept his opinion of himself really low. She had told him she liked the book, but what he really wanted to hear was what she didn't like. "She thinks the parts that fail are where I remember visually rather than make up," but he had heard all that before. He had expected her to say that the entire book was rubbish, and he would have preferred to hear that because it was such a great incentive to work. Her comment about his lack of vitality was rubbish as well, and he hadn't worried about it at all. "I don't worry — Who has vitality in Paris? People don't write with vitality — they write with their heads." When he was in great shape, he didn't feel like writing. He felt too good.

Hemingway's final advice to Scott: "Why worry? When they bawl you out ride with the punches."[26]

The second meeting that October night in 1929, the month the New York stock market crashed, was the last time Stein, Hemingway, and Fitzgerald would be together. Stein and Hemingway met on other occasions during the ensuing weeks before the year and decade ended, and Scott came to dinner with Ernest and Pauline on December 9. During this visit, Fitzgerald talked about Robert McAlmon being in New York where he was trying to interest Max Perkins in publishing one of his books. He was drinking a lot and spreading malicious stories about people as he often did when he was drunk. McAlmon had once told Hemingway that Scott was a homosexual. "I told him he was a liar and a damned fool," Hemingway recalled. "Frankly I think he is crazy."[27] Now McAlmon was in New York telling Perkins and others that Hemingway was a homosexual

F. Scott Fitzgerald (courtesy George Eastman House, International Museum of Photography and Film © Nickolas Muray Photo Archives).

and that Pauline was a lesbian. He said that Ernest had a "suppressed desire" for him, McAlmon, and that Hemingway had beaten Hadley during her pregnancy, causing her to deliver Bumby prematurely.

Ernest and Pauline sat for an hour listening to Fitzgerald recount McAlmon's slanders. Pauline finally said to her husband that it was his own fault for associating with such swine, and Ernest agreed. There would be no satisfaction in beating up McAlmon, he said, though he should have done it years earlier and would have if McAlmon weren't so pitiful. But he would have to go through with it now because physical correction was the only thing such people understood. They had no moral feelings to hurt.[28]

Apparently some of McAlmon's stories had reached Gertrude Stein. The last time she spoke with Hemingway before he and his wife sailed for Key West, she seemed particularly aggressive. She accused Ernest of having killed off many of his rivals and put them under the sod. "I never seriously killed anybody but one man," Hemingway lied, "and he was a bad man, and he deserved it, but if I killed anybody else I did it unknowingly, and so I am not responsible."[29] Stein then told him that she had heard of an incident proving conclusively that he was homosexual. She refused to say what it was, only that it was very credible. Formerly she had been against male homosexuality. Now she believed that homosexuals of both genders possessed inherently greater creative sensibilities. To prove her case, she carefully ticked off for Hemingway the names of male homosexuals who had contributed substantially to the arts. Stein had also been toying with the notion that Jews and Spaniards possessed unique creative gifts, she and Picasso being notable examples. Hemingway, who was neither Jew nor Spaniard, did not fit this theory, so she might have concluded that he must really be, perhaps unconsciously, homosexual, his great displays of masculinity, as Alice contended, being attempts to disguise the fact.

Hemingway felt more convinced than ever that the menopause had made Stein erratic and peculiar. She had grown increasingly more quarrelsome and resentful. He had been out in the world for a long time and was familiar with things like jealousy and slander. The kinds of stories Stein claimed to have heard, and that McAlmon was spreading, made him sore as hell when he first learned about them, but they soon die out, he told himself, if they're not true. He wasn't going to let such things disturb him unduly. It would be good, though, to get away from Paris and back to Key West, Florida.

Part II
Taking Patches of Skin Off

— 7 —

Poor Old Papa

By the early thirties, Paris had changed significantly from what it had been following the war. This was only natural Gertrude Stein said, yet the changes were mostly for the worse. Paris had become less Paris. The city was more peaceful but not so interesting. There were a lot young people around, but they seemed pretty old; that is, nothing really inspired them or anyone else for that matter.[1] Still, she and Alice were having "a nice peaceable time," she wrote to an acquaintance, "having really quarreled for keeps with all our young friends."[2]

Gertrude and Alice liked to spend the spring and summer months in the south of France. For years they stayed at the Hotel Pernollet in Belley, a town of five thousand inhabitants, situated three hundred seventy miles southeast of Paris. Appropriately named, Belley was the birthplace of the celebrated philosopher gourmet Jean Brillat-Savarin. Stein said that she and Alice liked simple living and good eating, and Belley supplied both.

In 1929 Gertrude Stein secured a lease on a seventeenth century manor house in the nearby farming hamlet of Bilignin, about a mile from Belley. The house, reached by a small country road, was spacious, looked out over a wide green valley, and contained furniture that once belonged to Brillat-Savarin. Next to the house lay a plot of land where Alice grew the fruits and vegetables that went into the excellent meals she prepared. The garden yielded more food than both could eat, so Alice canned, preserved, and made into liqueurs all that she was able. The rest she harvested just before returning to Paris, usually sometime in October, and had the produce crated and shipped home for use during the winter.

Gertrude Stein spent most of her time at Bilignin reading murder mysteries, taking long walks with the dog, talking to farmers and peasants, and writing. Despite the general public's lack of enthusiasm for her work, many people, including publishers, urged her to write her autobiography, but she always dismissed the notion. "No," she said emphatically. "I am not interested in autobiography messages experiments. I am interested in literature and I happen to be the first American since Whitman who is making literature."[3] She kidded Alice, though, saying that Alice should write an autobiography. Gertrude proposed several titles: "My Twenty-five Years With Gertrude Stein," "My Life With the Great," and "Wives of Geniuses I Have Sat With." Alice admitted to being a pretty good housekeeper, gardener, needlewoman, secretary, editor, and vet, but she didn't see how she had time enough to be a pretty good author as well. Gertrude finally said to Alice one day, "It does not look to me as if you were ever going to write that autobiography. You know what I am going to do? I am going to write it for you."[4] The result was *The Autobiography of Alice B. Toklas*, written in six weeks at Bilignin by Gertrude Stein.

Shifting the narrator's point-of-view from herself to Toklas was not an attempt to hide the author's identity; Stein explained how she came to write the book in the final paragraphs. Instead, she saw this as a fascinating experiment — writing autobiography from another's perspective. In doing so, she put aside her own cryptic, convoluted, repetitious style and adopted Alice's mannerisms, speech patterns, and modes of thought. Upon completing the manuscript, she sent it to her agent in Paris. He quickly sold it to the American publishers Harcourt and Brace. Before the book appeared, portions were to be serialized in the *Atlantic Monthly*, a circumstance that fulfilled a long-held ambition and brought the fifty-nine-year-old Gertrude Stein much satisfaction.

Ernest Hemingway's next book was also non-fiction — an American aficionado's look at Spanish bullfighting. As early as April 1929 Hemingway told Max Perkins that he hoped one day to do a serious study of the bull ring, something along the lines of Charles M. Doughty's *Travels in Arabia Deserta*. The book would contain wonderful pictures and would not be just a history and textbook, or an apologia for bullfighting, "but instead, if possible, bull fighting its-self."[5]

Hemingway worked diligently from the spring of 1930 until January 1932, Scribner's publishing *Death in the Afternoon* on September 23. The book described the author's initiation into the *corrida de torros* and analyzed his initial reactions to the spectacle. It explained the terminology of bullfighting and the equipment used, examined how fighting bulls were raised and what characteristics distinguished the best. It discussed the three stages of the *corrida*, defining the roles of banderilleros and picadors, and compared the techniques, merits, and shortcomings of matadors past and present. Hemingway carefully emphasized that bullfighting was not a sport in the Anglo-Saxon sense of the word, but a tragedy, a ritual representation of life and death. The book concluded with pictures of bulls and bullfighters, an explanatory glossary of terms and phrases used in bullfighting, and three appendices. The opening page mentioned Gertrude Stein, telling about the time in Paris she talked of bullfights and showed Hemingway pictures "of herself and Alice Toklas sitting in the first row of the wooden barreras at the bull ring at Valencia with Joselito and his brother Gallo below." It was a benign reference, showing no animosity or tenderness one way or the other.

Hemingway was now thirty-three years old and entered upon the main sequence of his literary career. His father's suicide three years earlier had been a defining event in his life. Whether rightly or wrongly, he came to view his father as having been a coward, as having been too weak in character to stand up to Grace Hall Hemingway's stronger, more ambitious will. Ernest began to understand what he had long intuitively felt—that ambition in women meant trouble. It made them a threat. It made them dangerous and malicious adversaries. It turned them into domineering, self-centered harridans. He intended to avoid, if possible, his father's failings in this regard, and he would certainly be wary of ambitious women like his mother, whom he designated an "all American bitch."[6]

Enjoying his current successes, he and his wife bought a comfortable two-story house in Key West, and Ernest planned to buy a large, custom-made fishing boat in which to cruise the Gulf Stream looking for tarpon, barracuda, and marlin. Pauline gave birth to another son, Gregory, delivered, like the last, by caesarian section. And in December 1932, at the Criterion Theater in New York City, Paramount Pictures premiered the movie *A Farewell to Arms* starring Helen Hayes, Gary Cooper, and Adolphe Menjou. Hemingway despised the film for the way it distorted his book, but the picture's success underscored his popularity as a writer. No longer the challenger, but the reigning champion of American letters, he had begun to experience all the fame, prosperity, and vexations that accompanied the title.

A major vexation was the lukewarm reviews *Death in the Afternoon* received. Critics acknowledged Hemingway's well-deserved literary stature and his credibility as an expert on bullfighting, yet they found a variety of faults in his latest work. One critic claimed that Hemingway's "extremely masculine style" barely saved readers from drowning in a flood of technicalities. Moreover, "Mr. Hemingway is guilty of the grievous sin of writing sentences which have to be read two or three times before the meaning is clear." This corresponded stylistically to "the later stages of Henry James."[7] Another reviewer thought *Death in the Afternoon* contained some of the author's best writing, though the volume was still "a strange book, childish, here and there, in its small-boy wickedness of vocabulary; bitter, and even morbid in its endless preoccupation with fatality."[8]

Granville Hicks, writing in the *Nation*, stated that if the book had been written by anyone else, there would be little to say about it. "Fortunately the author, fully aware of the interest in his personality, has made a vigorous effort to put as much of himself as possible into his book." Readers would be drawn to the work, said Hicks, not because of their interest in bullfighting, but due to their interest in Hemingway and the intimate revelations he makes about himself. These revelations "take the form of dialogues between the author and an old lady, dialogues that suggest both Frank Harris and A. A. Milne at their most objectionable."[9]

The most devastating review came from Max Eastman, Hemingway's former Paris friend. Principally a social and literary critic, but also a journalist and poet, Eastman had published some of his work through Scribner's. His review, titled "Bull in the Afternoon," began by acknowledging the many "gorgeous pages in Ernest Hemingway's book about bullfights." There was humor and "straight talk of what things are." Nevertheless, "there is an unconscionable quantity of bull — to put it as decorously as possible — poured and plastered all over what he writes about bullfights. By bull I mean juvenile romantic gushing and sentimentalizing of simple facts." Hemingway had built a reputation opposing such sentimental poppycock, the kind of stuff "dished out by those Art nannies and pale-eyed professors of poetry" that Hemingway purportedly despised. "Why then does our iron advocate of straight talk about what things are, our full-sized man, our ferocious realist, go blind and wrap himself up in clouds of juvenile romanticism the moment he crosses the border on his way to a Spanish bullfight? It is of course a commonplace that Hemingway lacks the serene confidence that he *is* a full-sized man."

Eastman continued by saying that Hemingway suffered from a persistent sense of self-doubt. This made it necessary for him "to put forth evidences of red-blooded masculinity. It must be made obvious not only in the swing of the big shoulders and the clothes he puts on, but in the stride of his prose style and the emotions he permits to come to the surface there." This trait in the author's character had created "a literary style, you might say, of wearing false hair on the chest."[10]

Hemingway, when he read Eastman's review, became furious. Here was another Paris friend questioning his manhood and accusing him of being a phony. He fired off a telegram to Max Perkins: "TELL YOUR FRIEND EASTMAN WILL BREAK HIS JAW."[11] In a follow-up letter to Perkins from Havana, where he had been fishing for marlin, Hemingway stressed that if he ever saw Eastman again, he would seek redress. "It certainly is damned fine to have friends." As soon as they learn you are out of the country they get brave and start talking. "You see what they can't get over is 1 that I *am* a man (2) that I can beat the shit out of any of them 3 that I can write. The last hurts them the worst." He promised that wherever and whenever he met up with any of these "professional male beauties of other years," they would have a hard time talking and repeating their slanders after he got through working them over.[12]

Almost as disturbing to Hemingway as the reviews of *Death in the Afternoon* was Janet Flanner's "Paris Letter" in the March 4, 1933, issue of the *New Yorker*. Flanner reported that a "Paris-written book of extreme interest to both sides of the Atlantic" would soon be published. *The Autobiography of Alice B. Toklas* (which Flanner hinted was actually written by Gertrude Stein) would be a "complete memoir of that exciting period when Cubism was being invented in paint and the new manner of writing being patented in words," a time when "everything we now breathe was already in the air and only a few had the nose for news to smell it — and with most of the odors of discovery right under the Toklas-Stein roof." Considerable mystery and secrecy still surrounded the book, said Flanner. Among those who had seen it, quarrels had already arisen over which section was the best, "the Picasso part, or the analyses of Hemingway."[13]

It was "the analyses of Hemingway" that worried Ernest. Despite his readiness to put real people in his own books, to exhibit their idiosyncrasies and shortcomings, he did not want others doing the same to him. Critics who tried to psychoanalyze him through his works horrified him, and he made every effort to keep people from poking around in his private life and evaluating what they found. "I am opposed," he said later, "to writing about the private lives of liveing [sic] authors and psychoanalyzing them while they are alive." Such things could damage a writer, make him self-conscious, and cause him great worry, annoyance, and interruption of work.[14]

He immediately wrote to Flanner, whom he had known in Paris, saying that he had once been very fond of Stein and had been loyal to her until she pushed his face in a dozen times. At their last meeting, Stein had told about an incident, "some fag story, which proved me conclusively to be very queer indeed." Stein would not say what it was.

"Poor old Papa," Hemingway said. Well, he would probably read all about it in her autobiography. He claimed he never cared what she did in or out of bed, and both had always liked each other very much. But once she reached menopause, "she got awfully damned patriotic about sex." Her attitude about homosexuality and creativity passed through several stages, the first being that no one was any good who wasn't that way. The second was that anyone who was that way must be good. And finally, anyone who was good had to be that way. Without knowing what Stein was about to say, yet anticipating that it would be uncomplimentary, he told Flanner that he was going to write his own memoirs one day when he couldn't write anything else. They would be accurate and funny, and he wouldn't be trying to prove anything.[15] He complained to others about Stein in similar fashion, hoping in this way to parry the criticism he felt was coming.

Arnold Gingrich, a man Ernest had met in New York a short time earlier, was another to whom he complained. A book collector from Chicago and publisher of *Apparel Arts*, Gingrich was about to launch a new quarterly magazine to be called *Esquire*. He wrote Hemingway that it would be for men what *Vogue* was for women, but there would be nothing effeminate about it. "It aims to have ample hair on its chest," he said, referring to Max Eastman's review, "to say nothing of adequate cojones."[16] Gingrich wanted Hemingway to write some articles on hunting and fishing to help set the proper tone for the magazine and to give it a boost. Hemingway, about to leave with his wife and two older sons for Spain, and from there continue on to Africa, promised four articles from various stops along the way, the first from Cuba.

In his letter to Gingrich, his anxiety about Stein's forthcoming book spilled out. He said that Stein had once been a fine woman until she went "goofy" with the menopause. After that she began taking herself too seriously instead of taking her work seriously. Finally she got the notion that any writer who was good had to be queer; "if they did not seem to be they were merely concealing it." Still, he confessed to having learned a lot from her before she went crazy.[17] Clearly Ernest was not looking forward to Gertrude Stein's "analyses of Hemingway." She could be pretty plain-spoken, and he expected a severe public scolding like he had sometimes received at 27 rue de Fleurus. But for all his apprehensions, he was still not prepared for the drubbing Gertrude Stein actually gave him.

The *Atlantic Monthly* ran *The Autobiography of Alice B. Toklas* in four parts beginning with the May 1933 issue. Parts one and two, titled "Discovering Picasso and Matisse" and "When We Were Very Young," covered the years before the war. Part one began with Toklas meeting Stein in Paris in 1907 but focused primarily on Gertrude and Leo Stein's early discoveries and purchases of modernist paintings, and the start of Gertrude's friendships with Picasso and Matisse. Picasso, when Stein first met him, impressed her as "small, quick-moving but not restless, his eyes having a strange faculty of opening wide and drinking in what he wished to see." Matisse, medium size with a reddish beard and glasses, was poor but single-mindedly dedicated to his art. His wife kept a small millinery shop and was a fastidious housekeeper. "She was a very straight dark woman with a long face and a firm, large, loosely hung mouth like a horse. She had an abundance of dark hair."[18]

Part two of the *Autobiography* stepped back in time, dealing with Gertrude Stein growing up in Oakland, California, her years at Harvard Annex and Johns Hopkins, her move with Leo first to London and then to Paris, and more about her friendship with Picasso. Part three, "The War and Gertrude Stein," detailed the relief efforts Stein and Toklas undertook during the war. Gertrude learned to drive, bought a Ford that she got modified into a small truck, and she and Alice transported medical supplies to outlying hospitals. Gertrude did the driving and Alice took care of everything else. Gertrude was good at the wheel so long as she drove forward, but she was not good at backing up. "She goes forward admirably," Alice is made to say, "she does not go backwards successfully. The only violent discussions that we have had in connection with her driving a car have been on the subject of backing."[19] Following the Armistice, Stein and Toklas drove to towns devastated by the war to distribute blankets, underclothing, and babies' woolen stockings and booties to returning refugee families.

So far there was nothing in the memoir to disturb Hemingway, but most of the critical remarks about contemporaries were reserved for the final installment. Part four, titled "Ernest Hemingway and the Post-War Decade," began by emphasizing the changes that had come to Paris following the war. There were many more people in the city, and everything seemed active, restless, and disturbed. Stein quoted Clive Bell as remarking, "They say that an awful lot of people were killed in the war, but it seems to me that an extraordinarily large number of grown men and women have suddenly been born."[20]

Many of these people began turning up at 27 rue de Fleurus, which had become a gathering place for painters and expatriate writers. An early visitor was Sherwood Anderson. He came "and quite simply and directly, as is his way, told her [Stein] what he thought of her work and what it had meant to him in his development." She, of course, was pleased. "Gertrude Stein and Sherwood Anderson have always been the best of friends but I do not believe even he realizes how much his visit meant to her."[21]

Stein and Toklas met Ezra Pound. "He came home to dinner with us and he stayed and he talked about Japanese prints among other things. Gertrude Stein liked him but did not find him amusing. She said he was a village explainer, excellent if you were a village, but if you were not, not." Besides Japanese prints, Pound talked about T. S. Eliot. This was the first time Stein had heard of Eliot, but soon he came to visit. He seemed a stiff, formal young man. "Eliot and Gertrude Stein had a solemn conversation, mostly about split infinitives and other grammatical solecisms and why Gertrude Stein used them."[22]

There was also Hemingway, twenty-three years old, shy and good-looking, "with a letter of introduction from Sherwood Anderson." Gertrude Stein and Hemingway had many interesting conversations. They became close and helped one another. "Later on when things were difficult between Gertrude Stein and Hemingway, she always remembered with gratitude that after all it was Hemingway who first caused to be printed a piece of *The Making of Americans.*" From that time forth she always had a weakness for Hemingway. "After all he was the first of the young men to knock on my door, and he did make [Ford Madox] Ford print the first piece of *The Making of Americans.*"

Her weakness for Hemingway and her sense of gratitude still did not cloud her perceptions or bridle her tongue. "Gertrude Stein and Sherwood Anderson are very funny on the subject of Hemingway," she continued. "The last time that Sherwood was in Paris they often talked about him. Hemingway had been formed by the two of them, and they were both a little proud and a little ashamed of the work of their minds."

Stein mentioned Hemingway having repudiated Sherwood Anderson's work. She talked about his sending Anderson a letter in the name of American literature which he, Hemingway, and his contemporaries were going to save. Anderson and Stein discussed these things and found them amusing. "What a book, they both agreed, would be the real story of Hemingway, not those he writes but the confessions of the real Ernest Hemingway. It would be for another audience than the audience Hemingway now has, but it would be very wonderful." Both agreed, still, to having a weakness for Hemingway because he was such a good pupil. Alice protested that he was a rotten pupil. "'You don't understand,' they both said, 'it is so flattering to have a pupil who does it without understanding it.'"

In those early days, wrote Stein, Hemingway easily got tired. "He used to get quite worn out walking from his house to ours. But then he had been worn by the war." Like most men, of course, he was fragile. "Recently a robust friend of his said to Gertrude Stein, 'Ernest is very fragile. Whenever he does anything sporting something breaks his arm, his leg, or his head.'" The memoir concluded with Stein offering to write Alice's autobiography for her, promising to do so "as simply as Defoe did the autobiography of Robinson Crusoe. And she has, and this is it."[23]

Hemingway read the final installment of the *Autobiography* in Key West while preparing to leave for Europe. At one time he had advised Sherwood Anderson, after attacking him in *The Torrents of Spring*, not to take what he said personally — friends should not have to pull their punches, otherwise nothing came of it but phony Great American Writers. He later told Max Perkins that you must never let the pack know you were wounded. Later still he counseled Scott Fitzgerald not to worry, but to ride out whatever punches were thrown at you. All that advice he now forgot in the aftermath of *The Autobiography of Alice B. Toklas*. Hemingway took what Gertrude said very personally indeed, and it was not in his nature to ride out punches quietly. Stein had buried a haymaker in the pit of his ego, and you could hear the cries of agony for years afterward.

"Poor old Gertrude Stein," Hemingway wrote to Perkins. "Did you read the August Atlantic?" Since the menopause, she had lost all sense of taste. She could no longer tell a good painting from a bad one, a good writer from a bad one — "it all went phtt."

"Poor old Hem the fragile one." He had just returned, he told Perkins, from ninety-nine days under a hot sun on the Gulf Stream where he had caught 54 swordfish, seven in one day. The biggest was a 468 pounder that put up such a colossal fight, a crew member had to hold Hemingway around the waist to prevent him from being pulled overboard while another man poured buckets of water over his head to keep him cool. "Poor fragile old Hem posing as a fisherman again. Weigh 187 lbs. Down from 211."[24]

Hemingway also wrote to Ezra Pound, telling him, "I learned more about how to write and how not to write from you than from any son of a bitch alive and have always said so." He had learned from Stein too

> — in conversation. She was never dumb — in conversation. Damned smart in conversation. But it seems she and old mother hubbard Anderson made me in their spare time. Well by Jesus that will be something for them to be remembered by if its true. I stuck by that old bitch until she threw me out of the house when she lost her judgement with the menopause but it seems that I'm just a fickle, brittle, brain-picking bastard. She gave me some damned good advice many times and much shit to boot.

Pound could perhaps see the steps in "my progressive loss of certain virtues." Nothing, he said, can compare to a self-appointed legendary woman. Ernest concluded, "Well gents it will be a big day when write my own bloody memoirs because papa isn't jealous (yet) and have a damned rat trap memory and nothing to prove. Also the documents."[25]

In a letter to Arnold Gingrich, Hemingway acknowledged that Stein "was a good psychologist." She knew that he did not get angry at being called anything he actually was but exploded like fireworks when accused of something he was not. Her piece in the *Atlantic Monthly* had been "damned intelligent malice."[26]

But how could he avenge her malice? He truly believed, as he said years later, that if someone sticks a thumb in your eye, you thumb him back. If he fouls you, you foul him back. You can't let the rotten bastards get away with anything. Yet Gertrude Stein presented a problem. Her comments pained and angered him more than anyone's. To be kicked in the ribs like this by one he had truly cared for, who had been so important to him during his formative years as a writer, really hurt. What frustrated him beyond all measure was that he could not vent his anger in the usual way. He could not promise to break her jaw or threaten to knock her down the next time he saw her. All he found to do over the next several years was to snipe at her occasionally in his writings. It was a petty response, but the length of time he persisted in it shows the depth of his pain and the frustration he felt at not being able to get back at her in a more meaningful way.

Sherwood Anderson, after reading the *Autobiography*, empathized with Hemingway to a degree. He understood how much Stein's comments would hurt him. "I have been reading with joy the autobiography as it came along in the magazine," he wrote to Gertrude, "a bit sorry and sad on the night after that number when you took such big patches of skin off Hemmy with your delicately held knife—But great joy in the whole performance."[27]

Shortly after its being serialized in the *Atlantic Monthly*, *The Autobiography of Alice B. Toklas* appeared in book form to mostly enthusiastic reviews. The *Paris Tribune* in a headline declared it the "Season's Most Brilliant Book."[28] The *Nation* stated that "among books of literary reminiscences Miss Stein's is one of the richest, wittiest, and most irreverent ever written."[29] The *New Statesman and Nation* said the *Autobiography* was "a perfect piece of narration ... delightful, and brilliant with sincerity."[30]

The four magazine installments had been abridged, but in the complete book version, Stein took an additional patch of skin off Hemingway by accusing him of cowardice. She wrote that when Sherwood Anderson came to Paris after publication of *The Torrents of Spring*, "Hemingway naturally was afraid. Sherwood as naturally was not." Sherwood and Gertrude were amused discussing the incident. "They admitted that Hemingway was yellow, he is, Gertrude Stein insisted, just like the flat-boat men on the Mississippi river as described by Mark Twain."[31]

The reference to the flatboatmen in chapter three of Mark Twain's *Life on the Mississippi* would not have been lost on Hemingway. The flatboatmen are a couple of phony toughs who get into an argument and begin threatening each other, swelling around in a circle, whooping and cussing and prophesying havoc and general desolation once they go into action. "I'm the old original iron-jawed, brass-mounted, copper-bellied corpse-maker from the wilds of Arkansaw!" exclaims one. "Blood's my natural drink, and the wails of the dying is music to my ears."

"Hold me down to earth," bellows the other, "for I feel my powers a-working! whoo-oop! I'm a child of sin, *don't* let me get a start. Smoked glass, here, for all! Don't attempt to look at me with the naked eye, gentlemen!" Both are finally shown to be "chicken-livered cowards" and are sent sprawling by the blows of a third party tired of their antics. In linking Ernest to these two characters, Stein was charging Hemingway with posing as a tough guy himself, she being the one to administer the blows, exposing him for the coward he was. From Stein's point of view, Hemingway's cowardice lay in his attempt to conceal his predominantly emotional, sensitive nature. In its place, to shield his vulnerability, he had erected a facade of baseness and brutality to hide behind. This, to her, was a cowardly thing for him to do.

— 8 —

Getting Even

Besides Sherwood Anderson, others wrote to Gertrude Stein, complimenting her and praising her book. She received many fan letters from the general public, something she had not expected but which thoroughly delighted her. Carl Van Vechten, novelist and critic, perhaps Stein's most enthusiastic supporter in America, wrote from New York saying that he had been reading *The Autobiography of Alice B. Toklas* in book form "and have nothing but words of praise for it. It seems to me, indeed, that I have talked about nothing else since the first part appeared in the Atlantic. What a delightful book it is!"[1] He urged her to come to America to enjoy her triumphs and to be photographed.

Henri Matisse, on the other hand, was not among Gertrude Stein's well-wishers. He aligned himself with George Braque, Eugene Jolas, Tristan Tzara, and other artists who denounced, in a special supplement to the publication *Transition*, certain statements made by Stein in her book. All refuted the notion that Stein played any part in shaping the modernist art movement in Paris. Matisse pointed out that Stein had a sentimental attachment for Picasso, but to the best of his recollection, it was Braque who invented Cubism, not Picasso, as Stein claimed. Matisse also wished to dispel the impression that his wife looked like a horse. She was, he said, "a very lovely Toulousaine, erect, with a good carriage and the possessor of beautiful dark hair, ... a pretty throat and very handsome shoulders."[2]

Stein found these hostile reactions to her book "a scream." She noted that compared to writers, artists tended to be exceedingly thin-skinned. Stein and Matisse, as a result of the *Autobiography*, never met again.[3]

Leo Stein, living in Italy and now completely estranged from his sister, thought Gertrude's book maintained a sprightly tone of gossip, rising occasionally to a high level of comedy — "But God what a liar she is!" Leo had witnessed many of the things Gertrude wrote about. He found her chronology unreliable and thought much of what she said concerning incidents prior to 1911 "false both in fact and implication."[4] Aside from her faulty memory and outright fabrications, her writing he thought dreadful. He was puzzled that so many regarded her as an important literary influence. "A lot of people find, like Sherwood Anderson, that Gertrude makes words fresh. As I have never found words grow stale ... this justification makes no appeal to me." He believed that Gertrude adopted her peculiar style and odd mannerisms because she could not give ordinary words and syntax any punch. "I doubt," he said, "whether there is a single comment or general observation in the book that is not stupid." Still, on rereading two paragraphs from *The Making of Americans*, he understood "how Hemingway could have learned from them another way of emancipation from habit formations, though his power of expression is sufficient to enable him to write decent English. I simply cannot take Gertrude seriously as a literary phenomenon."[5]

Conversely, Gertrude relished her position as a literary phenomenon. She had always told the young painters and writers who came to sit at her feet and hear her talk that being successful was not good for them, "and then I who was no longer young was having it happen."[6] She now found success more exhilarating than harmful. Never having made any money before, she found it truly exciting. Up until now she had lived on a modest pension derived from a family inheritance, but the brisk sale of the *Autobiography* put extra money in her pocket. The book quickly went through four printings, the first selling out nine days prior to publication. It made the best-seller list and was featured on the cover of *Time* magazine. Stein received $8,495 in American royalties, and though not a lot compared to what Hemingway and Fitzgerald regularly took in, she nevertheless felt famous and rich. With the extra money she purchased a new eight cylinder Ford and bought Basket the dog a new collar and a blanket coat custom-made by a man who specialized in coverings for race horses. Some time later she had an electric stove put in her apartment to replace an old one that burned coal.

Having been schooled in psychology, she wondered what lasting effect this good fortune might have on her. "It is funny about money. And it is funny about identity," she said. You are still you whether you become successful or not, "but when your public knows you and does not want to pay for you and when your public knows you and does want to pay for you, you are not the same you."[7] The principal danger of success lay in how it altered identity: "It is all a question of the outside being outside and the inside being inside. As long as the outside does not put a value on you it remains outside but when it does put a value on you then it gets inside or rather if the outside puts a value on you then all your inside gets to be outside."[8] Perhaps now, at least, the public would view her as a serious writer and not just a literary curiosity. It had always bothered her that people were more interested in her than in her work. She didn't see any sense in it because if it was not for her work they would not be interested in her.[9]

Perhaps, too, people would begin to recognize her for the influential genius she was. "I know that I am the most important writer writing today," she claimed. "Einstein was the creative philosophic mind of the century and I have been the creative literary mind of the century."[10] Although she freely admitted to being a genius, she wondered sometimes what a genius was precisely. "Picasso and I used to talk about that a lot. Really inside you if you are a genius there is nothing inside you that makes you really different to yourself inside you than those are to themselves inside them who are not a genius."[11] She eventually came to think that talking and listening had much to do with it. "One may really indeed say that that is the essence of genius, of being most intensely alive, that is being one who is at the same time talking and listening. It is really that that makes one a genius."[12] Of course it was a difficult thing to be talking and listening at the same time, but that is what it was. "That is what genius is to be always going on doing this thing at one and at the same time listening and telling really listening and really telling."[13]

Her concept of genius may have been influenced, as well, by William James's definition of the word. "Genius, in truth," James wrote in *The Principles of Psychology*, "means little more than the faculty of perceiving in an unhabitual way."[14] She and Picasso both perceived in unhabitual ways. This was part of the reason she was a genius and her brother was not, why Picasso was a genius and Hemingway was not. Hemingway was a skillful writer, to be sure, but he smelled of the museums. He continued doing things as they had been done in the past. He only looked like a modern.

Picasso told her that early in his career his family treated him with consideration as a genius until he became successful; then they treated him like anyone else who was successful and no longer with consideration as a genius. "It is funny this knowing being a genius," said Stein, "everything is funny."[15]

It was funny how people began inviting her to various social functions. She and Alice, who usually attended such events only occasionally, were now engaged everyday for at least a week in advance, sometimes for two events in the same day. Stein enjoyed the socializing, for she liked meeting people and going to new places: "It was pleasant being a lion and meeting the people who make it pleasant to you to be a lion."[16]

Another funny thing was the increasing call for her to lecture in America. She had considered the possibility several times before but always decided against it. Then, just before publication of the *Autobiography*, her Paris literary agent, William Aspenwall Bradley, brought a lecture agent to visit her. The lecture agent, who published religious books and school books in the States, and who came to Europe every winter looking for interesting people to speak in America, was an unusually solemn character. Bradley explained to him that *The Autobiography of Alice B. Toklas* would soon be a best-seller and that Gertrude Stein would be much in demand. The agent replied gravely, "Interesting if true."

Offended by his manner, Stein took an immediate dislike to the man. If all lecture agents were like this one, she did not want to lecture in America. She told the man not to bother and dismissed him. Mr. Bradley tried to convince her that she made a mistake in not taking advantage of the popularity her book would generate. Surely she wanted to get rich. Certainly she did: "I want to get rich but I never want to do what there is to do to get rich." Jo Davidson, the sculptor, advised her that an artist should sell his personality, but Stein objected; the artist sold his personality only insomuch as it expressed itself in his work. She admitted to being a person with no initiative. She liked to stay where she was so long as there were plenty of people around, and Paris always had plenty of people around. No, she decided again; she would not be lecturing in America.[17]

Gertrude Stein had previously maintained on the opening page of *The Making of Americans* that she wrote for herself and for strangers; but the success of *The Autobiography of Alice B. Toklas* forced her to rethink

8. Getting Even 103

her position. She now worried a lot about identity — who she was in relation to her audience. She could no longer regard her readers as distant and abstract entities to whom she owed no responsibility. They were the ones who currently invited her to social events, who sent her fan letters, and who encouraged her to come to America. "Inside and outside and identity is a great bother," she remarked. "And how once that you know that the buyer [audience] is there can you go on knowing that the buyer is not there. Of course when he is not there there is no bother."[18]

But Gertrude Stein knew the audience was there, watching and knowing about her, and that awareness made her uneasy. "The minute you or anybody else knows what you are you are not it, you are what you or anybody else knows you are."[19] These conditions made writing impossible. She acknowledged that she had always quarreled with a great many young men, and she quarreled with them most about success making them sterile. "And I blamed them. I said it was their fault. I said success is all right but if there is anything in you it ought not to cut off the flow not if there is anything in you. Now I know better." She knew that success did cut off your flow, and she found that frightening. "What happened to me was this," she continued:

> When the success began and it was a success I got lost completely lost. You know the nursery rhyme, I am I because my little dog knows me. Well you see I did not know myself, I lost my personality. It has always been completely included in myself my personality as any personality naturally is, and here all of a sudden, I was not just I because so many people did know me.

With so many people knowing her, she became too self-conscious to write:

> I began to think about how my writing would sound to others, how could I make them understand, I who had always lived within myself and my writing. And then all of a sudden I said there that it is that is what was the matter with all of them all the young men whose syrup did not pour, and here I am being just the same. They were young and I am not but when it happens it is just the same, the syrup does not pour.[20]

She then grew worried about not writing and being a genius. "And if you stop writing if you are a genius and you have stopped writing are you still one if you have stopped writing."[21]

Success of *The Autobiography of Alice B. Toklas* had brought on this debilitating self-consciousness, but the self-consciousness grew even more acute with news from her agent, Mr. Bradley, that *Four Saints in Three Acts* would soon be performed in America. About seven years had passed since Virgil Thomson completed scoring the opera, and finally, after much exertion, he had found, while in New York, a group willing to produce it. The Wadsworth Atheneum in Hartford, Connecticut, intended to present a Picasso retrospective, the first such exhibition of Picasso's work in the United States, and the director of the Atheneum felt that *Four Saints in Three Acts*, performed in the museum's newly-completed auditorium, would complement the show. Stein and Thomson, however, were not at the moment on speaking terms. They had earlier quarreled over a trivial matter involving the young French poet Georges Hugnet. Stein had done a free rendering or creative paraphrase in English of Hugnet's poem-sequence *Enfances*, the two versions to be printed together. But a difficulty arose over what to call Stein's contribution, since it was not, strictly speaking, a translation. Stein wanted to call it an *adaptation* or a *transposition* or a *reflection*.

When Hugnet later showed her a subscription blank for the forthcoming volume, Stein saw that his name and the title *Enfances* had been set in large type, and below that, in much smaller print, "*Suivi par traduction de Gertrude Stein*" ["Followed by the translation of Gertrude Stein."] Stein thought Hugnet deceitful and disloyal. She did not like "translation," and she especially did not appreciate her name being printed in smaller type than Hugnet's. She demanded that in the published book, her name appear on the same line of the title page as Hugnet's and in the same size type. Hugnet protested that this would indicate a collaboration, or it might lead people to think he had translated an original work of hers. He declined to change anything. Stein then refused to participate any further in the venture.

Hugnet finally asked Virgil Thomson to intercede and help negotiate a compromise. Thomson attempted to do so, but in discussing the matter with Stein, he encountered only demands and intractability, fomented chiefly by Alice Toklas. Thomson realized that Alice had to protect her territory and was doing all she could to keep Gertrude and Hugnet apart. It was a similar situation, thought Thomson, to Stein's breakup with Hemingway. Painters, sculptors, composers, historians, and newspaper people did not present a problem, but Alice felt threatened when other creative writers got too close to Gertrude.[22] At last growing impatient, Thomson made some remark to the two women that he later admitted was "an ugly thing," and he quickly apologized in a note for having "hurt you who I am ashamed to have hurt."[23] The apology seemed to have averted a serious quarrel, as all parties met amicably a short time later to celebrate Christmas Eve. The following morning, Thomson came down with the flu, which for two weeks prevented him from calling on Stein. He was also kept busy, despite his illness, preparing for a concert of his music that he was soon to perform. When he finally rang the bell at 27 rue de Fleurus, Stein answered. "Did you want something?" she asked.

"Merely to report on my absence," Thomson replied.

"We're very busy now," Stein said. They could not see him just then. And she closed the door. Thomson later sent her a printed announcement of his concert along with a personal note of invitation. In return, he received a card on which was printed the name "Miss Stein," under which Gertrude had written "declines further acquaintance with Mr. Thomson."[24]

"We were after that never friends or anything," said Stein following the incident.[25] She dismissed Thomson and Hugnet entirely from her life, except that in the following year she brought out her rendering of *Enfances* in a thirty-three page self-published book titled *Before The Flowers Of Friendship Faded Friendship Faded*. Under the title appeared the words "Written On A Poem By Georges Hugnet." And so matters stood until *Four Saints in Three Acts* obliged her to start corresponding again with Thomson in order to work out a legal agreement. Although normal practice allowed the composer of such a work two-thirds and the librettist one-third share of royalties, and even though Thomson had invested much time and energy finding a venue and financial backing, Stein demanded they split the profits fifty-fifty and Thomson agreed. Otherwise, Stein granted Thomson complete control over the production with the freedom to make whatever changes he deemed necessary.

Impressed by the Negro singers and dancers he had seen perform in Harlem, Thomson decided on an all-black cast. He found that black performers moved gracefully and took great care to enunciate their lines, a critical factor when dealing with a difficult text like Stein's. White performers tended to stand around like lumps and barely moved their lips.

Thomson also hired as production director John Houseman, a thirty-one-year-old former grain futures seller on Wall Street whose business had collapsed following the crash of '29. For several years afterward, Houseman barely eked out a living co-writing comedies for the stage. Although Houseman possessed no practical experience in theatre production, Thomson hired him because he seemed capable and motivated, and he appeared to have the right temperament. Best of all, he agreed to work gratis just to learn the business of directing. (Houseman afterward went on to direct many other things, heading up the Negro Theatre Project of Harlem and joining twenty-year-old Orson Welles to create the Mercury Theatre. At age seventy-one he took up screen acting, winning an Oscar in the Best Supporting Actor category for his portrayal of Professor Kingsfield in the motion picture *Paper Chase*.)

Four Saints in Three Acts opened in Hartford on the night of February 8, 1934, and played successfully for six performances.[26] Thomson was pleased at how eagerly the singers took to Stein's unusual text, bringing out the humor and vigor of the lines and enunciating everything so clearly that not a word was missed: "If a magpie in the sky on the sky can not cry if the pigeon on the grass alas can alas and to pass the pigeon on the grass alas and the magpie in the sky on the sky and to try and to try alas on the grass alas the pigeon on the grass the pigeon on the grass and alas."

Thomson was also pleased with the opera's generally enthusiastic reception by audiences and critics alike. Still, he noted a pattern that had already begun to emerge whenever a joint work of his and Stein's was performed in America: "The literary consensus is always that the music is lovely but the poetry absurd; whereas the music world, at least nine tenths of it, takes the view that Stein's words are great literature but that my music is infantile."[27] After its run in Hartford, the opera moved to New York for what was intended to be a week on Broadway. George Gershwin and Arturo Toscanini attended the premiere. The week stretched into six. By every measure, the opera was a theatrical triumph. "For six months and more," wrote Thomson later, "the show was named at least once every week in every New York paper and in some paper somewhere in the United States every day. There were constant editorials, cartoons, and jokes about it; all the music and drama critics in the East reviewed it."[28]

Gertrude Stein's fan mail increased. Carl Van Vechten sent her a photograph showing her name in lights on the marquee of the 44th Street Theatre in New York, and he urged her again to come to America. Her Paris literary agent, Mr. Bradley, wrote to her that summer at Bilignin imploring her to make the trip, saying that a lecture tour in America would do much to promote her work. Anticipating her acceptance, he had already made arrangements. The agency handling the matter was the same as that represented by the solemn man who published religious books and said "Interesting if true." Stein became angry. To Bradley she sent back word that she had no intention of lecturing in America, none at all.

That summer at Bilignin, Alice planted her vegetable garden as usual. Gertrude did little writing. The syrup still would not pour. But she read, took long walks in the country, entertained a number of visitors, and thought over her decision not to lecture in America. She simply did not want to be selling her personality. She wanted her fame to rest on her works alone. Yet supposing she *had* decided to lecture — what would she have talked about? The more she thought, the more things she found to say — things that an intelligent audience might like to hear. As she began sorting out various topics and meditating on them day after day, it eventually became clear to her that she and Alice would be going to America after all.[29]

Ernest Hemingway had a natural gift for selling his personality. He possessed a knack for promoting an image the public wished to buy. Nearly all that he wrote seemed to underscore a fascinating aspect of his adventurous life, while everything people read about him in the press appeared to illuminate a facet of his writing. In his first article for *Esquire*, appearing in the premiere issue dated Autumn 1933, he gave an account of his recent fishing expedition in the Gulf Stream. Titled "Marlin Off the Morro: A Cuban Letter," the article, accompanied by photographs, resembled *Death in the Afternoon* in its overall treatment and attention to detail. In discussing, for instance, the various types of marlin found in the waters off Cuba, and in describing the four ways in which a marlin hits a trolled bait, Hemingway displayed a mastery of subject that marked him as a true aficionado of the sport.

The Hemingways, after returning briefly to Key West to prepare for their trip to Europe, sailed from Havana on August 7, arriving ten days later in Spain. There Ernest wrote his second *Esquire* piece, "The Friend of Spain: A Spanish Letter." He noted the many changes that had taken place in Spain over the past several years. People seemed more prosperous yet were taxed more heavily than ever. Bull fighting was in bad shape. The present crop of matadors was disappointing overall, and the bulls "were uniformly poor, colorless, without force, bravery or style."[30]

During his two months in Spain, Hemingway read proofs for a new collection of stories, titled *Winner Take Nothing*, scheduled for publication by Scribner's in October. Also while in Spain, he saw the book version of *The Autobiography of Alice B. Toklas* accusing him of being yellow. He wrote Max Perkins that he had "no reaction to the Stein thing at all." He reiterated what he had told others, that he had been loyal to Stein until she practically threw him out of her house and that she had lost all taste and judgment with the menopause. He mentioned how she had quarreled with nearly all her former friends, after which, she "Took up with a 4th rate lot of fairies." But it was fine with him — "she certainly invented some fine apochryphal incidents about me But what the hell I'm only sorry for her. It was a damned pitiful book."[31]

Several months earlier, about the time the *Atlantic Monthly* published the final installment of the *Autobiography*, the *New Yorker* began running James Thurber's *My Life and Hard Times*, a memoir Ernest found more entertaining than Gertrude's. Hemingway considered Thurber one of the best writers working in America and had sent him a humorous letter saying how much he liked his latest piece. Thurber appreciated the note and later used a portion as a blurb on the dust jacket of his memoir when it came out in hardcover. The blurb read, "Even in the earliest days when Thurber was writing under the name of Alice B. Toklas we knew he had it in him if he could only get it out."[32] Thurber's hardbound memoir appeared almost simultaneously with Stein's.

Despite Hemingway's claim that he had no reaction to Stein's book at all, his conduct in the months following publication showed how much it really galled him. In an article he wrote for a popular French art magazine telling how he came to buy Joan Miró's painting "The Farm," he got in a couple of digs, the first alluding to Stein's sexuality. He wrote,

> No one could look at it [Miró's painting] and not know it had been painted by a great painter and when you are painting things that people must take on trust it is good to have something around that has taken as long to make as it takes a woman to make a child (a woman who isn't a woman can usually write her autobiography in a third of that time) and that shows even fools that you are a great painter in terms that they understand.

After Miró painted "The Farm," Ernest continued, and after Joyce wrote *Ulysses*, both had the right to expect people to trust their future works, even if they didn't understand them, so long as the artists continued to work hard. "If you have painted 'The Farm' or if you have written *Ulysses*, and then keep on working very hard afterward, you do not need an Alice B. Toklas."[33]

In addition to these little jibes, Hemingway resorted to his old practice when anyone seriously irritated him and he needed to blow off steam — he began writing a satire. He called his pastiche "The Autobiography of Alice B. Hemingway." In the six-page typewritten piece, which he initially planned to submit to the *New Yorker* but never did, the narrator, called Alice, says that she met her husband, Hemingway, in Paris. In those days he wore a black leather coat, and there was a rumor, "which I believe he fostered, that he was Marshal Petain's chauffeur. He did not look to me to be a genius. He looked like Marshal Petain's chauffeur. But even then he was going to Gertrude Stein's atelier regularly."

Alice asks her husband what he does there. "I look at the pictures and I listen to her talk," he says. "The pictures are very good. She's smart too. She makes some good cracks." Alice wants to know what Stein thinks of his work. They don't talk about his work, he says. "We talk about her work and how to get it published." He never gets tired of listening to her, though. "The other one tells some funny stories too." The other one is also named Alice, the same as his wife. "She runs the show you know. She's a very severe disciplinarian. I've heard a little of it, coming in unexpectedly. I'll tell you sometime. She's very charming. Picasso told me she ruined Gertrude. She is very ambitious, especially socially. I like her but she doesn't like me."

Gertrude wrote some fine things once, the husband remarks, better than anyone at the time. But she wasn't appreciated. So to avoid feeling herself a failure, she devised a new way of writing that was easy. It didn't have to mean anything, and it didn't, but it made her happy just to turn out words every day. "She makes up all sorts of reasons for writing this way but the real reason is because she is cockeyed lazy and can write that way every day and never fail." Alice, the wife, encourages her husband to write about this, yet he doesn't want to because he really likes Gertrude. "She is often very smart about things that have happened and she talks well. But she doesn't know anything about the way things are going to happen." The wife decides to write about it herself in her autobiography, "only Hemingway has written it for me and here it is and I am it."[34]

The real Hemingway left for Paris on October 20, his real wife, Pauline, having gone ahead to book lodgings, do some shopping, and arrange for the two older boys to be properly cared for while she and Ernest were on safari in Africa. The family put up at the Paris-Dinard Hotel on rue Cassette near their former apartment in the rue Férou and only five or six minutes' walk from 27 rue de Fleurus. Morrill Cody, newspaper man and long-time Hemingway acquaintance, recalled years later that during his stopover in Paris, Hemingway remained "very secretive about his goings and comings, swearing the few of us who saw him to the utmost secrecy." Cody thought this odd behavior an early sign of the paranoia that afflicted Hemingway in the years just prior to his death. Perhaps so, though another reason seems more likely.

Hemingway had begun writing his third *Esquire* article. He had not mentioned Stein in the previous two. The reason may have been that at least one of the articles would be published before he arrived in Paris, and so he wished to move cautiously. He knew how small the city could be — how easily one might run into almost anybody on the street. He may have thought it best not to risk antagonizing Gertrude until he was well out of the country and on his way to Africa. It would be embarrassing enough to bump into her accidentally, given their strained relations, without having just slanged her in a popular magazine. He probably swore the few who saw him, like Morrill Cody, to the utmost secrecy because he did not want Stein even to know he was in town. There was no telling what she might do, no telling what pretext she might find to confront him. Hemingway knew how to deal with unpleasant men, but assertive, ambitious women frightened him.

His third *Esquire* article would not run until February of the coming year, long after he was gone; consequently, he felt safe in now taking a jab at Stein. He began his piece, titled simply "A Paris Letter," recalling pleasant memories of the fall hunting season in Montana. "This year, at the same time," he wrote, "we are in Paris and it is a big mistake. All I do is go out and get depressed and wish I were somewhere else." It was only for three weeks, but Paris conjured up gloomy thoughts of all that had happened since America entered the Great Depression. "This old friend shot himself. That old friend took an overdose of something. That old friend went back to New York and jumped out, or rather fell from, a high window. That other old friend wrote her memoirs. All of the old friends have lost

8. Getting Even

their money. All of the old friends are very discouraged. Few of the old friends are healthy." Montparnasse and its cafés had been taken over by the respectable French bourgeoisie. Instead of Americans, the only foreigners you saw were refugees from the Nazi repressions in Germany.

"What really makes you feel badly here though is not any of the things I mentioned earlier. People must be expected to kill themselves when they lose their money, I suppose, and drunkards get bad livers, and legendary people usually end by writing their memoirs. What makes you feel bad is the perfectly calm way everyone speaks about the next war. It is accepted and taken for granted." If they were right, once the war starts, he warned, America had better stay out of it.

The reference to Stein came off as mild and tentative to be sure, but *Esquire* was not the proper arena to fully voice the bitterness he felt. Morrill Cody said that Ernest in private spoke violently against Stein and promised to "get even" with her. "He was particularly infuriated," said Cody, "by her claim that she had 'discovered' him and had helped him find a publisher. 'It is we who tried like hell to find a publisher for *her*,'" exclaimed Ernest. He seemed to be whipping himself into greater fury as time went on, and whatever restraints he may have felt about getting even with Stein in the first three *Esquire* pieces vanished as he prepared to leave for Africa.

Cody had recently taken the job of ghost-writing a memoir for Jimmy Charters, former barman at the Dôme. Cody asked Hemingway to write an introduction for the book. Ernest agreed to do so, but as the book had not yet been written, he used the opportunity to attack Stein. Although he did not mention her by name, the first sentence made clear the person he meant:

> Once a woman has opened a salon it is certain that she will write her memoirs. If you go to the salon you will be in the memoirs; that is, you will be if your name ever becomes known enough so that its use, or abuse, will help the sale of the woman's book. Even if your name means nothing to those strange folk who pay cash for literary reminiscences (I understand they have been banded into clubs or guilds, perhaps for their own protection) you will still have your place in the memoirs if you will devote yourself loyally enough and long enough to serving the cause of the woman and of her salon, and quite too often, of her art.

The best way to get extensively mentioned "is to have the woman be fond of you and then get over it." The reasons for her getting over it could be that you were no longer young, that you had lost your teeth, your hair, your money, your shoes, your shirt.

> Or you may get very tired of seeing the woman or of hearing her talk. It may be that the getting over it is induced by domestic compulsion [Alice Toklas], or by the changes of the seasons [menopause], or it may be anything you say, but the memoir writer will usually prove that a lady's brain may still be between her thighs, even though those thighs — but let us not make jokes about thighs — and will treat you in her memoirs exactly as any girl around the Dôme or the Select would.

Hemingway then expressed mock surprise and grief that Jimmy Charters intended writing his memoirs. If you go to a literary lady's salon, he continued, you can plan on showing up in her memoirs, but a saloon or a bar is different. "You should expect to be able to go into a saloon or bar and pay for your drinks without appearing in the bartender's memoirs." Still, "Jimmy served more and better drinks than any legendary woman ever did in her salon, certainly Jimmy gave less and better advice." If his memoirs succeeded in capturing only part of his knowledge and charm, it should be a very entertaining volume. "I wish it were not about Montparnasse because that is a dismal place. But Jimmy could make it very cheerful when he was behind the bar. Here's luck to him putting it in a book!"

Handing Morrill Cody the introduction, Hemingway still felt dissatisfied with it. "He thought that the introduction to my book was not strong enough," Cody said, "but since he was leaving for Africa in a few days, I was afraid that if he took it away, I would wind up without any introduction at all."[35] The piece, therefore, remained as written and appeared as the introduction to *This Must Be the Place; Memoirs of Montparnasse*, by "Jimmie, the Barman," published the following year.

Once in Africa, Hemingway found Tanganyika much like Montana and Wyoming only with more roll and vastness to it. The Serengeti remained green after a nine-month drought except where it looked black from the great migrating herd of wildebeest, estimated at three million head, reaching as far as the eye could see to the blue hills in the distance. Working the edge of the herd were the lions, spotted hyenas, and jackals. Climbing into the highlands above the plain, Ernest thought the land resembled an abandoned New England orchard, but an orchard that ran on for fifty miles. Africa was more beautiful than he had imagined.

8. Getting Even

Camped on one side of the Serengeti next to the Serenea River, the Hemingway entourage consisted of native guides, gun-bearers, porters, cook, driver, a noted white hunter, Pauline, Ernest, and Charles Thompson, a Key West friend Hemingway invited along, all expenses paid. The safari cost hundreds of dollars a day, but it was Pauline's rich uncle, Gus Pfeiffer, who picked up the tab. Uncle Gus owned controlling interest in Hudnut, the perfume company, and he had given Ernest and Pauline twenty-five thousand dollars worth of company stock to finance the trip. He considered it an investment toward Hemingway's next book.

Not long into the safari, Ernest came down with amoebic dysentery and had to be flown four hundred miles to Nairobi, Kenya, for treatment. At the peak of his illness he passed a pint and a half of blood a day. "That's a hell of a lousy disease," he wrote Max Perkins. "Your whole damn intestine tries to come out. Feels as though you were giving birth to a child."[36]

While recovering in bed, he wrote the final article promised to Arnold Gingrich for his magazine. Titled "a.d. in Africa: A Tanganyika Letter," it was from "Your amoebic dysentery correspondent." Hemingway described the beauty of the country and noted the quantity of game it contained. Even with his head full of Africa's vast magnificence, and with his body full emetine to treat his illness, he still could not resist taking a poke at Gertrude Stein. He mentioned how slow he had been to diagnose the dysentery. "Symptoms of a. d.," he wrote, "run from weakly insidious through spectacular to phenomenal." For ten days he felt progressively weak and ill before the symptoms got so bad that he sought help. "I became convinced that though an unbeliever I had been chosen as the one to bear our Lord Buddha when he should be born again on earth." He felt flattered by this and wondered "how much Buddha at that age would resemble Gertrude Stein."[37]

Hemingway sent Gingrich the article accompanied by a letter apologizing for it being late, but he explained that he had been sick as hell with no pep to write. He said to Gingrich, "One of Gertrude's feathered friends told her Papa was always breaking things, getting sick etc. But wonder what would happen to G. and friends if they went where papa goes and did what papa does."[38]

Despite Hemingway coming down with amoebic dysentery, the safari still proved successful. At the end of eight weeks, the group had collected many impressive heads. They had killed four lions, three cheetahs, four buffalo, two leopards, two rhinos, four Thompson gazelle, eight Grant, seven wildebeest, seven impala, two klipspringers, four roan, two bushbucks, three reedbucks, two oryx, four topi, two waterbuck, one eland, and three kudu. In addition, they bagged a serval cat, two warthogs, thirteen zebra, and one cobra. And just for fun, they had shot forty-one hyenas.[39]

The Hemingways arrived in Paris from their African trip near the end of February, the month *Four Saints in Three Acts* was enjoying runs in Hartford and New York. After a brief stay in Paris, the Hemingways were to return home to Key West. Before departing, Ernest made an appearance at the Parisian, a new bar just opened by Jimmy Charters, for whom Morrill Cody was working as ghost writer. Robert McAlmon was also there, and Hemingway remembered that he had a score to settle with him. He approached McAlmon, led him outside, accused him of spreading malicious rumors, and quickly dropped him with a short left to the head. The episode raised only a mild protest among those who learned of it. McAlmon may have deserved chastising, but Hemingway's method appeared brutal. Said one disapprovingly, "Hemingway weighed over two hundred pounds, and Bob about a hundred and fifteen soaking wet."[40]

Not seriously hurt, McAlmon made no fuss about the incident. He still doubted, however, that Hemingway was yet the rugged tough guy he so much wanted to be. His actions contained too much swagger to be entirely genuine. McAlmon recalled Hemingway's days as a shadow boxer and how, upon returning from his first trip to Spain, he had taken up shadow-bullfighting. McAlmon wondered if after living in Key West he had taken up "shadow-barracuda-fishing, or coming back from Africa he would shadow-lion-hunt."[41]

—9—

Knowing the Vital Spots

Gertrude Stein and Alice Toklas sailed from Le Havre aboard the French liner *Champlain* on October 17, 1934. They arrived in New York one week later. Among those awaiting their arrival were Carl Van Vechten, Bennett Cerf of Random House, and a crowd of reporters. Cerf was to be Stein's American publisher, though he claimed not to understand a word Stein wrote. He had already agreed to republish *Three Lives* in the Modern Library and later announced that he would publish one Gertrude Stein title a year, Stein to choose the book herself.

Before disembarking, Gertrude Stein spoke to reporters about her writing. She insisted that it was clear and simple; it just needed getting used to. One must learn to hear her work with the ears, not just see it with the eyes. She claimed to write as she talked, naturally as the words came to her. "You are accustomed to see with your eyes differently to the way you hear with your ears," she explained, "and perhaps that is what makes it hard to read my works for some people." She maintained, for example, that *Four Saints* was easy to understand, "a perfectly simple description of a Spanish landscape." She went on to express pleasure at the popular recognition *The Autobiography of Alice B. Toklas* had brought her, and in response to a question, she stated that her affection for Ernest Hemingway continued unabated.[1]

Throughout her American visit, Stein generated much controversy in the press. The debate focused on her literary status and why she wrote the way she did. One correspondent considered her "the great, brilliant amateur of modernity in her special field."[2] Another spoke of her as "a phenomenon for which we may be thankful."[3] Others, however, felt that she was the perpetrator of a literary prank, her writing sheer gibberish. A columnist sarcastically rejoiced that he had finally found the key to understanding Stein — she was one of America's prime humorists. Even the *Journal of the American Medical Association* weighed in. The *Journal's* editor wondered whether Stein's "literary abnormalities" represented a literary hoax or were "distortions of the intellect." He advanced the theory that Stein might suffer from palilalia, "a form of speech disorder in which the patient repeats many times a word, a phrase or a sentence which he has just spoken."[4]

Reporters also took an interest in Stein's appearance. They usually wrote of her as being short, solid, and simply dressed, some noting that she had a pleasant voice. A writer for the *New Republic* described her as possessing a "Well shaped masculine head chopped from a big block, vigorously modeled, striking as Stonehenge, posed as an image, carrying a close skull-cap of short thick iron-gray hair."[5] Reporters found Alice Toklas decidedly more peculiar, one describing her as "a small, thin-faced, mouselike woman."[6] Another also described her as "mouselike, in her gray fur cloak and her little astrakhan cap pulled low over her brow. Her hair was dark and curly, her eyes gray and rather sad. Her voice seemed tired. She was nervous."[7]

Again in her native country after an absence of thirty-one years (twenty-seven for Alice), Stein found everything at first unreal. The cabs and trucks looked so different from those in France. Even the streets looked different. Lights blazed everywhere. She wondered why Paris was called the City of Lights when there were so many more in New York.

During her month's stay at the Algonquin Hotel, from which location she traveled to neighboring towns and cities to lecture, she met Virgil Thomson. He was in the States preparing *Four Saints* for a week-long run in Chicago. This was their first face-to-face meeting since Stein closed her door on Thomson two years earlier. The encounter proved amicable, if not warm. Thomson told a friend, "Gertrude and I have kissed, I wouldn't quite say made up, but kissed."[8]

On November 12, a little more than two weeks following her arrival, Stein gave a radio interview in which the questions and her responses to them had been written out beforehand. As she discussed some of her works and her writing style, her delivery sounded awkward and stiff to those who had heard her talk and laugh spontaneously. She gave her views on parts of speech and said that she often omitted capital letters and question marks because they were useless — hangovers from a time when people did not read very well and needed help. "[I]f you don't know that a question is a question without a question mark being there what is the use of writing the question."⁹

After giving talks at the Museum of Modern Art (opened five years earlier), the Colony Club on Park Avenue, and Columbia and Princeton universities, Gertrude and Alice flew to Chicago for the opening night of *Four Saints*, Virgil Thomson conducting. This being the first time the two women had ever been in a plane, they felt extremely nervous, so Carl Van Vechten accompanied them to help ease their fears. Once Gertrude got in the air, she very much enjoyed the flight. Going over America like that, she said, seeing the ground from high above, she knew why post-cubist painting was what it was: "I saw there on the earth the mingling lines of Picasso, coming and going, developing and destroying themselves, I saw the simple solutions of Braque, I saw the wandering lines of Masson."¹⁰

Alice Toklas, 1934 (Beinecke Rare Book and Manuscript Library, Yale University).

Once in Chicago, Stein found the opera delightful. Sitting near the back of the theatre in a private box, she liked everything she saw and heard:

> To know to know to love her so.
> Four saints prepare for saints.
> It makes it well fish.
> Four saints it makes it well fish.
> Four saints prepare for saints it makes it well well fish it makes it well fish prepare for saints.

Having grown increasingly deaf in recent years, the condition aggravated by the flight from New York, she moved closer to the stage after the first act so as to see and hear things better:

> Pigeons on the grass alas.
> Pigeons on the grass alas.
> Short longer grass short longer longer shorter yellow grass Pigeons large pigeons on the shorter longer yellow grass alas pigeons on the grass.

Thomson's music provided a structure and continuity to Stein's libretto that the words alone did not possess. Some found this an advantage, others a limitation.

> If a magpie in the sky on the sky can not cry if the pigeon on the grass alas can alas and to pass the pigeon on the grass alas and the magpie in the sky on the sky and to try and to try alas on the grass alas the pigeon on the grass the pigeon on the grass and alas.

Stein said later that it all looked very lovely, "and the movement was everything they moved and did nothing, that is what a saint or a doughboy should do they should do nothing, they should move some and they did move some and they did nothing it was very satisfying."[11]

The next six months hurried along in a flood of activity. Traveling mostly by automobile, Stein lectured at about thirty schools across the country from New England, down through the South, and into California. She also attended many informal discussions, private parties, and celebrations. To those who expressed puzzlement and even exasperation with her writing, she responded to their questions and comments with her usual patience on such occasions. In Cleveland, when someone remarked that her writing must be hard to do and must require a particular state of mind, she replied, "Think of something, concentrate and write it exactly as it looks to you." Then after referring to several passages from one of her books, she said, "It is accurate, descriptive, realistic and NOT a state of mind. It is not hard to write. It is exactly as it is." Asked about the magpie in the sky and the pigeon on the grass alas, she explained, "It's like this. The magpie is in the sky while the pigeon is on the grass. The magpie is flying over and trying to pass the pigeon. The pigeon can't fly, it is on the grass. I felt sorry for it."[12] Later on the tour, in response to a question at Wesleyan University in Georgia, she reportedly said, "I don't care to say whether I'm greater than Shakespeare, and he's dead and can't say whether he's greater than I am. Time will tell."[13]

Eventually the talks and lecturing became tedious although she liked seeing the country. The wooden houses in all the American towns she passed through excited her, and she particularly liked the Burma Shave signs along the highways. Yet she felt disappointed by the ten cent stores. She had looked forward to buying things in ten cent stores, but she could never find anything she wanted, and nothing sold for ten cents anyway. On the other hand, she liked nut stores and drug stores a lot. Seeing people eating and drinking at the counters in drug stores fascinated her. She would often go into a drug store to buy detective novels and to watch the people eating and drinking at the counter. It looked to her like a slice of provincial life set in the midst of a city. "The people sitting on the stools and eating in the drug store all looked and acted as if they lived in a small country town."[14]

On Christmas Eve, she and Alice visited Scott Fitzgerald and his wife at their rented home in Baltimore. Zelda Fitzgerald was on holiday leave from a sanitarium where she was being treated for recurring episodes of mental illness. Scott had been drinking heavily. At the close of the evening, Fitzgerald walked his two visitors to their car through the slush and snow. He thanked Stein for coming by and blurted out that it was just as though Jesus Christ had stopped in.[15]

In New Orleans, Gertrude Stein met Sherwood Anderson. He took her to see the Mississippi River, which she found disappointing. The river was not as wide as she had imagined it from reading Mark Twain.

Weeks later, in Beverly Hills, Stein met Dashiell Hammett, her favorite detective writer. She asked Hammett why men authors all wrote about themselves like women did in the previous century. Men adopted central characters who were idealized versions of themselves. Hammett told her that in the nineteenth century men were confident. The women were not confident, "but in the twentieth century the men have no confidence and so they have to make themselves as you say more beautiful more intriguing more everything."[16]

Of all the celebrities Stein met in Hollywood, Charlie Chaplin pleased her most. She thought him gentle. He reminded her of a typical Spanish gypsy bullfighter. She and Chaplin talked about the cinema, Chaplin explaining something that especially intrigued her. He said that in earlier silent films you could always change the rhythm of the action, but now you could not; you were always bound by the rhythm dictated by the voice.

She told Chaplin about writing *Four Saints*, saying that what was most exciting was when nothing happened. Saints naturally should do nothing. Being a saint was enough, and a saint simply existing was everything. Once you made saints do anything, they were just ordinary people. Chaplin said yes, he understood that.[17]

From Beverly Hills and Hollywood, Gertrude and Alice drove north through the San Joaquin Valley, through the remaining snow and spring rain of Yosemite, and finally west to the Bay Area for visits to scenes of their childhoods. Stein had been raised in Oakland and Alice across the bay in San Francisco. They eventually flew back to the East Coast and prepared to return to Europe on the *Champlain*, the same ship that had brought them.

In her hotel room at the Algonquin the morning before she and Alice Toklas sailed for France, Gertrude Stein gave an interview to a writer from the *Atlantic Monthly*. The writer described Stein as strong and round, built close to the earth, with marvelous brown eyes, and close-cropped grey hair, "like the hair of the Roman emperors." Stein talked freely about America, writers, and writing.

She had looked at things in America for a long time now, the interviewer observed. What did she think happened to American writers once they reached thirty-five or forty? It seemed to him that they lost their juice and dried up. "The trouble is a simple one," said Stein. "They become writers. They cease being creative men and soon they find that they are novelists or critics or poets or biographers." By defining and thereby limiting themselves in this way, they lost their creativity and passion. "If Mr. Robert Frost is at all good as a poet, it is because he is a farmer — really in his mind a farmer, I mean." Sherwood Anderson was truly great because he did not care what he was other than a man. He therefore managed to retain his freshness of creativity and passion. "Scott Fitzgerald, you know, had it for a little while, but — not any more. He is an American Novelist."

"What about Hemingway?" asked the interviewer.

"He was good until after *A Farewell to Arms*. No, he was not really good after 1925. In his early short stories he had what I have been trying to describe to you. Then — Hemingway did not lose it; he threw it away."

In *The Autobiography of Alice B. Toklas*, Stein had been purposely coy in discussing what she meant by the *real* Ernest Hemingway. It appeared to be a secret she shared with Anderson, a secret that Hemingway tried diligently to hide, but one the reader was left to puzzle over. Part of her meaning had to do with her suspicion at the time that Hemingway was a homosexual, and wouldn't his audience be surprised to read "the confessions of the real Ernest Hemingway." But more important from the perspective of his being a successful author was the other thing he attempted to hide. In her most extensive public remarks on Hemingway since the *Autobiography*, she made clear the critical points underlying his character.

"When I first met Hemingway," she said, "he had a truly sensitive capacity for emotion, and that was the stuff of the first stories; but he was shy of himself and he began to develop, as a shield, a big Kansas City–boy brutality about it, and so he was 'tough' because he was really sensitive and ashamed that he was. Then it happened. I saw it happening and tried to save what was fine there, but it was too late. He went the way so many other Americans have gone before, the way they are still going. He became obsessed by sex and violent death."

She warned the interviewer not to misunderstand what she meant. Sex and death were valid human emotions to write about. "But for Hemingway everything became multiplied by and subtracted from sex and death." From the very start she recognized that Hemingway did not write about these things to find out what they were; he used them to disguise what "was really gentle and fine in him, and then his agonizing shyness escaped into brutality." But, no, she said after a pause, Hemingway was not really brutal —

> the truly brutal man wants something more than bullfighting and deep-sea fishing and elephant killing or whatever it is now, and perhaps if Hemingway were truly brutal he could make a real literature out of those things; but he is not, and I doubt if he will ever again write truly about anything. He is skillful, yes, but that is the writer; the other half is the man.[18]

And it was the other half, the truly sensitive, emotional side of his personality that Hemingway tried to conceal.

Still in pain from the thrashing Gertrude Stein had given him in *The Autobiography of Alice B. Toklas*, Hemingway continued to plot ways of paying her back. He would not have tolerated a man calling him yellow, and with a man he would have known immediately how to respond, but with Gertrude, what could he do? His initial response, once he returned

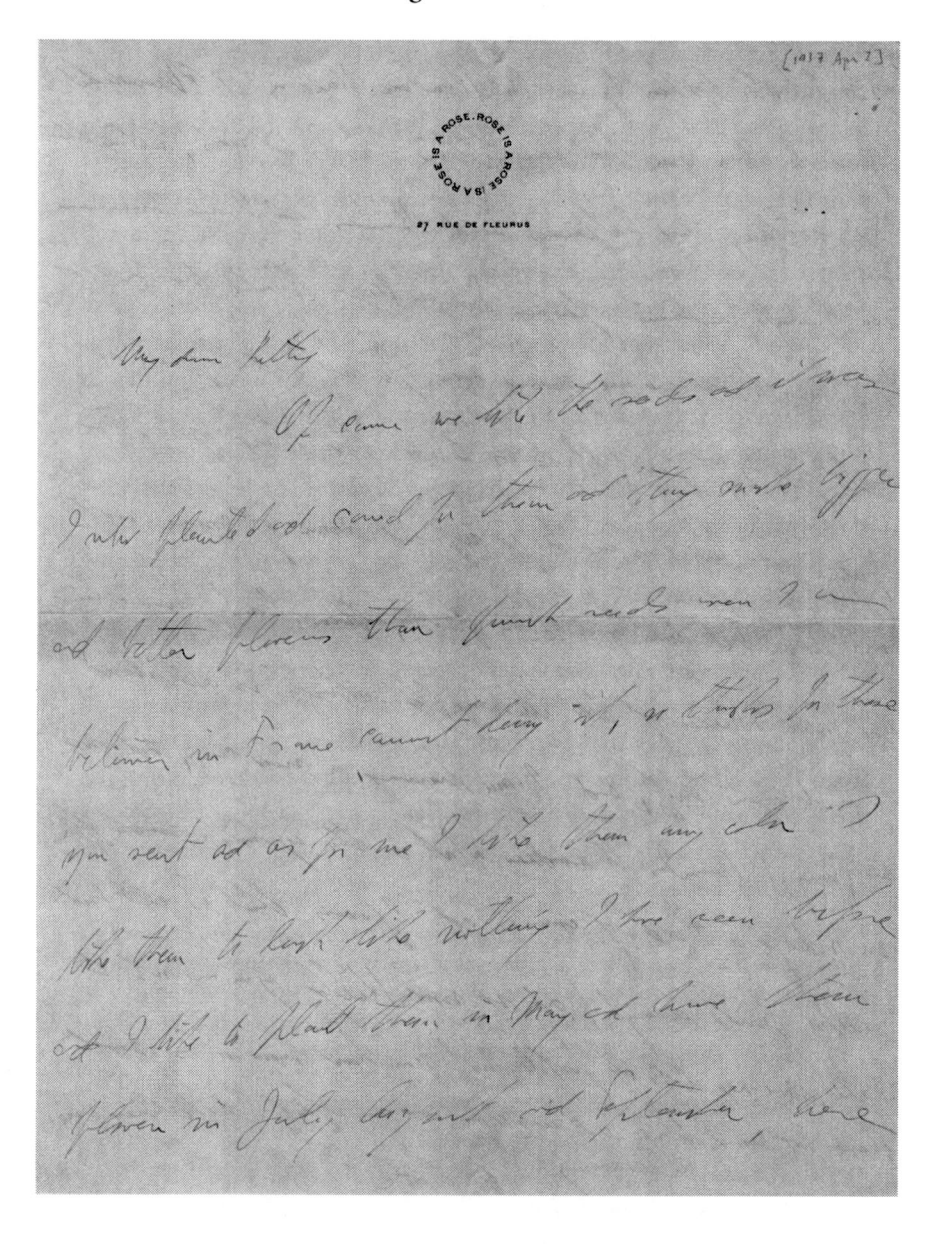

Gertrude Stein's letterhead stationery (Beinecke Rare Book and Manuscript Library, Yale University).

9. Knowing the Vital Spots

to Key West from his African safari, was to inscribe a copy of *Death in the Afternoon* "To Gertrude Stein from her pal Ernest Hemingway." Then, mimicking Stein's personal stationery, in which "rose is a rose is a rose is a rose" was printed in a circle at the top, he hand-printed in a circle, just beneath the inscription, "a bitch is a bitch is a bitch is a bitch." At the bottom of the page he scrawled in quotation marks, "Before the fruits of marriage came, marriage came," a play on the title *Before The Flowers Of Friendship Faded Friendship Faded*, Stein's rendering of Hugnet's poem, published three years earlier. Hemingway apparently never sent Stein his personally inscribed book, hoping, perhaps, that a better opportunity to get even would eventually present itself.

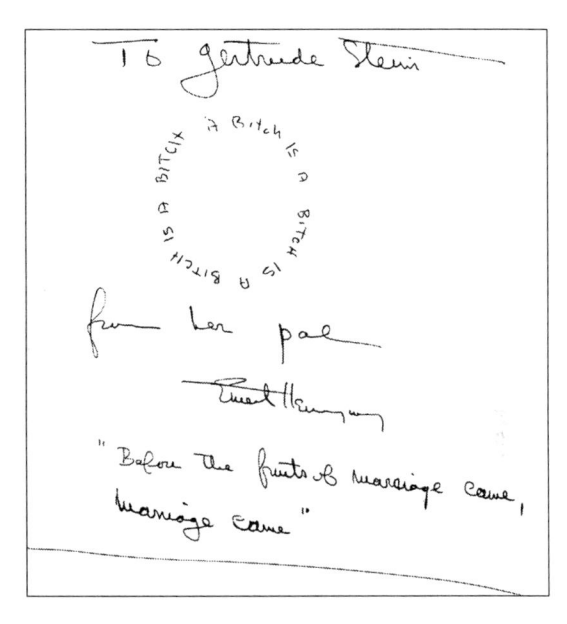

Hemingway's inscription to Stein in a copy of *Death in the Afternoon* (courtesy Lilly Library, Indiana University, Bloomington, Indiana).

He agreed to write twelve new articles for Arnold Gingrich's magazine *Esquire*, using the $3000 advance he received to help pay for a custom-fitted thirty-eight-foot fishing yacht he took possession of in May. He wrote two of the new *Esquire* articles on Africa and another on marlin fishing before deciding to put his remaining African material into a longer work he then started to write. Each day during the next six months, with appropriate breaks to go fishing with friends aboard his yacht *Pilar*, he relived his African adventures, turning out 492 handwritten pages by fall. About the time Stein arrived in New York to begin her lecture tour, he was nearing completion of the work.

Having put his African adventures into a book, and saying all he had to say for the moment on marlin fishing, he did not know how to fulfill his commitment to *Esquire*. Gingrich suggested he do a piece on Stein.

"She is getting the most sickening kind of adulatory play in the press right now —" Gingrich wrote, "maybe more nauseating in Chicago than elsewhere because she was here for the opening of the 4 saints in 3 acts last night — most comments refer to her fight, or misunderstanding, with you her erstwhile pupil." If Ernest could get a piece ready for the next issue, due on newsstands in December, he could call it "Merry Christmas to Gertrude."[19]

Hemingway replied that he did not want to write about Gertrude although such a piece would be a definite success. She had sounded so terrible on the radio a few nights back that it would be "like socking a dummy or a ghost." He assured Gingrich again that Stein had been a pleasant woman before the menopause, and anyway he did not feel right about taking shots at people who had been friends, no matter how rotten they eventually became. "Besides," he added, "I've got the gun and it's loaded and I know where the vital spots are." One always felt a great sense of superiority in just knowing "you can finish anybody off whenever you want to and still not doing it." He had written down all the facts about Gertrude so they would be safe and available if anything happened to him, "but I don't like to slam the old bitch around when she's here having a wonderful time."[20]

Being able to finish Gertrude off any time he liked was largely fantasy. His posthumous memoirs of Paris in the twenties would later show that the loaded gun he mentioned was not as devastating as he boasted. As for not wanting to slam Gertrude around, Hemingway did not let on to Gingrich that he had already slammed her in his new African book, soon to be serialized in *Scribner's Magazine*.

The first part of *Green Hills of Africa* appeared in the May 1935 issue. In a brief forward, Hemingway stated that none of the characters or incidents in the book was imaginary and that he had "attempted to write an absolutely true book to see whether the shape of a country and the pattern of a month's action can, if truly presented, compete with a work of imagination." For the magazine segments, though not for the printed book, he supplied a list of characters. Among them were

    Pop— Mr. Jackson Phillips, called Mr. J. or Mr. J. P.— a white hunter or professional guide. Not to be called Pop to his face
    Mr. Hemingway— A braggart
    Mrs. Hemingway— Wife of the above known as P. O. M. or poor old mama. Known to the natives as Mama

9. Knowing the Vital Spots 125

No reference to Stein appeared in the initial installment. But the opening chapter of part two, printed in the June number of *Scribner's*, contained a passage in which Hemingway represented himself talking to P. O. M. about the bravery of Mr. J. P., the white hunter:

> "Mr. J. P. is really awfully brave [says P. O. M.], you know he really is. He's *so* lovely."
> "Yes, and he doesn't have to read books written by some bitch he's tried to help get published saying how he's yellow."
> "She's just malicious. She knew that would make you angry."
> "It did all right. She's skillful when she's malicious, with all that talent gone to malice and nonsense and self praise. Well, she's cashing in now."[21]

Later in the year, as Scribner's prepared to publish the hardbound version of *Green Hills of Africa*, Max Perkins requested that Hemingway reconsider the passage about Stein. "I'm not afraid of libel," wrote Perkins, "+ I don't care a hang about her, but what she has said [in *The Autobiography of Alice B. Toklas*] was plainly spiteful + jealous + not worth so much notice from you, + almost all readers will not know what she said anyway but will sympathize with a bitch because she gets called a bitch. I simply submit this for Your consideration."[22]

Reluctant to alter what he had written, Hemingway told Perkins that he was only trying to be completely honest:

> I don't mention her name and what proves it is Gertrude? what would you like me to put in place of bitch? Fat bitch? Lousy bitch? Old Bitch? Lesbian Bitch? What is the modifying adjective that would improve it? I don't know what word to replace bitch with. Certainly not whore. If anyone was ever a bitch that woman was a bitch. I'll see if I can change it.

Later in the same letter, Hemingway returned to the word Perkins found objectionable:

> Would you prefer fat female? That is possible. I'll change it to fat female. or just female. That's better. That will make her angrier than bitch, will please you by not calling a lady a bitch, will make it seem that I care less about her lying about me, and will please everyone but me who cares only about honesty.[23]

By the time the book version appeared in New York on October 25, 1935, Hemingway had changed the passage — actually expanding it — to read as follows:

> "Don't you think he's wonderful [P. O. M. says of Mr. J. P.]?"

"Yes, and he doesn't have to read books written by some female he's tried to help get published saying how he's yellow."

"She's just jealous and malicious. You never should have helped her. Some people never forgive that."

"It's a damned shame, though, with all that talent gone to malice and nonsense and self-praise. It's a god-damned shame, really. It's a shame you never knew her before she went to pot. You know a funny thing; she never could write dialogue. It was terrible. She learned how to do it from my stuff and used it in that book. She had never written like that before. She never could forgive learning that and she was afraid people would notice it, where she'd learned it, so she had to attack me. It's a funny racket, really. But I swear she was damned nice before she got ambitious. You would have liked her then, really."

"Maybe, but I don't think so," said P. O. M.[24]

Initial sales of the African book were disappointing, and the reviews came in mixed. Bernard DeVoto, writing in the *Saturday Review of Literature*, observed that while the characters in the new book were well drawn, the literary discussion was mostly bad. Moreover, the descriptions of things were long, confusing, over-written, and tiresome. Hemingway had attempted a new stylistic technique and failed. Having given up the short, clear sentences of *The Sun Also Rises*, he now wrote a great many long, meandering ones, producing "a kind of etymological gas that is just bad writing." In his early days, Hemingway had "carefully pondered Gertrude Stein to his own gain. The repetitious Stein of 'Tender Buttons' doesn't show up here, but Stein who is out to get four or five dimensions into prose is pretty obvious." Hemingway, said DeVoto, had once tried to simplify his vocabulary; now he simplified his grammar "till the result looks like a marriage between an e. e. cummings simultaneity and one of those ground-mists of Sherwood Anderson's that Mr. Hemingway was burlesquing ten years ago."[25]

Even though Sherwood Anderson did not notice his own ground-mists in Hemingway's latest opus, he wrote to a friend that he had been reading "Hemmy's *Green Hills of Africa* and thinking of him.... It's really a lousy book, and the god awful thing is that he doesn't know it and never will." According to Anderson, Hemingway had got the notion in his head that you became a great writer by "chucking the imaginative world" and writing about the real. The only thing was, Hemingway knew little about the "real" world because it was not *his* world. "He can't feel his way around in it, can't get it." A whole world of people existed out there that Hemingway knew nothing about, so he declared his superiority to it, cried "Kiss my ass" and "The hell with it," and that's how he got out of the problem. "Then you see what he does. He romanticizes what he calls the real world, gets ecstatic about shooting and killing, guts and dung."[26]

Edmund Wilson thought *Green Hills of Africa* far and away Hemingway's weakest performance to date, "the only book I have seen that makes Africa and its animals seem dull." Wilson cited a newspaper reviewer who criticized Hemingway for using the book as an opportunity to get back at Stein for what she said about him in the *Autobiography*. The reviewer noted that Hemingway had gone all the way to Africa to hunt, "and then when he thought he had found a rhinoceros, it turned out to be Gertrude Stein."[27]

Ernest complained to Max Perkins that Scribner's had not pushed *Green Hills of Africa* hard enough. He also complained about the critics ganging up against it. His stuff, he said, was no longer judged by whether it was good or bad, interesting or dull, but whether it was *In Our Time* or *The Sun Also Rises* or *A Farewell to Arms* or *Death in the Afternoon*. "It all gives me a pain in the ass." He later apologized to Perkins for flying off so. "I feel sort of bitter about a lot of things but I always get over that."[28] His bitterness about Stein, however, would take longer to get over than most things.

In the summer of 1935, during an extended fishing expedition in the Gulf Stream aboard the *Pilar*, Hemingway spent time on the small island of South Bimini. Situated forty-five miles east of Florida's southern tip, Bimini served as layover point and victualling and refueling stop for small craft in the area. One evening on the wooden dock shortly after sunset, Hemingway encountered several men, one being Joseph Knapp, a large man about Ernest's size, part owner of *McCall's*, *Collier's*, and other magazines. Knapp recognized Hemingway from his pictures and began taunting him and goading him to fight. "I think he had read in Stein that I was a phony and picked the fight," Ernest later wrote Arnold Gingrich.

Hemingway warned Knapp that he didn't know what he was getting himself into, but Knapp persisted, and the two men began to grapple. Hemingway connected with three left jabs and wondered why Knapp did not go down. Knapp instead lunged forward, grabbing Hemingway in a clinch, Hemingway clubbing him twice behind the ear with his right fist before stepping back and landing a solid punch that caused Knapp to "hit ass and head almost same time on planks." Hemingway was untouched, but being barefoot, he had lost two toenails in the scuffle. Knapp sailed for Miami early the next morning seeking medical treatment.[29]

The encounter gave Hemingway the reputation on Bimini of being a pretty tough character, a reputation he thoroughly enjoyed. He told Gingrich that since his clash with Knapp, when anyone had too much to drink or felt like living dangerously, he asked Ernest to fight. It had become a local pastime called "Trying him." Said Ernest, "Have fought 4 times in last 2 weeks — twice with bare fists, twice with gloves. All knock outs."[30]

An incident similar to the Knapp affair occurred eight months later in Key West. Hemingway's sister Ursula was visiting from Illinois, and one evening she attended a cocktail party where another guest was the poet Wallace Stevens. With probably more than one drink under his belt, Stevens started berating Ursula about her brother, saying what a chump he was and how he wasn't really a man. If Hemingway was there right now, Stevens claimed, he would knock him out with a single punch. Although twenty years older than Hemingway, Stevens was considerably larger and fancied himself a good brawler.

Ursula ran home crying and told her brother what had happened. This was evidently the third time Stevens had shot his mouth off like this in public, and Ernest had had enough. He rushed outside into the gathering dusk and the rain, and encountered Stevens just as he emerged from the party. The clash was violent and conclusive. Hemingway knocked Stevens down several times, but Stevens kept getting up. Ernest had on glasses, and an onlooker told him to take them off so that it would be a clean fight, which Hemingway did. Stevens then delivered a crushing blow to Hemingway's jaw, but instead of injuring Hemingway, the punch broke Stevens' hand in two places. Ernest then gave the larger man a beating that left him bruised and swollen, and needing the assistance of a nurse.

Ursula, who witnessed the fight, was scared Stevens might die. Ernest feared being arrested and jailed. But no one pressed charges, and next day Stevens, wearing dark glasses, showed up at Hemingway's house, where he apologized to Ursula and asked for Hemingway's promise not to tell anybody about the incident. The official story was that he had fallen down stairs. Yet despite his promise, Hemingway could not keep the incident entirely secret. He assured a friend that due to his size, Stevens had gone down "in spectacular fashion into a large puddle of water in the street." Stevens was probably only a mirror fighter anyway, said Ernest, one of those who flex their muscles and practice devastating punches in the bathroom. But maybe he was wrong. "Anyway I think Gertrude Stein ought to give all these people who pick fights with poor old papa at least their money back."[31] She had convinced them he was a fake, but they were learning otherwise. He was getting damned tired of it though, he said, "but not nearly as tired of it as Mr. Stevens got."[32]

If only settling scores with Gertrude were as easy and as straightforward.

Once again in France, Gertrude Stein and Alice Toklas resumed their usual routine of spending the summer at Bilignin and the rest of the year in Paris. Stein continued having trouble writing. Words still did not ooze up from deep inside and down onto the page as easily as before. She continued to worry about identity and felt hampered by the constant awareness of an audience knowing her. At least she had resolved the issue of a genius not working. "It is always astonishing," she said, "that Shakespeare never put his hand to his pen once he ceased to write." Can genius exist, then, without activity — "does it still exist, yes or no." Her answer — "Rather yes, a genius is a genius, even when he does not work."[33]

To help get the syrup to pour again and help get the worry out of her system, she began a series of meditations inspired by her trip to America. In something of a compromise between her cryptic, repetitious style and the clearer style of the *Autobiography*, she wrote reflections on geography, human nature, the human mind, identity, audience, and more. The result was *The Geographical History of America, or The Relation of Human Nature to the Human Mind*, published by Random House the following year.

In February of 1936, Stein and Toklas flew to England where Gertrude delivered a lecture at Oxford and Cambridge universities titled "What Are Master-Pieces and Why Are There So Few of Them." She also addressed the French Club at Oxford with a talk called "An American and France," later expanded into the book *Paris France*. While staying at the home of composer Lord Gerald Berners in Oxford, Stein agreed to furnish Berners with a scenario for a ballet. She eventually adapted for the purpose a play she had written in 1931 called *They Must. Be Wedded. to Their Wife.*

The following month in Paris, she began writing *Everybody's Autobiography*, a continuation of what had happened in her life since *The Autobiography of Alice B. Toklas*. This time Stein wrote from her own point of view but still in the clear style that had distinguished the first memoir. She later told a friend, "The style in the autobiographies is what I call my moneymaking style. But the other one is the main one, the really creative one."[34] The new memoir contained no mention of Hemingway.

Near the end of *Everybody's Autobiography*, Stein noted the undercurrent of social unrest that had been running through France for some time. There was even talk of revolution. The French were used to such grumbling and it did not badly scare them. What really frightened people though, according to Stein, was the outbreak of civil war in neighboring Spain. That scared everybody, "really scared them, scared them because it was so near."[35] Fighting between fascist and Loyalist forces began in mid-July of 1936. Yet Stein did not think this portended another general European war. War, she maintained, must be conducted on a large scale, and Europe had grown too small. Everybody could tell what everybody else was doing. "Therefore Europe is too small to wage war since anybody now can see it all and if anybody really anybody can see it all then they cannot wage war. They can have a great many troubles but they cannot wage war. Not wage war."[36]

— 10 —

To Be One Succeeding

"War is coming in Europe as surely as winter follows fall," wrote Ernest Hemingway in a 1935 *Esquire* piece. This was a year before Gertrude Stein declared there would be no war.[1] Countries do not want war, Hemingway had written. Wars now were made by individual men. "France is a country and Great Britain is several countries but Italy is a man, Mussolini, and Germany is a man, Hitler."[2] These men wanted war. The civil war in Spain was just a dress rehearsal. The big conflict lay ahead and was already planned. Only the starting date remained uncertain. "If we want to stay out now is the time to decide to stay out. Now, before the propaganda starts."[3]

Hemingway personally did not want anything more to do with war. He had seen enough the first time around. He felt content to write, fish in the Gulf Stream, and hunt big game in Africa or birds and antelope in Wyoming. He was now at work on two stories set in Africa. One concerned a writer named Harry who, in marrying a rich woman, had sold himself out. Instead of writing, he had lived the good life on his wife's money. Several days earlier, while on safari, Harry had scratched his leg and forgot to put iodine on it. The wound became infected and moist gangrene set in. Although painless, the infection spread rapidly. Realizing he was about to die, he began thinking of all the things he had meant to write but now never would. He had traded his talent for comfort and security until it was too late. Now he lay helpless on a cot in a tent on the Serengeti Plain, rotting away literally as a man and figuratively as an artist.

The story served in part as a cautionary tale exploring some of Hemingway's own apprehensions. Married to a woman with money, Ernest lived in a big house in Key West, took expensive trips, and fished from his own yacht in the Gulf Stream. He had not published a novel in almost seven years. He drank too much and had ballooned to almost 300 pounds. How much of his own artistic integrity had he traded for comfort and security? A great deal he apparently felt.

Scott Fitzgerald, meanwhile, had completely gone to pot. He had faded nearly as fast as the writer in Hemingway's story. Fitzgerald had just published a three-part essay in *Esquire* titled "The Crack-Up." It comprised a brief personal account of how the big sudden blows from outside and the small subtle blows from within had taken their toll on him. He disclosed how a year before turning forty he realized "that I had prematurely cracked," mentally and physically, like an old plate.[4]

Hemingway thought Scott's article appalling. He found it shocking that Scott had given up so young and that he spoke so openly about his self-destruction. Yet Ernest figured that if Scott could discuss his humiliation publicly, he would not mind if others did too. Consequently, in his first African story, Ernest included a passage in which the dying writer Harry "remembered poor Scott Fitzgerald" and his romantic awe of the rich. Harry remembered how Scott "had started a story once that began, 'The very rich are different from you and me.' And how someone had said to Scott, Yes they have more money. But that was not humorous to Scott. He thought they were a special glamorous race and when he found they weren't it wrecked him just as much as any other thing that wrecked him."[5]

It was then Fitzgerald's turn to be shocked. After reading "The Snows of Kilimanjaro" in the August issue of *Esquire*, Scott wrote Hemingway complimenting him on the story overall, saying it was one of his best, though "poor Scott Fitzgerald" spoiled it for him and had cost him a night's sleep. He asked Ernest to lay off him in print and to drop his name when he included the story in a book. Hemingway, in his reply, said that he had not written about any of his friends for five years because he felt sorry for them, but now he was going to stop being a gentleman and resume being a novelist. When the story later appeared in a book, Scott's name had been changed to Julian.

Writing to Max Perkins, Fitzgerald mentioned the "crazy letter" Hemingway had sent him. Ernest, he said, had bragged about what a great writer he was and how much he loved his children. "Somehow I love that man, no matter what he says or does," Fitzgerald admitted, but one more smart remark and Scott would have to join those lining up against him. "No one could ever hurt him in his first books," Scott told Perkins, "but he has completely lost his head and the duller he gets about it, the more he is like a punch-drunk pug fighting himself in the movies."[6]

As fighting between Loyalist and fascist forces in Spain intensified, Hemingway decided that he should be there to see firsthand what was actually going on. News received in the States was often vague and contradictory. Perhaps he could write a series of dispatches that would help keep the United States out of the next big war. First, though, he must finish a novel he had started about contraband-running between Cuba and Key West. Getting this book out after such a long fallow period was important to him.

As he had indicated in his letter to Fitzgerald, Hemingway did not spare his friends. He described in his novel one character, clearly meant to be John Dos Passos, as "the incorruptible novelist," a man who often borrowed money from rich people without paying it back. "When he started he always paid every one back and he really was incorruptable [sic]. Then he began to work at it. Of course every once in a while he has a book out but he never pays anyone anymore." Another character in the novel speaks of Fitzgerald, using his real name, as never having had good sense. "All charm and talent and no brains.... He was romantic about money and about youth. Jumped right from youth to senility. Didn't think there was anything between. Didn't even bother to pass through manhood. Thought old age came after youth. Turned out it did for him." The same character labels Harry Crosby, who had recently committed suicide, a "silly ass ... crazy as a coot half the time," a terrible writer who should have killed himself sooner. Hart Crane, another suicide, who jumped off a ship in the Caribbean, "was an unfortunate buggar. Always propositioning the wrong sailors and getting beaten up. Had a dreadful beating in Havana the night before his boat sailed."

Hemingway did not even spare himself. As a character passes by a big white house with yellow shutters nearly hidden by large date palms, he thinks of the "big slob" who lives there. He had written a novel years earlier, a tour de force, "but all he writes now is that tripe in Esquire." He just seemed to quit. He had let everyone down. Easy living had probably softened him up. Key West was a tough town to write about. Still, you could find good stories and interesting people, "but that slob has lived here six years and he's never written a thing about them, he's too drunk I guess. Well that's the way they go when they get in the money. He stinks and his stuff stinks."[7]

Hemingway did not mention Gertrude Stein in the book.

After Hemingway finished his novel, he sent the typescript to Arnold Gingrich in Chicago, asking Gingrich to look it over. Gingrich soon wrote back, saying he had misgivings about portions being libelous. Hemingway invited Gingrich down to Key West where they could fish and talk about potential problems. Once Gingrich arrived, he and Ernest reviewed the novel, Gingrich contending that the personal references had to go. Hemingway argued vehemently for retaining them.

Despite Ernest's passionate insistence on keeping the passages, by the time Scribner's published *To Have and Have Not* in October of 1937, Hemingway had removed them, cutting out great chunks of text and leaving the gaps unfilled. "The book, as it came out," recalled Gingrich, "was rather malformed as the result of such major excisions without any sort of replacement of the deleted elements." Surprised at the lack of craftsmanship this revealed, a craftsmanship Hemingway had always prided himself on, Gingrich thought Hemingway's confidence as an artist was fast eroding. Hemingway had started to believe his own press clippings about being the great American author, and his writing suffered as a result.[8]

Although *To Have and Have Not* sold well, Hemingway still complained to Max Perkins that critics reviewed it unjustly.[9] Unlike Gertrude Stein, Hemingway took hostile reviews badly. To him they were personal attacks. While the awareness of audience made Stein self-conscious for a time and interfered with her writing, and while she could get pretty warm when attacked face-to-face, she remained almost entirely indifferent to negative criticism in the press. Over the years she had been accused of everything from charlatanism to being mentally impaired. Yet she believed so completely in herself and in the importance of her work, that hostile criticism had little effect on her. People who wrote disparaging remarks simply did not understand what she was doing. Hemingway, on the other hand, could not endure hostile criticism. Every disapproving word lacerated his mind, leaving a festering sore. Though many of his works dramatized the quality of "grace under pressure," a trait he often exhibited in real life under difficult and sometimes dangerous situations, he never mastered the art of grace under criticism. An unfriendly review stirred up feelings of persecution and rage that rankled for years.

An example took place in New York as he was passing through the city on his way to Spain. This was the second of his three trips to cover the Spanish Civil War for the North American News Alliance. He dropped in to visit Max Perkins at the Scribner's building on Fifth Avenue. As he entered Perkins's office, he found the editor seated behind his desk, and next to it, on one side, Max Eastman, who, four years earlier, had written "Bull in the Afternoon," the scathing review of Hemingway's bullfighting book.

Apparently delighted to see his former Paris friend again, Hemingway said to Eastman, "Hello, you great big son-of-a-bitch." With Perkins looking on, the two writers chatted briefly about Ernest going to Spain and about Eastman having missed Hemingway in Key West the previous winter. Ernest then moved closer and said, "I want to show you something." He unbuttoned his shirt to reveal the abundant dark hair on his chest. "Is that false hair?" he asked. He next undid the top button of Eastman's shirt revealing a somewhat sparse growth.

"I guess you have me there," said Eastman, and all three men laughed.

But Ernest's laugh quickly vanished. "Look here, what did you say I was sexually impotent for?" Taken aback, Eastman denied making any such statement. "Yes, you did, and you played right into the hands of the gang that were saying it." If he had the article, he would show him. Coincidentally, a volume of Eastman's essays, containing "Bull in the Afternoon," lay on Perkins's desk. Eastman picked up the book and handed it to Hemingway, inviting him to show Perkins where it was stated or implied that Ernest was impotent. Perkins could be the judge. Ernest found the passage about circumstances making it necessary for Hemingway "to put forth evidences of red-blooded masculinity" and the passage claiming that Hemingway had initiated a literary style "of wearing false hair on the chest."

"What does that mean —" said Hemingway, "some circumstance?" As Eastman tried to explain that those remarks carried no implications of sexual impotence, Hemingway, growing increasingly agitated, said, "You know damn well what you meant," and he shoved the open book into Eastman's face. Eastman, who did not box, but who knew something about wrestling, grabbed Hemingway and bent him back onto Perkins's desk, both men sliding off onto the floor, Hemingway on his back and Eastman on top. Eastman had some vague notion of going for Hemingway's throat, but then he saw Ernest smiling up at him. Hemingway next reached up and patted Eastman on the shoulder. He seemed to be saying that Eastman was not as soft as he first thought.

With people gathering at Perkins's door to see what the commotion was about, the two combatants quickly got to their feet and started picking things up off the floor that had fallen from the desk. When Eastman sat back down, Hemingway, still smiling, patted him again on the shoulder. He then walked away a few steps, turned around, and started shouting insults. "Ernest," said Eastman, "I think you're a lunatic."

Hemingway finally left the room, allowing Eastman and Perkins to conclude their business. As Eastman walked out of Perkins's office a short time later, Hemingway stood in a nearby room from which he began taunting Eastman and shouting more insults. "I hit you in the face with your own book," he yelled; "I let you off easy, see?"

Eastman was amazed by the entire episode. He decided that Hemingway's erratic behavior — his sudden shifts of emotion — "were simply crazy."[10] The incident also showed how personally Hemingway took negative criticism and how long he nursed a grudge.

"Sammy," said Gertrude Stein, "do you think that Alice and I are lesbians?"

Samuel Steward, visiting for a few days at Bilignin, was one of Stein's current young protégés. The question embarrassed him, coming so unexpectedly, and he recalled a hot fire going up his spine. "I don't see that it's anybody's business one way or another," he replied.

"Do you care whether we are?"

"Not in the least," he said, starting to perspire.

She asked if *he* was queer or gay or different "or whatever they are calling it nowadays." Steward reluctantly admitted that he was bisexual.

"It bothers a lot of people," said Stein. "But like you said, it's nobody's business." She pointed out that prejudice against homosexuals came from the Judeo-Christian ethos, "especially Saint Paul the bastard, but he was complaining about youngsters who were not really that way, they did it for money." Everybody suspects or knows those who are homosexual, but nobody says anything about it.

"We are surrounded by homosexuals," Stein continued; "they do all the good things in all the arts, and when I ran down the male ones to Hemingway it was because I thought he was a secret one."[11] Stein told Steward that the chief reason for her split with Hemingway was that she and Alice could not stand drunks. Hemingway drank a lot, and one night he turned up at her flat completely intoxicated and had to be ejected by two men who were visiting her.[12] That is what triggered the final break.

In late April of 1937, Gertrude Stein and Alice Toklas again flew to London. They attended the premier of *A Wedding Bouquet*, the ballet for which Stein had written the scenario for Lord Berners. Following the performance at Saddlers Wells Theatre, the audience called Stein, Berners, and the cast members out onto the stage where they took repeated bows. Stein remarked later that she guessed it was a great success. "And then we went somewhere [to the opening night party] and we met every one and I always do like to be a lion, I like it again and again, and it is a peaceful thing to be one succeeding."[13] Little did she realize that her succeeding in London was about the last peaceful thing she would enjoy for some time.

Early in 1938 the lease on 27 rue de Fleurus expired, and the landlord asked Stein to leave. He wanted the apartment for his son, who was soon to be married. A friend found Stein and Toklas another apartment on the rue Christine, a small street between the rue Dauphine and rue des Grands Augustins near the Palais de Justice. Gertrude Stein tried to view the change optimistically. For one thing, she and Alice "were tired of the present which also was the past." Besides, no servant at the old place could stand the kitchen, and after the people next door built a garage, no air circulated in the house.[14] The new apartment was smaller than the old one. Of the 131 paintings she owned, Stein could find space on the walls for only 99 of them. The rest had to be stored in closets.[15]

Not long after the move to the rue Christine, another misfortune occurred when Basket the dog died. Gertrude and Alice found this loss especially hard to bear, Stein saying that they "just cried and cried and cried." The vet advised getting another dog as much like Basket as possible, but Picasso argued against it. Getting another Basket, he said, would create only more torment. Imagine if he, Pablo, should die, and Gertrude went out and got another Pablo. It would just not be the same.[16] As she considered whether to follow the vet's advice or Picasso's, Gertrude Stein continued her walks about Paris, only now she ventured out alone. One afternoon as she strolled up and down the streets in her usual manner, she suddenly ran into Ernest Hemingway.

Each appeared genuinely delighted to see the other. Without evident signs of embarrassment, they talked and laughed just as though the decades of acrimony and name calling had never occurred. Hemingway assumed no tough guy posses, but displayed instead the shy, sensitive side of his character that Gertrude Stein had found so attractive twenty-five years earlier. In writing to Carl Van Vechten a short time later, Stein mentioned her "funny encounter with the real Ernest Hemingway" and how "we loved each other for an hour obstructing traffic on the Faubourg Saint Honoré." Hemingway, she said, "was funny really funny."[17]

Van Vechten, in his reply to Stein's letter, said that the meeting should produce literature on both sides: "I can't wait to see what you write about this."[18] Yet Van Vechten's expectations came to nothing. Perhaps the encounter seemed anticlimactic following the years of public sniping. Perhaps the dramatic events lying just over the horizon would drive the incident from their minds. Or perhaps the meeting revealed a foundation of genuine affection that showed how foolish their previous hostility had been. Whatever the reason, neither Stein nor Hemingway later wrote about their chance meeting one winter afternoon in 1938 on the Faubourg Saint Honoré.

Hemingway was in Paris on assignment again for the North American News Alliance. This was his fourth trip to Europe in the past year and a half. Germany had been massing troops along the French border and conducting summer war games. Many suspected that Hitler might be planning to invade France by the end of September, and Hemingway was there in case hostilities erupted. Accompanying him much of the time was a tall, attractive blond named Martha Gellhorn. The two had met in Key West two years earlier, had covered the Spanish Civil War together, and were presently continuing an affair they began in Madrid in 1937. Like Hemingway's first wife, Gellhorn came from St. Louis. The current wife, Pauline, had grown up there. Martha, at age thirty was a seasoned traveler, a journalist, and the author of two highly-acclaimed novels and several short stories. Like Hemingway, she was headstrong, professionally ambitious, and restlessly impatient at remaining in one place too long.

Ernest found himself again in a domestic quandary — attached to two women and not knowing which way to turn. One woman represented the possibilities of an exciting new relationship, the other a marriage gone stale. With winter closing in and no European war to write about, he decided to return to the States and think it over. Back again in Key West, he spent much of his time bickering with his wife and growing more discontented with the life around him. He had been in this place, surrounded by these people, long enough.

He also began turning over in his creative mind the knowledge and experiences he had acquired in Spain. One of his projects began as a story about an American college professor named Robert Jordan from Montana, expert in the use of high explosives, who finds himself in Spain at the outbreak of the civil war. He aligns himself with the Loyalist cause and is sent into the Guadarrama mountains to join a guerrilla band led by Pablo, an intelligent but ruthless fighter, who has recently turned coward. Jordan carries a backpack filled with dynamite and has orders to blow an important bridge that spans a deep gorge. He must get Pablo to help him. Hemingway told Perkins that after working steadily on the piece for many days, "[I] found I had fifteen thousand words done; that it was very exciting; and that it was a novel."[19]

To escape from his domestic problems and to gain the privacy he needed to write, Hemingway took a ferry across to Cuba where he got a small room at the Sevilla-Biltmore in Havana. He laid in a stock of cured meats and tinned foods, set up his typewriter, arranged his papers, and set to work. This was the simple, spartan life that appealed to him just now. He wanted no more of Pauline's wealthy friends and family, no more expensive African safaris on other people's money, no more big house in Key West with all its attendant responsibilities.

Martha Gellhorn, at work on her own novel, joined him in April. Dissatisfied with Ernest's cramped and cluttered hotel room, she scouted the vicinity and found a place to rent where she and Ernest could work in comfort. La Finca, "The Lookout," was a run-down farmhouse with a swimming pool on fifteen acres of land high up in the hills overlooking Havana. Martha used her own money to fix up the place, and when Ernest moved in with her, he knew that his life with Pauline was over. He did not feel the same remorse in leaving her that he had felt in parting from Hadley. Pauline had stolen him from his first wife; now Martha was stealing him from her. It seemed only fitting.

With the coming of summer, Martha visited her mother in St. Louis while Ernest headed for Wyoming and Idaho where he could fish, hunt, and continue to write about the American dynamiter. The problems posed by Hitler and Mussolini seemed far away. For now he lived only in his novel.

As Hemingway drove west across the United States, Gertrude Stein and Alice Toklas drove south through France to spend the summer as usual at Bilignin, not far from Belley. Alice had the garden to plant and take care of. Gertrude looked forward to reading, writing, chatting with farmers and shopkeepers, and taking long walks in the country. They had taken the vet's advice and gotten another dog, a large white male poodle they called Basket II. It looked identical to the first Basket. They contrived a harmless little fantasy in which Basket II was the offspring of Basket I, almost the reincarnation, so that both Baskets were really the same one, and now there was no more cause to grieve.

Talk of impending war dominated conversations and the news. Gertrude Stein continued to maintain that it was only talk. "Hitler will never really go to war," she told a young journalist, Eric Sevareid.

> He is not the dangerous one. You see, he is the German romanticist. He wants the illusion of victory and power, the glory and glamour of it, but he could not stand the blood and fighting involved in getting it. No, Mussolini — there's the dangerous man, for he is an Italian realist. He won't stop at anything.

Sevareid thought Stein politically naive. She had the best flow of talk he had ever heard — with the possible exception of Artur Schnabel, the pianist — but she did not understand Fascism.[20]

By August 1939, the situation looked ever more discouraging. Italy had recently annexed Albania. Germany had occupied Austria, the Sudetenland, Bohemia, and Moravia. Yet Gertrude Stein still argued that there would be no general European war. She seemed to think it a breach of etiquette to mention the possibility. "Oh, no, no," she told an acquaintance. "War isn't logical, no one wants a war. Yes, of course Hitler is making a speech tomorrow. He's always making a speech. Of course, Roosevelt's going to talk. Ha, ha, he's always talking. No, no, things aren't serious."[21] But when German troops invaded Poland a month later, on September 1, with Great Britain and France declaring war on Germany two days after,

10. To Be One Succeeding

Gertrude Stein became horribly frightened. "I had been so sure there was not going to be war and here it was, it was war, and I made quite a scene." She and Alice were spending the day visiting French friends when they learned that France had declared war. Stein began shouting, "They shouldn't! They shouldn't!" and her friends tried to console her. "I apologized and said I was sorry but it was awful, and they comforted me — they, the French, who had so much at stake, and I had nothing at stake comparatively."[22]

Gertrude and Alice decided that it would be safer to spend the winter in the country than in the capital, though they made a quick motoring trip up to Paris to retrieve some winter clothing and to shut up the apartment. Besides the clothing, they brought with them several paintings, including Picasso's 1906 portrait of Stein and Cézanne's portrait of his wife. They wanted to place the remaining pictures on the floor to help protect them from possible shelling and bombing, but there was not enough room on the floor, so they left the paintings on the walls. Gertrude figured that it would be a short war anyway, and that she and Alice would be returning to Paris in the spring to resume their normal lives. Little did she imagine that it would be five years before they saw Paris again.

Gertrude Stein had not lived in the country during the winter since she was a girl in northern California, and she enjoyed the experience. Gasoline became harder to get and the large stone manor house proved impossible to heat, but she liked the snow, the moonlight, and the task of sawing wood. She even began helping Alice by cutting box hedges around the property. Food was not a problem at first, and Gertrude had plenty of detective and adventure novels to read.

With the spring came renewed war activity. The Germans invaded France in May. Alice and Gertrude could hear bombs exploding in the distance, and there was a general uneasiness among the people in the area, but still things were not bad. Then on June 10 Italy declared war on France, and Gertrude Stein got really scared, "completely scared, and my stomach felt weak, because — well, here we were right in everybody's path; any enemy that wanted to go anywhere might easily come here. I was frightened; I woke up completely upset. And I said to Alice Toklas, 'Let's go away.'" They were less than eighty miles from the Italian border and things could get ugly fast. They viewed the Italians as less disciplined and therefore more dangerous than the Germans.

Gertrude telephoned the American consul in Lyon, who told her to leave immediately. The *préfet* at Bourg said the same thing. "Well, I don't know," Gertrude told Alice, "it would be awfully uncomfortable and I am fussy about my food. Let's not leave." She returned to cutting box hedges and tried to forget about the war. But two days later, Alice, who had been following news on the radio, said that sooner or later they would have to go. Besides the danger that every civilian in the region faced, Alice and Gertrude ran the additional risk, being Jews, of falling into German hands.

They drove to Lyon to obtain Spanish visas. On the way back, they were stopped several times by the French military who were setting up anti-aircraft guns and getting ready to blow up bridges. Before reaching Belley, they met a couple they knew, a doctor and his wife. Gertrude and Alice spoke about their indecision whether to leave or to stay. The doctor was staying, but doctors were like soldiers, he said, they had to stay. "But now how about us?" asked Gertrude. "Should we or should we not?"

The doctor thought carefully and said that in the last war he had friends who stayed during the German occupation and saved their homes while people who left lost theirs. He thought that unless your home was actually destroyed by bombardment, it was best to stay. Besides, he told the two women, "Everybody knows you here; everybody likes you; we all would help you in every way. Why risk yourself among strangers?"

"Thank you," Stein said, "that is all we need. We stay."[23]

About the time German troops surrounded Warsaw, and while they prepared to invade France, Ernest Hemingway and Martha Gellhorn were staying at Sun Valley Lodge in Idaho as non-paying guests. Celebrities were often invited to stay at the lodge free of charge. Their presence helped boost the prestige of the new vacation resort. Hemingway spent the mornings at work on his novel and the afternoons hunting pheasants and ducks in the surrounding hills. Martha sometimes participated in the hunt, Ernest having taught her how to shoot, but she was growing impatient to be in Europe now that the war had started. As an ambitious journalist, she always wanted to be where the action was. She got an assignment with *Collier's* and soon left for Finland. Hemingway stayed behind.

"I don't care about going to war now," Ernest wrote to Max Perkins

10. To Be One Succeeding 143

from Cuba where he had returned for the winter. "Would like to live a while and have fun after this book and write some stories." He wanted to spend more time with his sons as well. "Also would like to have a daughter."[24]

Martha returned to Cuba in mid–January 1940 to find Ernest still at work on his Spanish Civil War novel, which he finished in July. "It is a hell of a book," Hemingway wrote to Perkins. "I hated to have that damned Jordan get what he got after living with the son of bitch for 17 months. Felt worse than if it were me."[25]

A central character in the novel, Pilar, Pablo's woman, takes control of the guerrilla band once Pablo proves a coward. Pablo, in his cowardice, becomes unpredictable and poses a danger to Robert Jordan's mission and hence to the Loyalist cause in general. Pilar then decides to turn against Pablo and aid Robert Jordan in blowing the bridge. As a robust, assertive woman, Pilar shows striking similarities to Gertrude Stein. Hemingway describes Pilar as about fifty years old, "almost as big as Pablo, almost as wide as she was tall, in black peasant skirt and waist, with heavy wool socks on heavy legs, black rope-soled shoes and a brown face like a model for a granite monument. She had big but nice looking hands and her thick curly black hair was twisted into a knot on her neck."[26] Besides being shrewd, earthy, and domineering, she has a deep voice with a "tongue that scalds and that bites like a bull whip"; yet at times she can be warm and caressing as well. She becomes Robert Jordan's main support, offering astute advice and helping him get through difficult situations.

Even though Hemingway fashioned the character Pilar on the features that appealed to him in Gertrude Stein in the 1920s, Pilar does not seem at all intended as a commentary on Stein. Hemingway got in a direct jab at Stein elsewhere in the book, though. A passage in chapter twenty-four was evidently meant to be a reflection on Stein's diminishing importance to him personally and to literature in general. Unintentionally it reveals a lingering resentment toward a woman whose strong will and assertiveness he still found intimidating.

Robert Jordan is putting slices of onion on a sandwich early one morning when Agustín, one of the guerrilla fighters, asks if he always eats onions for breakfast. "When there are any," Robert Jordan replies. "What hast thou against the onion?"

"The odor. Nothing more. Otherwise it is like the rose."

Robert Jordan grinned at him with his mouth full.

"Like the rose," he said. "Mighty like the rose. A rose is a rose is an onion."

"Thy onions are affecting thy brain," Agustín said. "Take care."

"An onion is an onion is an onion," Robert Jordan said cheerily and, he thought, a stone is a stein is a rock is a boulder is a pebble.[27]

— 11 —

In Time of War

Germany invaded France on May 13, 1940, and France surrendered less than six weeks later. "It is funny about wars," Gertrude Stein observed, especially those involving the French. "In one war they upset the Germans by resisting unalterably steadily and patiently and valiantly for four years, in the next war they upset them just as much by not resisting at all and going under completely in six weeks. Well that is what makes them changeable enough to create styles."[1]

Before Germany and France signed an armistice, the mechanized German *Wehrmacht* rolled into Belley. Soldiers arrived in trucks and armored vehicles, some on motorcycles. To Gertrude Stein it seemed unreal to see German soldiers in their gray uniforms on the streets of this small French town. "They did not look like conquerors; they were very quiet." The soldiers did a lot of shopping, buying pastries, silk stockings, perfumes, and women's shoes. "They went up and down, but they were gentle, slightly sad, polite." They caused no trouble at all. "They were polite and considerate; they were, as the French said, correct. It was all very sad; they were sad, the French were sad, it was all sad, but not at all the way we thought it would be, not at all."[2]

The French avoided the Germans as much as possible and spoke of them among themselves only as "they." It was unpleasant having them there, but not as unpleasant as it might have been. Life did not change drastically. Alice put up a great quantity of raspberry jam, raspberries growing plentifully that year. Gertrude Stein continued to write. She wrote a piece for the November 1940 issue of the *Atlantic Monthly* titled "The Winner Loses: A Picture of Occupied France." She also wrote *The World*

Is Round, a children's book; *Ida A Novel*, published in 1941; and *Mrs. Reynolds*, published after the war. Ironically, *Paris France*, expanded from her earlier lecture "An American and France," was published in London on the day German troops marched into Paris — June 14, 1940.

Food, fuel, clothing, and other items became scarcer as the war progressed. Like others in the area, Gertrude went about the countryside, walking nine or ten miles a day, talking with friends and farmers, foraging for bread, a couple of eggs, or a little butter. Some peasants gave her a cat they called Hitler due to a marking that resembled a mustache, but Basket soon chased the cat off. Gertrude wondered if it was an omen.

She missed the Paris gossip. She liked hearing what everyone was doing. Despite her prolonged absence from the capital, she learned that Scott Fitzgerald had died suddenly of a heart attack in Hollywood at age forty-four. "Poor Fitzgerald," she wrote to a friend in the States, "I would have liked to have done something for him in memoriam, the three out of that old time together whom I really care for were Sherwood Hemingway and Fitzgerald." She wanted to know what had become of Hemingway. She had heard nothing about him in a long time.[3]

A little more than two months after Fitzgerald's death, she read that Anderson had died as he set out on a cruise to South America. "I wish he might have had his South America trip," she said, "he was so looking forward to it, he had written me about it just before he started, dear Sherwood."[4] She asked her stateside friend to keep her informed and also to put a few yards of white darning thread in every letter he sent. New clothes were hard to find. Everyone had to make his old clothes last, but there was no thread to mend them when they needed repair. Laundry soap was another item impossible to get. Gertrude and Alice were always especially delighted to receive a letter in which the sender had thoughtfully sprinkled some Ivory Soap flakes into the envelope. But even if clothes, thread, and soap had been available in shops, the women had no money to buy them. Eventually, in order to raise cash, Gertrude had to sell her Cézanne painting. They ate Cézanne for the remainder of the war she later remarked. Gertrude also had her Ford converted from burning gasoline to alcohol, but when alcohol became hard to get and there was not much reason to go anywhere anyway, she sold the car. She thought that people now lived much as they had in the Middle Ages. Still, things were not entirely bad. In many ways this was the most pleasant and peaceful time of Stein's life.

Everything had become simpler. "One day is the same as another day and yet every day is different."⁵

In February of 1943 the lease expired on the Bilignin house, and Gertrude and Alice had to move. Someone offered them a modern house in Culoz, a town of about 2,000 people, some twelve miles from Belley, and they took it. While saying goodbye to friends in Belley, they met the former *sous-préfet* of the town. He warned them to leave immediately for nearby Switzerland; otherwise the Germans would put them in a concentration camp. Stein protested that they were just moving to Culoz. Besides, the Swiss border was closed. The *sous-préfet* assured her that the matter could be arranged.

"You mean pass by fraud?" she asked.

"Yes," he replied, "it could be arranged."⁶

Alice and Gertrude discussed the proposition during supper. They both felt funny about leaving. Stein thought that anti–Semitism was silly and illogical, and she could not believe that it posed any real danger to them. Finally she said, "No, I am not going we are not going, it is better to go regularly wherever we are sent than to go irregularly where nobody can help us if we are in trouble, no I said, they are always trying to get us to leave France but here we are and here we stay."⁷

Culoz being an important railway center, especially for trains running to and from Italy, the town was occupied by 250 soldiers of the German Occupation Force. Gertrude and Alice moved among them, trying not to call attention to themselves. Nevertheless, soldiers appeared at the door one day demanding quarters for two officers and their orderlies. Rooms were quickly prepared, but there was not time enough to remove all the English language books scattered around the house. Also of concern was an English engraving, hanging in a guest room, of Benjamin Franklin demonstrating one of his inventions on a lake in an English park. Fortunately, the Germans took no notice of these things, nor of the women's American accents, and, to Gertrude and Alice's relief, left after two weeks. For the most part, Stein found the Germans more a nuisance than a danger. She later claimed they were like a fog — "something that was always there but which you walked right through and hardly saw or thought about."⁸

Close to Christmas there came a lull in the war, and Stein thought the conflict might be nearing an end. Food became less scarce and people began to move about more. One day Gertrude and Alice rode the train to

Aix-les-Bains to do some shopping. The town contained many German soldiers. In one shop the two women spotted an officer who looked just like Hermann Göring, Hitler's second-in-command. Stein decided, though, that it probably was not him. Göring would not be in a small French town drinking chocolate and eating bread and jam.

Earlier in the day, the women had gone into a small café just outside Aix-les-Bains. Two German soldiers were there. One of them looked to Stein very much like Hemingway when he was young. He might actually have been "a Czech or something," Gertrude thought, but in a German uniform he was still the enemy, "and like Hemingway he was drinking, he had a brandy and then he had an eau de vie and then he had a glass of sparkling wine and then he had an Amer Picon, and then he had a glass of sparkling wine and he looked more and more like Hemingway" the more he drank. Finally, as the two soldiers prepared to leave, "the good-looking one who looked like Hem when he was young" held out his hand to shake hands with the proprietress. The proprietress, although greatly embarrassed, could not refuse. After the soldiers left, no one in the café said anything, though Stein realized that all understood and felt the same way: "to sell and take money is one thing but to shake hands is another thing and the proprietress knew it was not her fault and still she knew it should not have happened."[9]

On the first anniversary of the start of the Second World War, Ernest Hemingway and Martha Gellhorn left Cuba to vacation once again in Sun Valley, Idaho. With the typescript of his book safely in Perkins's hands, Ernest looked forward to some relaxation. *For Whom the Bell Tolls* appeared the following month to strong critical acclaim. Typical was the review in the *Atlantic Monthly*, the reviewer stating that *For Whom the Bell Tolls* was "a rare and beautiful piece of work." Hemingway had succeeded magnificently. "He has done his finest work, and, what is perhaps more important, he has dispelled any fears concerning his own limitations."[10]

With his career and reputation revitalized, his private life improved as well. At least it became less complicated. Pauline had filed for divorce in May on grounds of desertion. The divorce became final six months later, and less than three weeks after that, Ernest and Martha got married in Cheyenne, Wyoming. Martha was scheduled to leave for China at the end of January to cover the Sino-Japanese War for *Collier's*, and Ernest agreed to go with her. He was not altogether keen on the trip, but he had nothing better to do at the time. He was going more as a companion than as a working writer, though just before leaving, he agreed to write a series of articles for the liberal New York newspaper *PM*. Also before leaving, he made a quick trip to Cuba to spend time with his sons over Christmas. While on the road, he learned of Scott Fitzgerald's death. Not long before, Ernest had reread Fitzgerald's novel *Tender Is the Night*, and he wrote to Max Perkins saying how amazingly excellent much of it was. "Reading that novel," said Hemingway, "much of it was so good it was frightening."[11]

Hemingway was pleased with the reception of his own latest book. Even with the war in Europe and the poor economic conditions at home, it was selling well. He jokingly wrote former wife Hadley of his promise to son Patrick "that every time we sold 100,000 copies I would forgive a son of a bitch and when we sold a million I would forgive Max Eastman."[12]

By the time Ernest and Martha arrived in China, Ernest learned that Anderson had died. "Writers are certainly dying like flies," Ernest wrote to Perkins from Hong Kong. "It is a damned shame about old Sherwood. He always liked living very much. I suppose finally no one will be left alive but the Sitwells."[13]

Martha later recounted the China trip in her book *Travels with Myself and Another*, the other being Hemingway, whom she referred to only as U.C. (the Unwilling Companion). She did not use his name.[14] The book describes half a dozen "horror journeys" she experienced during the course of her extensive travels. This particular trip to China was a horror primarily due to the widespread poverty and disease they encountered, the smell of sweat in the crowded cities, and the stench of human waste just about everywhere. Despite her own revulsion, Hemingway remained sanguine throughout. He seemed always at his temperamental best under physically adverse and challenging conditions.

After returning home, and with entry of the United States into the war following the Japanese attack on Pearl Harbor, Martha became more eager than ever to be where the action was. Cuba seemed about as far from the war as one could get. It is true that German submarines had begun operating in the Caribbean. Reports circulated that German U-boats sometimes stopped fishing vessels at sea and requisitioned their supplies. Martha set off in a 30-foot sloop, along with three crew members, on a two-month excursion to research and write about the situation for *Collier's*. She had been encouraging Ernest to get more involved in the war. As a writer, he had an obligation to witness what was happening and to report on it. Hemingway felt that he would have to go to the war eventually though he was in no hurry. The war would last five years he said in July of 1942, "maybe ten, maybe always."[15]

Growing restless at being in one place so long, and becoming discontented with Ernest's lifestyle — especially with his Cuban cronies and his increasingly heavy drinking — Martha sailed for Lisbon in October 1943 to report on the war for *Collier's*. Her departure annoyed Hemingway. Part of his annoyance was guilt, for while he had written little during the previous few years, Martha had been chasing all over and publishing one magazine article after another. Feeling deserted and lonely with Martha gone, he resented that she cared more about advancing her career than being his wife. When Martha returned home in March 1944, she again urged Hemingway to stop squandering his time and talent, and to get involved in the war effort. Hemingway, jealous that Martha had been to the war and he had not, railed at her for being war crazy, for seeking danger and excitement, and for being selfish and having no responsibility to others. "I put it to him," Martha said later, "that I was going back, whether he came or not."[16]

Hemingway finally yielded and accompanied Martha to New York, all the while continuing what she termed his "hideous and insane reviling" of her conduct. He claimed not to have the slightest interest in going to the war in Europe. He felt no excitement at all about the prospect. "Just feel like horse, old horse, good, sound, but old, being saddled again to race over the jumps because of unscrupulous owner." As always, he would make the race as best he could, even though he was neither happy nor interested. He was sure he would be killed and hoped Martha would be satisfied at what she had done. Martha responded that he was making it impossible for her to love him.[17]

Hemingway, before leaving for Europe, signed a contract with *Collier's* to be its chief war correspondent. Martha regarded the act as calculated treachery designed to put her in her place. Magazines were allowed only one frontline correspondent, and this relegated her to secondary status. She would now be authorized to visit only non-combat zones. On March 13 Hemingway left for England by plane while Martha made the zigzag crossing (to avoid German U-boats) in a ship loaded with dynamite. The trip took seventeen days. During the crossing, she had time to think matters through and reach a conclusion. She wrote a friend while at sea that as far as she was concerned, it was all over. Ernest was rare and wonderful; he was a mysterious type and wise in so many things; and he was a good man overall. "He is however bad for me, sadly enough, or maybe wrong for me is the word; and I am wrong for him." She didn't know how it happened or why, but "it will never work between us again."[18]

Upon arriving in port at Liverpool, Martha learned that Ernest had been in an automobile accident three days earlier. Receiving a severe concussion and lacerations to the head requiring fifty-seven stitches, he was now recovering at the London Clinic. She also learned that prior to the accident he had been attending an all night drinking party. The man driving him back to his hotel at three in the morning through blacked out streets, had piled into a steel water tank. Martha was livid that Ernest should be partying in a time of war. She arrived at the hospital in an ugly mood but broke into laughter when she saw him with a mound of bandages on top of his head like a turban. He had been entertaining friends and was shocked at Martha's lack of sympathy. "If he really had a concussion," Martha said later, "he could hardly have been drinking with his pals or even receiving them. He did not look the least ill anyway." Hemingway's injuries were real enough, but Martha by this time was entirely fed up and could not muster any compassion for him. She told Hemingway she was through, completely finished, and walked out.[19]

Hemingway soon wrote to his son Patrick complaining of Martha's "Prima-Donna-ism" and her lack of humanity. He had made a great mistake with her, or else she had changed — perhaps both. He later complained to a friend that Martha did not care for pictures, music, nor good books but liked to read detective and crime fiction. Since he corrupted easily, he also started reading those things. "I was basically unhappy much of the time I was with her," he said, "because I knew I was a damned fool and a shit to have left my wife and children no matter how much I tried to rationalize it and I drank too much, using it as an anaesthetic on my conscience, and as I said I even read detective stories." As for Martha in particular, "I can say M. was the most ambitious girl I ever met. That doesn't mean much because I have not met many ambitious girls as they frighten me and I dislike them. I was in love with Martha but I never liked her too much."[20]

While Martha Gellhorn was by nature more restless and peripatetic than Grace Hall Hemingway and Gertrude Stein, all three, due to their assertiveness and ambition, produced in Hemingway complex feelings of love, fear, dislike, and respect. All three, in addition to being self-assured and headstrong, were Hemingway's intellectual equals. Ernest could not dominate them nor impress them with his "matador poses." He being an ambitious, headstrong individual himself, such personalities were bound to create friction as they interacted. But while Martha retained a life-long aversion to Hemingway following their breakup and wanted nothing more to do with him, Stein harbored no such feelings. She could drop friends quickly enough, but nursing personal hatreds was not part of her character.

Gertrude and Alice Toklas remained in Culoz, even as conditions there became more dangerous. Several times the war appeared to be winding down only to pick up again. The Germans, after a series of easy victories at the start, were now suffering defeats — in Russia, North Africa, and the Crimea. In the area around Belley and Culoz the Germans grew more desperate and menacing. They began intimidating local civil servants and started arresting enemy aliens. Gertrude and Alice hunkered down and awaited better times. Alice recalled, "By the autumn of 1943 food was no longer a subject. We were impatiently waiting for the invasion and liberation."[21]

The expected invasion started the following June when Allied forces landed at Normandy and slowly, during the ensuing months, fought their way inland. In mid–August another invasion force of U.S. and Free French troops landed in southern France between Cannes and Toulon. Alice wrote, "Just when the communiqués were getting almost unbearably exciting, two officers and thirty soldiers of the Italian army were billeted upon us." The officers took up quarters in the house while the soldiers made do with the garage and the chauffeur's quarters.[22] Contrary to their earlier fears, Gertrude and Alice found the Italians more sociable than the Germans. The Italians recognized the women as Americans, but that presented no problems. The soldiers were soon supplying Alice with tobacco from the black market, tobacco being something she had long been without, and the officers sent the women three pounds of Parmesan cheese.

The war news, meanwhile, continued heartening as Allied forces advanced eastward from their beachhead at Normandy. Tanks of the French

11. In Time of War 153

2nd Armored Division entered Paris from the southwest at about seven in the morning on August 25. U.S. soldiers marched in from the south a short time later. By mid-afternoon the German commander in Paris surrendered to French officers. "Glory hallelujah Paris is free," exclaimed Gertrude Stein upon hearing the news, "imagine it less than three months since the landing and Paris is free."[23]

"When we heard over the radio that Paris was liberated we were wild with excitement," wrote Alice Toklas later. "The end was near."[24] Gertrude and Alice might have been surprised to know that among those helping to liberate Paris that August day in 1944 was Ernest Hemingway.

Hemingway had long resisted going to the war. Before Pearl Harbor he had urged in various magazine articles that America stay out. But once the United States entered the conflict, and once he got personally involved, he threw himself wholeheartedly into the action. Twelve days after his automobile accident, and still not fully recovered, he got a close-up look at the D-Day landing at Normandy. He watched from the stern of a landing craft carrying troops and ammunition through mine fields to a sector of Omaha Beach. As the craft tried to land, it drew heavy salvos from two German machine-gun emplacements. "The machine-gun fire was throwing water all around the boat," Hemingway wrote in a *Collier's* dispatch, "and an antitank shell tossed up a jet of water over us." He could see bodies strewn along the beach and tanks burning near the shore. Destroyers attempted to take out German pillboxes with their deck guns. "I saw a piece of German about three feet long with an arm on it sail high up into the air in the fountaining of one shellburst." The landing craft Hemingway was on managed to discharge its troops and ammunition, and get out.[25]

Back in England, Hemingway flew on several bombing missions with the Royal Air Force. He also went on two flights in which the pilot attempted to shoot down German rockets headed across the Channel toward the English coast. The missions were dangerous and exhilarating, and they allowed Ernest to forget for a time his problems with Martha.

Six weeks after the D-Day landing, Hemingway returned to Normandy, linking up with General Patton's tank division. From there, near the end of July, he transferred to the 22nd Regiment, 4th Infantry Division. Many colleagues were puzzled, some greatly impressed, and a few disgusted, to find this well-to-do, middle-aged, world-renowned author enduring the rigors of war along with men nearly half his age. Hemingway appeared to enjoy battlefield conditions and even to thrive on them. This followed a recurring pattern in his life: irritable when bored and lonely, he invariably grew more focused, composed, and good-natured under physically challenging circumstances.

Over the next four months Hemingway saw a good deal of fighting. He took part in some of it, always showing courage under fire. His active participation in combat violated Geneva Convention rules, which prohibited journalists from carrying arms or from engaging in warfare. Yet for the moment he seemed less interested in being a journalist than in experiencing combat firsthand.

In August he learned that Paris was soon to be taken and that General Eisenhower had given the task and the honor to the French 2nd Armored Division under General Leclerc. Hemingway joined Leclerc's army at Rambouillet, twenty-three miles southwest of Paris. Over the next week he helped interrogate prisoners and helped coordinate information on enemy troop positions. He also gathered about him a small circle of French guerrilla fighters who began addressing him as Captain. When Leclerc's army moved on Paris, Hemingway and the guerrillas, in their jeeps, accompanied the advancing column. The armored division quickly penetrated the protective screen of German tanks and artillery set up to impede the French and allow the bulk of German troops to evacuate. When the French army reached the outskirts of the city, Hemingway's group raced ahead. Ernest wanted to be the first American to enter Paris.

German commanders were already prepared to surrender, but small pockets of resistance remained. Small arms fire crackled throughout the city, and the streets continued dangerous. Hemingway and his group first made their way to the Traveler's Club to ensure that it was free of Germans, and then they moved on to the Café de la Paix and the Ritz Hotel. Next day they "liberated" the Negro de Toulouse and Lipp's Brasserie before pulling in to the rue de l'Odéon. Sylvia Beach heard someone outside repeatedly calling her name, and soon people in the street took up the call of "Sylvia!" Adrienne Monnier, Sylvia's companion, cried, "It's Hemingway! It's Hemingway!" Sylvia ran downstairs and collided with Ernest. He picked her up and swung her around and kissed her. Shakespeare and Company had been liberated.[26]

Hemingway later often embellished his exploits in helping to free the city. Yet he also wrote that taking Paris was nothing much. "It was only an emotional experience. Not a military operation." The Germans, he said, in fleeing the city, had left behind a lot of office workers as soldiers, figuring that typists would not be needed any longer.[27]

As Allied divisions continued dislodging German troops from northern France, U.S. forces moved up from their beachhead in the south. About the time Allied troops moved into Paris, American soldiers arrived at Grenoble, some fifty miles from Culoz. "[O]h, if they would only come by here," Stein said. "We must see them. There is no way of getting there."[28]

Except for a handful of railway men, the Germans had pretty much cleared out of the Belley/Culoz region. When the military left in mid-July, Gertrude was sitting with the mayor's wife near the main road out of Culoz. "There were quite a few motor cycles rushing up and down with German soldiers," she wrote, "and then there was a lull and then there came along hundreds of German soldiers walking, it was a terribly hot day and in the mountain heat is even hotter than below, and these soldiers were children none older than sixteen and some looking not more than fourteen." Gertrude thought it unbelievable that the once feared German motorized army had been reduced to this—"childish faces and the worn bodies and the tired feet and the shoulders of aged men."[29]

When the Italians departed, Alice said later, "they tore up their military papers and left singing. There were about six hundred Italian soldiers in the neighbourhood and the frontier was only 125 kilometres away. We hoped they would cross it safely. Later we heard that they had all been killed by the Germans."[30]

Gertrude and Alice routinely visited Belley once a month to shop and to bank. On the last day of August they went to town as usual and were told that Americans had arrived—they were in the hotel. Greatly excited, Gertrude and Alice hurried to the hotel and entered a room filled with French resistance fighters, the mayor, and various others. Gertrude asked in a loud voice, "Are there any Americans here." Three men stood up and said they were Americans. They came from the 120th Engineers. "We held each other's hands and we patted each other and we sat down together and I told them who we were, and they knew."[31] Gertrude offered to put them up for the night at her house, and they accepted.

Next day, the fifth anniversary of the war's beginning, as everyone sat down to lunch, four more Americans showed up at the house. They were war correspondents and included Eric Sevareid, who had purposely come looking for Stein and Toklas. "Gertrude greeted us with a shout and a bearhug," wrote Sevareid. "We talked, of course, for hours and hours. Rather, Gertrude talked and we listened, and the process was as agreeable as ever before." Stein wanted to hear all the gossip she had missed during her years of isolation. She inquired about many of her friends. She asked about Hemingway. When they told her they had just seen Hemingway's wife, Martha Gellhorn, "Alice sniffed and said: 'That makes his third wife. Tch, tch, tch.'"[32]

As Stein began talking about Hitler, Sevareid interrupted to remind her of their prewar discussion in which she had insisted that Hitler was not dangerous being only a German romanticist. "Miss Stein hesitated only a moment, then went on with the thread of her conversation, pretending not to have heard me."[33]

In relating the experiences she and Alice had been through, Gertrude said that the Germans "were unpleasant at times but never really bad while they were here." They had a terrible habit, however, of carrying off the keys. One German soldier used to come to the door and ask politely if he could walk in the garden.

Their French neighbors had been truly marvelous. The mayor, for instance, a small man with a bald head and a huge mustache, had conveniently forgotten to list their names when the Germans were rounding up enemy aliens. He told Gertrude, "you are obviously too old for life in a concentration camp. You would not survive it, so why should I tell them?"[34]

Even with the Germans gone and Paris liberated, Gertrude and Alice did not leave Culoz right away. For several months, said Gertrude, "we were so busy just feeling free and talking to everybody who was feeling free too, that we almost forgot about going back to Paris." Besides, the capital was said to be dark and dreary with no electricity, gas, or food. During the occupation, she had kept herself from talking about the apartment that had lain vacant for five years. She was afraid to think about the pictures that were now worth a great sum. There was nothing she could do about the situation, and talking about it would only have worried her unnecessarily. She did, however, get friends in Paris to go by the apartment and investigate. Gertrude and Alice learned, much to their relief, that the place was dirty but otherwise undamaged. The pictures all seemed to be there. It had been a close call, though, for in the waning days of the occupation, just two weeks before Paris was liberated, four members of the Gestapo entered the apartment, apparently looking for Stein. A neighbor girl heard the men moving around on the floor above, rushed upstairs, and confronted them. The Germans were going through personal belongings and had worked themselves into a fury over the Picasso pictures, saying they were examples of degenerate art. The men threatened to cut up the pictures and burn them. The girl ran back downstairs and phoned the French police, who showed up in force ten minutes later. When the Germans could produce no written authorization for being there, the gendarmes ordered them out. But the Germans returned the following day and entered the apartment using a key they had lifted the day before. They stole linen, dresses, shoes, and some kitchen items, but they left the pictures alone.[35]

Gertrude and Alice returned to Paris in mid–December. They were home at last. "It was all over," wrote Gertrude, "it was very frightening, the apartment was very lovely, the treasures were all there, and we went to sleep, quite a little frightened, but still asleep, not warm nor cold, a little tepid, and on the whole very happy."[36]

Following the liberation of Paris, Ernest Hemingway rejoined the 22nd Regiment. It was now fighting in the Hürtgen Forest near Aachen as part of an enormous Allied effort to push the Germans out of France and Belgium and back into Germany. The drive had bogged down at the Siegfried Line, a series of fortified positions running along Germany's western border. The fighting was brutal, taking place at close quarters and in hostile terrain. The campaign proved one of the costliest of the war. The U.S. lost more than twenty-five percent of its men engaged in the battle. Besides lacking adequate supplies and combat support, soldiers suffered from the rain, snow, cold, and mud. Many contracted pneumonia, trench foot, and other ailments related to the severe winter conditions. In three months more than 33,000 Americans were killed, wounded, captured, or disabled by disease.

Under these difficult conditions, Hemingway displayed the same composure, the same courage under fire, that he had shown on previous occasions. One evening in the living room of a farmhouse that served as headquarters, Ernest joined the regimental commander and other officers for dinner. Just as the meat was served, a German artillery shell smashed through the wall facing Hemingway and went out the opposite wall without exploding. Everyone but Hemingway scrambled for the cellar. As the commander reached the head of the stairs, he looked back. "Hemingway was sitting there quietly, cutting his meat," the officer wrote later.

> I called to him to get his ass out of there into the cellar. He refused. I went back and we argued. Another shell came through the wall. He continued to eat. We renewed the argument. He would not budge. I sat down. Another shell went through the wall. I told him to put on his goddamned tin hat. He wouldn't, so I removed mine. We argued about the whole thing but went on eating. He reverted to his favorite theory that you were as safe in one place as another under artillery fire unless you were being shot at personally.[37]

Hemingway eventually contracted pneumonia and returned to Paris on December 4 to recuperate. When the Germans launched a massive counterattack on the 16th, Hemingway, although still running a fever, decided to rejoin the regiment. First, however, he had to see Gertrude Stein. He learned that she had just returned to Paris, and, according to Sylvia Beach, he wanted to patch up their quarrel. But he was "skeered," wrote Beach, and "couldn't get up the courage to go alone. I encouraged him in his plan, and promised to accompany him to the rue Christine, where Gertrude and Alice were then living. I thought it better for Hemingway to go up alone, so I took him all the way to her door and left him with my best wishes. He came to tell me afterward that it was 'fine' between them again."[38]

Ernest Hemingway as war correspondent, 1944.

His conversation with Stein had been brief. "There wasn't a hell of a lot of time then," Ernest remembered, "and so I just told her I had always loved her and she said she loved me too which was, I think, the truth from both of us."[39] That was all Hemingway said of the incident, and Gertrude Stein wrote nothing. It was the last time the two would meet.

— 12 —

Three-Cushion Shots

Hemingway remained too sick to participate in the final action in Hürtgen Forest. Yet confident the Allies would soon win the war in Europe, he decided to return home. On the way to New York, he stopped in London for a brief visit with Martha to initiate divorce proceedings, and by mid–March he was back in Cuba, having been gone fifteen months.

Gertrude Stein, after returning to Paris, became a favorite among American GI's in the city. She stopped to talk with them on the streets, asking them about their families, where they came from, how they liked the Army, what they planned to do on returning home, and many other things. She signed autographs, posed for pictures, and invited many of the soldiers to her apartment. It seemed to Alice Toklas that she invited them all. Alice served refreshments while Gertrude lectured, scolded, and asked questions as she had formerly done with the young men who came to visit her following the First World War. "Our home again became a salon," wrote Alice. "There were almost constant visits from American GI's."[1]

The young soldiers fascinated Gertrude Stein. Their language and their attitudes especially intrigued her. She felt generally optimistic about the young men's futures. "After the last World War there was the lost generation," she wrote in an article for *New York Times Magazine*; "they were very successful but I called them sad young men because their life was finished by 30." The young men coming out of this world war were different. They were sad already, even before leaving home, so "there is a fair chance that life will begin at 30 instead of ending at 30 and I think more or less that is what is going to happen to this generation."[2]

Throughout the war, Gertrude Stein had kept a journal of her thoughts and experiences under the German occupation. Early in March, 1945, Random House published the work, titled *Wars I Have Seen*. Stein once confided to a friend that she had envied the financial success of writers like Hemingway and Louis Bromfield. She wrote, "The Hem Louis made me sad because they earn so much money, when I think Paris France brought me less than a thousand and Winner Loses $250 and yet it was read all over the world and Ida which seems much loved only $350, it is sad ... it would be nice to make money, so nice, well anyway...."[3]

Now Bennett Cerf wrote her that *Wars I Have Seen* was doing extremely well. The book had sold 10,000 copies less than a month after publication. "This will undoubtedly be by far the most popular success you've ever had in America," he said.[4] In addition, Batsford Ltd. was set to bring out a British edition in the fall. Added to the royalties these editions would bring her, she received $2,000 for allowing *Collier's* magazine to print portions of the book. At seventy-one, Gertrude Stein thoroughly enjoyed her popularity and good fortune. She looked much thinner than when in her prime, and she had begun having intestinal problems, but she still appeared healthy and showed little inclination to slow down. At the suggestion of one of her new soldier friends, a corporal with the 441st Troop Carrier Group, she and Alice Toklas boarded a troop transport plane and, over a period of several days, flew to German cities devastated by the war. Stein observed the destruction and met with American GI's everywhere she went. Back in Paris she began a book called *Brewsie and Willie*, named after the two main characters. The work attempted to capture the language and the attitudes typical of American soldiers stationed in Europe.

Gertrude Stein also began another collaboration with Virgil Thomson. She and Thomson had communicated little during the late thirties and not at all during the war. In 1945, however, Columbia University offered Thomson $1,000 and Stein $500 for another opera, and both accepted. It had been eighteen years since Thomson asked Stein to write the libretto for their first opera, *Four Saints in Three Acts*. Stein again wanted to do something on George Washington and again Thomson vetoed the idea. He argued once more that the costumes would make everyone look the same. Stein then selected for her subject Susan B. Anthony, the nineteenth century suffragette. She called her work *The Mother of Us All*, a title some regarded as referring not only to Anthony, but to Stein as well. Thomson saw how much Stein identified with Anthony. "When she showed her in a scene of domesticity," said Thomson, "that might as well have been herself and Alice Toklas conversing about Gertrude's career."[5] Susan B. Anthony's final speech sounded like Stein speaking of herself:

> In my long life of effort and strife, dear life, life is strife....
> Life is strife, I was a martyr all my life not to what I won but to what was done.
> (Silence)
> Do you know because I tell you so, or do you know, do you know.
> (Silence)
> My long life, my long life.[6]

Gertrude Stein had never been one to resurrect discarded friendships. Her association with Virgil Thomson therefore remained congenial but fragile with only mutual business interests holding it together. During discussions about their new opera, the two often talked, as they had in the past, about their differing childhood experiences and their respective religious conditioning. Thomson, although not religious, had been born into a strongly Southern Baptist family. Whenever he mentioned heaven, hell, salvation, and so on, Stein would say, "When a Jew dies he's dead." Their cultural attitudes toward friendship differed as well. Thomson established long-lasting friendships that survived many difficulties. Yet he noted with some bewilderment how often his Jewish acquaintances suddenly broke with their friends and never made up. He thought it might be a distinctly Jewish trait. Thomson was especially struck by Gertrude's permanent break with her brother Leo. Since their split years before, the two had never spoken or even exchanged letters, and they had crossed paths only once: in 1931 as Gertrude paused in her open air Ford at the intersection of a Paris street, Leo crossed the boulevard just ahead. He saw her and raised his hat; she stood and bowed to him. That was it.[7]

Thomson suggested that the Jewish religion offered no mechanics for personal forgiveness, whereas a Christian was obligated to forgive and to reconcile. Gertrude Stein liked Thomson's explanation, though years later Alice amended the theory. "You and Gertrude had it settled between you as to why Jews don't make up their quarrels," she told him, "and I went along with you. But now I've found a better reason for it. Gertrude was right, of course, to believe that 'when a Jew dies he's dead.' And that's exactly why Jews don't need to make up. When we've had enough of someone we can get rid of him. You Christians can't, because you've got to spend eternity together."[8]

12. Three-Cushion Shots

Working diligently and confidently, Gertrude Stein, in March of 1946, finished the libretto for *The Mother of Us All* and sent it to Thomson, then in New York. Thomson wrote back that it was "sensationally handsome" and much easier to dramatize than *Four Saints* had been. He found the entire work "very dramatic and very beautiful and very clear and constantly quotable."[9]

If, after completing the opera, Gertrude sometimes felt tired and edgy, she still loved to talk, especially about people. She mentioned to a friend that Hemingway had taken much from her literarily and paid her back with ingratitude. To another friend she observed that passing years had not brought Hemingway any greater understanding of life: "Anyone who marries three girls from St. Louis," she said, "hasn't learned much."[10]

Hemingway had been home about six weeks when Mary Welsh, a journalist with *Time* magazine, joined him in Cuba. Ernest had met her in London shortly after his arrival in May 1944. Mary Welsh was small, shapely, bright, and energetic. Unlike Hemingway's three wives, she did not come from St. Louis. She hailed from Walker, Minnesota.

Following Hemingway's car accident in London, Mary had shown Ernest the sympathy Martha Gellhorn refused to give. Mary pampered him with attention and adulation. She easily deferred to Hemingway's wishes and appeared willing to subordinate her personal ambitions to his. Mary wrote in her journal at the time, "Whatever else the critics say about him, they certainly [are] right about him and women — he wants them like Indian girls — completely obedient and sexually loose. That I think I might learn to handle."[11] This was just the type of woman Hemingway felt that he wanted, a woman not only intelligent and lively, but also compliant.

Ernest wrote to his sister Carol that he was finally cured of Martha. One writer in the family, he said, was enough, "and I need wife who will be in bed at night instead of in some different war. Need a wife very much, very badly and immediately and hope have same in Mary Welsh. She wants to quit writing and journalism and I am going to try very hard to be good husband to her whenever we can be married." He added that writing was a tough racket, "and you need somebody to help you instead of compete with you." He conceded that Martha was a lovely-looking girl who shot well in the field and who wrote a hell of a good magazine piece. But she was also a "very selfish and imperious girl and as I say what I wanted was wife in bed at night not somewhere having even higher adventure at so many thousand bucks the adventure. I loved her very much but finally got cured of it flying [with the RAF]."[12]

Although Martha later tried to forget the humiliating experience of having been the third Mrs. Hemingway, she tried at the time to be conciliatory. "My dear Bug," she wrote Ernest four months before their divorce became final, "I may not have been the best wife you ever had, but at any rate I am surely the least expensive don't you think? That's some virtue." She felt sad that she probably would never again see his three boys, to whom she had grown close. "However; I think I have learned all there is to know about amputations; one has to learn all the time, doesn't one? I never want to learn again; it seems to me a terribly enduring kind of knowledge."[13]

By contrast, Ernest long continued bitter and resentful, his usual reaction to people he felt had wronged him in some way, like his mother, most critics, Gertrude Stein, and others. Nearly a year after their divorce, he wrote Martha saying that during the years 1943 and 44, due to her tremendous ambition, he "felt like something that had been run over by a career bulldozer." He accused her of slacking off when the going got tough, of speaking with a phony accent, and of having "a queer, limited and imitative talent which it was possible to win races with when the imitation was carefully removed by the imitee." He further accused her of being tight with money and sometimes lying about financial matters. He signed off, "Good night, Marty. Sleep well my beloved phony and pretentious bitch." Perhaps wisely he decided not to post the letter. It is marked "unsent" in his hand at the top of the first page.[14]

About the time Ernest's divorce from Martha became final in December, Gertrude Stein made another trip by plane, this time to visit American GI's stationed in Brussels. While on the trip, her intestinal complaints grew worse. "Suddenly, Gertrude Stein was no longer well," wrote Alice, "and the doctor who came to see her said she should see a specialist because he thought her illness might become grave. But Gertrude rejected the idea and went on as usual. She even bought herself a little car."[15] The car was a French Simca, a low-slung, fully-enclosed vehicle, a great departure from the open, high-mounted Fords she had always owned. Perched atop one of her Fords, seated as if on a moving throne, her resemblance to a Roman

12. Three-Cushion Shots

emperor became much enhanced as she motored about Paris streets. Her new car, while sportier, made her less conspicuous. It was not what Picasso had advised her to get, but she seldom heeded Picasso's advice.

Driving down the rue des Grands Augustins in her Simca, she spotted Picasso outside his home and stopped. "Is this the car you have bought?" he asked.

"It is not the car you wanted me to buy," she said.

"Oh dear no."

"I don't like second-hand cars and that's what you proposed." Looking up at him from the driver's seat, she said, "Why are you so cross?"

Surprised, Picasso answered, "I'm *not* cross."

"Oh yes you are."

But it was Stein who seemed unusually out of sorts. Picasso asked Alice, "What's the matter with Gertrude?" Alice said that it was nothing; she just did not agree with him about the car.

"It's what I wanted and I've gotten it," Gertrude snapped. "So goodbye Pablo." And off she went down the street.[16]

Virgil Thomson was also finding Stein unusually irritable. One evening he gave a small dinner party, to which he invited Gertrude and Alice. Pleased with the food and the quality of wine he was able to serve, Thomson felt cheerful, and he began teasing a couple of his guests, one of them Gertrude. Alice cautioned him, "Don't scold her. She may cry."

Thomson had noticed how small and thin Stein looked, but, he said later, "I had not realized that her strength was low."[17] Stein felt that her lack of energy resulted from the constant stream of GI's showing up at her door at all hours. She loved the attention and the conversation, but constantly entertaining guests had grown tedious and exhausting.

A French friend offered Gertrude and Alice the use of his country house in Sarthe, some 125 miles southwest of Paris. There Stein could relax and recover her strength. Another friend drove the women down in Gertrude's Simca, intending to take the train back to Paris in a day or two. Once in Sarthe, the three took a leisurely sight-seeing drive through the surrounding countryside, but near Azay-le-Rideau Stein fell ill. "Gertrude's illness was frightening," said Alice. They got a room at the inn at Azay and sent for a doctor. The doctor told Alice, "Your friend will have to be cared for by a specialist, and at once!"[18]

Alice telephoned Gertrude's nephew Allan Stein in Paris, asking him to meet them next day at the train station. "When we went to board the train," said Alice, "Gertrude Stein refused to have a nurse or anyone take care of her, but ran around from one side of the train to the other to look out on the landscape."[19]

Upon arriving in Paris they found an ambulance waiting to carry Stein to the American Hospital at Neuilly. The following morning doctors discovered that she had uterine cancer and was not strong enough to undergo an operation. The doctors told her that surgery would have to be postponed until she built up her strength. Several days later they refused to operate at all. They had determined that the cancer was too far advanced. Disgusted by their cowardice, Stein grew angry and dismissed them all — she never wanted to see them again she said. Alice wrote to Carl Van Vechten, "She was furious and frightening and impressive like she was thirty years and more ago when her work was attacked." Stein's only enjoyment during this time came from receipt of two advance copies of the slim volume *Brewsie and Willie*, published by Random House. Alice remarked later that Gertrude read both copies with great pleasure.

Two other medical specialists were called in, and Stein demanded they do something. She had started to experience much pain. "I was not meant to suffer," she told them.

One of the surgeons, moved by her entreaties, decided to go ahead. "I have told Miss Stein that I would perform the operation," he announced, "and you don't give your word of honor to a woman of her character and not keep it."[20]

On the day scheduled for the operation, Alice noted that "Gertrude Stein was in a sad state of indecision and worry. I sat next to her and she said to me early in the afternoon, What is the answer? I was silent. In that case, she said, what is the question?"

The rest of the day passed for Alice in confusion and uncertainty; "later in the afternoon they took her away on a wheeled stretcher to the operating room and I never saw her again." Gertrude Stein died at 6:30 in the evening, July 27, 1946. She was seventy-two years old.[21]

Gertrude Stein's remains were interred in the Père Lachaise Cemetery on the Quai d'Orsay. This was the resting place of such notables as Brillat-Savarin, Balzac, Delacroix, Oscar Wilde, and Daumier. Obituaries appeared in major newspapers throughout the world, and over the next several months some who had known Stein, and others who only appreciated her work, published tributes to her. Janet Flanner, writing in the *New Yorker*, underscored Stein's association with painters, though she concluded by stating, "Miss Stein had her greatest literary influence on young Ernest Hemingway, when he was writing 'In Our Time.' It is now her epitaph. She was in our time."[22]

Carl Van Vechten acknowledged that it was too early to appraise Gertrude Stein's work. Still, he claimed, Stein was one of the great personages of her epoch; no more startling figure would likely shake the literary world in the twentieth century.[23]

Ernest Hemingway furnished no tributes. His extant correspondence for this period does not even mention Gertrude Stein. Her death occurred six days after Hemingway's forty-seventh birthday and four months after he wed Mary Welsh at a civil ceremony in Havana. Since the start of the year, he had been deeply immersed in the opening portion of what he envisioned as a monumental work covering the war years and immediately after. Its focus would be the personal wars fought by twentieth century man, primarily the artist, and it would incorporate the four elements of earth, air, fire, and water. The work never materialized as Hemingway first envisioned it, though over the course of time the water portion evolved into *Islands in the Stream* and *The Old Man and the Sea*. The earth segment would appear as *Across the River and Into the Trees* and as a work he began in January 1946, six months before Gertrude Stein's death, the posthumous and never completed *The Garden of Eden*.

Max Eastman and his wife were vacationing in Havana in 1946. One day they stepped in to the Bar Floridita and paused to watch a sober, slender, dexterous man expertly making daiquiris.

> He made them as though he were playing a violin [wrote Eastman]. Glancing in the mirror behind the bar, I saw standing four feet behind me a thick, stern-faced character with big glasses, beetle-black eyes and graying black hair. Something familiar about him ... yes, it must be ... but so heavy-glaring, sad, brutal, unillumined ... Ernest Hemingway. A kind of Ernest Hemingway. [Ellipses in the original.]

Remembering their last encounter in Max Perkins's office in New York before the war, Eastman measured the distance between Hemingway and the open door behind him: "he was in a position, if tackled, to be thrown through the door to the sidewalk on his back. This calculation insured me against the bewilderment which had been so painful when he insulted me before, and I was untroubled when I turned around and said, 'Hello, Ernest.'"

Hemingway merely stared at Eastman for a time. "I waited as one waits for a radio to warm up and say something. Finally he said: 'Hello, Max,' and we shook hands." Eastman introduced his wife, whom Ernest had met before. Eliena Eastman told Ernest she had not recognized him.

"How have I changed so much?" asked Hemingway.

"You used to have blue eyes," she replied. His eyes now looked black, like disks of obsidian.

The three sat down to sip cocktails and talk about mutual friends. They were all awfully nice people Ernest observed. "He seemed awfully nice himself," thought Eastman, "although every little while he would stare beyond us in an unseeing way that suggested inward tension to my perhaps too diagnostic eye."

"'I'll be seeing you around,' he said when we parted."[24]

While writing almost every morning at the Finca, and while contemplating the many challenges the artist faced in the twentieth century, Hemingway naturally thought about his own experiences as a struggling young author in the 1920s and after. He had always been good at fictionalizing personal experience, always adept at rewriting and embellishing private history. He now believed, or at least claimed to believe, that he had not been unduly troubled by Gertrude Stein's assault on him in *The Autobiography of Alice B. Toklas*. He said he couldn't understand why she had attacked him like that, but he really didn't give a damn. His not getting even with her he attributed to gentlemanly restraint rather than inability. He boasted to W. G. Rogers, who had just published a book on Stein, that he could have put her away anytime he wanted, but "I never counterpunched when she left herself wide open."[25] Hemingway now blamed Alice Toklas for all his past difficulties with Gertrude Stein. "Alice Toklas broke up our friendship with Gertrude as she did all friendships Gertrude had," he said. The reason was that "Toklas was a very jealous bitch and, too, Gertrude changed very suddenly when she had change of life. She became not simply lesbian ... but *patriotically* lesbian." He pointed out that Toklas was the dominant one of the pair; all the malice in the *Autobiography* actually came from her. "Alice had the ambition of the devil and was very jealous of Gertrude's men and women friends."[26]

12. Three-Cushion Shots 169

Hemingway said that in the war just past, he had been nice to Gertrude "and acted as though we had never not been friends because I had always been fond of her through faults, treason, bad judgement, ambition, lying, ostrich egg size egoism, lack of metier (*absolute*) etc and I also enjoyed making Alice jealous."[27] Due to her jealous and malicious nature, Alice could be extremely wicked to Gertrude. Ernest described to several friends an incident that took place in the twenties, an incident he referred to in passing in his 1933 pastiche "The Autobiography of Alice B. Hemingway." Stein and Toklas were leaving on a trip, and he stopped in at 27 rue de Fleurus to say good-bye. He was shown in by the maid, who told him to wait. Stein would be right down. As he stood looking at the pictures on the walls, he started to hear Alice talk to Gertrude in the bedroom upstairs. She was saying terrible things to Stein and Stein was pleading with her. He would not be specific about what Toklas said, though he quoted Stein as imploring in a loud and anguished voice, "Pussy! Pussy please don't. Oh please don't say you will do that. I'll do anything if you won't. Please Pussy. Please-." Hemingway said that he was out the front door in an instant. He did not want to hear anymore. It was just too awful.[28]

As Hemingway continued to recollect characters and incidents from his early Paris years, Alice Toklas took on the role of chief villain in the piece. He still maintained that Gertrude Stein had been lazy. She had invented a way of writing that allowed her to work every day and that gave her a sense of accomplishment. Then she entered a long period of megalomania coinciding with her "patriotic homo-sexual" phase. This was the time when she felt that one had to be queer to be any good. Finally she lost all judgment when she reached menopause. Gertrude could be difficult, yet Alice brought out her worst traits. Alice had been Gertrude's "evil angel as well as her great friend."[29]

Not that Alice Toklas remembered Ernest Hemingway with much greater fondness. In an interview on German radio, when pressed by the interviewer for her reaction to Hemingway, she responded, "Oh, Hemingway was a horror."[30] But why talk about him? That generation of writers was finished. It ended with Fitzgerald. "However good Faulkner may be," she wrote to Carl Van Vechten, "he isn't virile — and as for poor Hem and Steinbeck and the rest of them — the least said the better for one's digestion."[31]

Her hostile feelings toward Hemingway did not, however, keep her from discharging her duties as godmother to his eldest son. When twenty-six-year-old Jack Hemingway got married in Paris in 1949, Alice attended the reception. As a wedding gift, she gave the married couple an antique silver chalice. Jack had remembered Alice Toklas only "as one of the two giant women gargoyles of my childhood." Now he found her "a chattering little bird who moved without cease and came through the reception line three times, pouring out an endless cacophony and sparkling conversation laced with questions she never gave either of us time to answer."[32]

Ernest did not attend his son's wedding in Paris. The distance was too great and the time too short. He was then at work on *Across the River and Into the Trees*. This was a novel, set in 1948, about a fifty-year-old American Army colonel, dying in Venice of heart disease, who is in love with an eighteen-year-old Italian girl, a countess. Hemingway began the book in April and finished it less than twelve months later. His editor, Max Perkins, had died suddenly of pneumonia nearly two years before, thus depriving Ernest of a good friend and the best literary advisor a professional author could have. It is impossible to say what guidance Perkins might have provided as Hemingway worked on his book. It seems certain that it could not have made the result any worse. The novel, when published by Scribner's in September of 1950, drew the sharpest condemnation Hemingway had ever received.

Martha Gellhorn found it revolting. It made her sick, she remarked, how through the main character, Ernest continued to project a fictional image of himself and to worship that image. At least he would not have to write his autobiography "because he has been doing it, from the first novel, chapter by chapter, each book keeping pace with his calendar years, building up this dream vision of himself." Furthermore, "I weep for the eight years I spent, almost eight (light dawned a little earlier) worshipping his image with him."[33]

Critics nearly unanimously condemned the book. They found it tedious. Nothing happened they said. Not since *To Have and Have Not* had the author turned in such a weak performance. One critic stated, "It is not only Hemingway's worst novel; it is a synthesis of everything that is bad in his previous work."[34] In the "Books" section of the *New Yorker*, Alfred Kazin expressed pity and embarrassment "that so fine and honest a writer can make such a travesty of himself." He also noted that "Hemingway's prose has been getting pretty gamy."[35]

John O'Hara, writing in the *New York Times*, tried to be as generous as candor would allow. Still, about the only positive things he could find to say about the book were that it did not employ big block paragraphs as *A Farewell to Arms* had done, and it displayed "real class." One other positive feature is that the novel showed "Miss Gertrude Stein ... did Hemingway no harm." She, in fact, probably had been a good influence on him in his formative years. "Whatever influence Gertrude Stein had on Hemingway has been accepted, studied, utilized and rejected," said O'Hara. "Ernest Hemingway is and really always was, his own man. We now can forget about Gertrude Stein. Thank you very much, and so long." O'Hara concluded by having to admit that Hemingway "may not be able to go the full distance, but he can still hurt you. Always dangerous. Always in there with that right cocked."[36] These were the most commendable things O'Hara, or any other critic, could say about the novel.

Mary and Ernest Hemingway, 1950.

Hemingway was furious. "Sure, they can say anything about nothing happening in *Across the River*," he exclaimed in an interview, "but all that happens is the defense of the lower Piave, the breakthrough in Normandy, the taking of Paris and the destruction of the 22d Inf. Reg. in Hurtgen forest plus a man who loves a girl and dies. Only it is all done with three-cushion shots." Critics wanted him to repeat himself, but he was not going to. "In writing I have moved through arithmetic, through plane geometry and algebra, and now I am in calculus. If they don't understand that, to hell with them."[37]

By three-cushion shots, Hemingway meant the depth, dimensions, and subtle nuances he had always sought in his writing and that he achieved in his best work. The problem was, as some critics noted, the famous Hemingway style had become bloated. Hemingway once told Max Perkins, "It wasn't by accident that the Gettysburg address was so short. The laws of prose writing are as immutable as those of flight, of mathematics, of physics."[38] But somewhere along the way he had lost sight of those laws; he had strayed from the clear, crisp, condensed prose that conveyed more than appeared on the surface. In abandoning the short declarative sentence as the foundation of his idiom — in rejecting whatever influence Gertrude Stein, Ezra Pound, and others had in shaping his style — he now often indulged in what he earlier abhorred: elaborate scrollwork.

Critics thought Hemingway finished as a significant author. Just as Sherwood Anderson had predicted, he was ending up burlesquing himself. But at the time critics were heaping scorn on *Across the River and Into the Trees* and mourning the loss of a once great writer, Hemingway was finishing a four-part narrative set in the Gulf Stream. Parts one through three were published posthumously in 1970 as *Islands in the Stream*, another sprawling novel that lacked focus and concision. While working on chapter XI of the Bimini section, Hemingway couldn't help putting in a joke at Gertrude Stein's expense. The character Roger Davis, a writer, pretends to be drunk before a group of tourists. Young Tom Hudson participates in the gag, telling Davis, "You know if you get so you can't see you won't be able to write."

"I'll dictate," Roger said. "Like Milton."

"I know you dictate beautifully," young Tom said. "But this morning when Miss Phelps tried to take it off the machine it was mostly music."

"I'm writing an opera," Roger said. "Pigeons on their ass alas."

Hemingway later scratched out the last line.[39]

Part four of the Gulf Stream narrative was a relatively short, compact piece that Hemingway had considered writing since the mid–1930s. It was, on the surface at least, a simple tale about an old Cuban fisherman who rows far out to sea in a small skiff hoping for a truly big fish. He has not caught anything for eighty-four days, but even with the worst kind of bad luck, he is not discouraged. "His hope and his confidence had never gone." He realizes he may not be as strong as he once was, "But I know many tricks and I have resolution." With faith in his abilities and determination to succeed, he sets out in his skiff before dawn. "The old man knew he was going far out."

In crafting this tale of Santiago, the old fisherman, who finally hooks a huge marlin and battles it for three days and three nights, Hemingway seemed once more to have found his way; he had rediscovered the valuable lessons Gertrude Stein once taught him about immediacy, rhythms, and the use of words in repetition:

> He [Santiago] woke with the jerk of his right fist coming up against his face and the line burning out through his right hand. He had no feeling of his left hand but he braked all he could with his right and the line rushed out. Finally his left hand found the line and he leaned back against the line and now it burned his back and his left hand, and his left hand was taking all the strain and cutting badly.[40]

The old man, during his struggle with the huge marlin, remains humble and compassionate yet resolute. "He is my brother," says Santiago. "But I must kill him and keep strong to do it." Owing to his experience and determination, the old man at last prevails. The fish, however, is too big to fit in the boat, so Santiago lashes it to the side. "With his mouth shut and his tail straight up and down we sail like brothers," thinks the old man.

> If I were towing him behind there would be no question. Nor if the fish were in the skiff with all dignity gone, there would be no question either. But they were sailing together lashed side by side and the old man thought, let him bring me in if it pleases him. I am only better than him through trickery and he meant me no harm.
> ... It was an hour before the first shark hit him.[41]

Despite the old man's heroic efforts to beat off repeated attacks from sharks, they succeed in devouring the fish, leaving only the bare spine connecting the great head and tail.

In large measure, the adventure of the old fisherman alone on the sea represents the challenges faced by twentieth century man, the artist in particular. It is a parable epitomizing the difficulties the artist must endure and the courage, dignity, and resolution he must bring to bear in order to survive at his calling. Even then he may not be commercially successful. Sharks will sometimes devour what he has been at great pains to accomplish. Failure may likewise result from attempting too much. "And what beat you," the old man thinks to himself. "'Nothing,' he said aloud. 'I went out too far.'" Yet only by going out beyond where anyone else has gone can you hook the truly big fish.

Those who read the manuscript of *The Old Man and the Sea* thought it among Hemingway's finest achievements. A decision was made to publish the piece separately from the other three sections. *Life* magazine devoted its entire September 1, 1952, issue to the work, selling 5,318,650 copies in only forty-eight hours. Scribner's brought out the book one week later on September 8. The American trade edition enjoyed an advance sale of 50,000 copies and sold 3,000 copies a week for some time after. In London, the book sold 20,000 copies initially and then about 2,000 copies a week.[42] Reviews were universally favorable. William Faulkner called it simply, "His best. Time may show it to be the best single piece of any of us, I mean his and my contemporaries."[43] In May of 1953, *The Old Man and the Sea* won the Pulitzer Prize, and based largely on the strength of the one-hundred-forty-page novella, Hemingway received the Nobel Prize for Literature in 1954.[44]

Ernest Hemingway had recaptured the heavyweight title. He demonstrated that in writing he had moved through not only arithmetic, plane geometry, and algebra, but also through calculus and into a region few authors ever attain. In a letter to Charles Scribner, Hemingway said *The Old Man and the Sea* was the prose he had been aiming for his entire life, a prose that reads easily and simply, seems short, yet has "all the dimensions of the visible world and the world of a man's spirit. It is as good prose as I can write as of now."[45]

13

Broken Beyond Repair

Robert McAlmon — sick, poor, bitter, and long forgotten by the world — was living in the small arid town of Desert Hot Springs, one hundred miles east of Los Angeles, California. People had started writing him lately, asking for information about Joyce and Stein and Hemingway, "about the so-called writers of the so-called lost generation." It made him think that current writers must be pretty barren. He thought about Ernest, about the man he knew in the 1920s, contrasted with the image the public had of him. He wrote to Bill Bird that "there are so many articles on Papa Hemingway, the great game hunter, the stern and staunch and heroic, the unflinching. I wonder if they are talking about the same guy."[1] McAlmon told another friend that he early thought Hemingway a faker and "felt Fitzgerald, Hemingway, et al.; their heroes and heroines were the bitches of the time, misdrawn."[2] When rumor spread that Hemingway would probably receive that year's Nobel Prize for Literature, McAlmon hoped Ezra Pound would get it instead, "but the phonies win the prizes."[3]

The Nobel committee considered Pound, as well as Frenchmen Paul Claudel and Albert Camus, but on October 28, 1954, it announced that the prize would go to Ernest Hemingway "for his mastery of the art of narrative, most recently demonstrated in *The Old Man and the Sea,* and for the influence he has exerted on contemporary style."[4] The United States ambassador to Sweden accepted the award on Hemingway's behalf. Ernest did not attend the ceremonies in Stockholm himself. The main reason is that he did not wish to be put on exhibit, he said, like an elephant in a zoo. Besides, his own health was poor. He was still recovering from two near-fatal plane crashes earlier in the year.

He and Mary had been on a five-month African safari at the time. In some ways it was the best African trip yet. Besides collecting trophies, Ernest served the Nyrok area for a time as honorary game warden, a job he took seriously. Every day he faced a new challenge such as running off elephants that had trampled a farmer's corn field, checking on the welfare a lioness and her new cubs, and shooting a leopard that had been killing someone's cattle. Every day, he said, was like knowing you were to pitch in a big league game. It was a first class life, and he felt supremely happy. He was shooting well and, as usual, he liked to boast about his triumphs. He told his wife, "I'm not a phony but I'm a terrible braggart."

Mary did not think him a braggart, "Only full of joy," she wrote in her journal. "He has been shooting doubles on the sandgrouse, no paltry trick, and he has a right to be pleased about it."[5]

In January the couple began what Mary called an "air safari," a journey by single engine Cessna that was to take them across the Serengeti Plain, Lake Victoria, and northern Uganda, then down the Congo River to Stanleyville in Zaire. As they flew over Murchison Falls on the Victoria Nile, the pilot came in low so that Mary could take photographs. On the third pass, the pilot had to make a sudden dive to avoid a flock of ibis, but in so doing he grazed an abandoned telegraph wire. The wire sheared off the rudder, forcing the Cessna down in scrub not far from the river. Aside from Mary going into shock and Ernest spraining his right shoulder, the three occupants were not seriously hurt. They spent a watchful night in the jungle, however, close to a herd of elephants. Next day a small privately-chartered river boat took them aboard and carried them to Butiaba.

There the Hemingways boarded a twelve passenger De Havilland Rapide that was to fly them to Entebbe. As the plane bumped along the furrowed runway on takeoff, it suddenly stopped and burst into flames. The passengers barely made it out. The crash had jammed shut the solid metal door, but Mary and the pilot managed to get out through a small window. Hemingway, too large to fit through the opening, repeatedly rammed his head and sprained right shoulder against the jammed door until he got it open far enough to escape.

Ernest was the most seriously injured. He ended up with a fractured skull; ruptured liver, spleen, and kidney; two cracked vertebrae; sprained right arm and shoulder; burns on his arms, face, and scalp; loss of hearing in the left ear; and temporary loss of vision in the left eye. After convalescing for little more than a month in Nairobi and Mombassa, followed by layovers in Venice and Spain, Hemingway returned with Mary to Cuba in June. Four months later he learned that he had won the Nobel Prize for Literature.

Mary subsequently wrote that following the plane crashes, "a plague began to descend upon us, an evil miasma, a foul-smelling deafening raucous bird of destruction and disaster enfolding us."[6] She referred to Ernest's steadily deteriorating mental and physical health. He never fully recovered from the second plane crash. What he gained on his injuries he lost to the encroachment of other disorders. He suffered at various times in the ensuing years from recurring liver infections, hepatitis, high blood pressure, high cholesterol, severe depression, and the beginnings of diabetes. People who had not seen him in some time were surprised at how much he had aged. Although still in his fifties, he looked much older.

In 1957 the editors of the *Atlantic Monthly* prepared to bring out their one hundredth anniversary issue and asked Hemingway for something. Hemingway did not want to excerpt anything from one of his books nor submit a story he was not sure of or that would be unsuitable for the magazine. Instead, "I started to write about Scott and how I first met him and how he was; writing it all true and it was tough to write and easy to remember and I thought it was very interesting." Yet he had misgivings about publishing these reminiscences in the *Atlantic* following the controversial and damaging portrait of Dylan Thomas by John Malcolm Brinnin in the same magazine two years earlier. "People would think I was doing that to Scott and him dead," Hemingway remarked.[7] So he put aside the article and gave the *Atlantic Monthly* two stories, "A Man of the World" and "Get a Seeing-Eyed Dog," both published in the November 1957 centenary issue. Still, the Fitzgerald piece had again roused his interest in those early apprenticeship years, and soon he began work on a book of sketches focusing on his life in Paris and on some of the people he had known there during the twenties. He finished three new sketches by December. One described a cold, blustery day in fall when he took refuge in the warmth and cleanliness of a café on the Place St.-Michel and, over a *café au lait* and a rum St. James, wrote "The Three Day Blow." Another vignette dealt with Ford Madox Ford, portraying him as foolish and slightly pathetic. The third described the time Ernest and his wife Hadley first called on Gertrude Stein at 27 rue de Fleurus.

Other sketches followed over the next several years. All attempted to capture that golden period when most of Hemingway's life and career lay before him. The sketches emphasized the happiness he and his wife shared, the desires and aspirations of youth, the hardships and discipline of becoming a writer, and the disappointments and disillusionment that slowly entered his life. Although he never finished the Paris sketches to his satisfaction, Hemingway came up with nineteen of them, three dealing with Gertrude Stein. In these three, he showed Stein to be outspoken and domineering, though he credits her with being a significant influence on him. Nowhere does he mention Alice Toklas by name. He refers to her only as Stein's "companion" or "the friend who lived with her." Neither does he quote Toklas speaking directly. The impression of the "friend" that emerges is of something small, dark, and slightly sinister moving quietly along the edge of Gertrude Stein's life.

The last sketch dealing with Stein is titled "A Strange Enough Ending." It recounts the spat Hemingway overheard when he dropped in to say good-bye to Gertrude Stein before a trip. It was the episode he had already described in several letters to friends. Only now it became the key event marking the end of the Stein/Hemingway friendship. "The way it ended with Gertrude Stein was strange enough," the sketch begins. Ernest arrived at the apartment before noon. The maid showed him in, poured him a glass of *eau-de-vie*, and asked him to wait. He had just taken a sip "when I heard someone speaking to Miss Stein as I had never heard one person speak to another; never, anywhere, ever." He does not specify who the "someone" is. "Then Miss Stein's voice came pleading and begging, saying, 'Don't, pussy. Don't. Don't, please don't. I'll do anything, pussy, but please don't do it. Please don't. Please don't, pussy.'" Hemingway wrote that he swallowed his drink, put down the glass, and headed for the door. Only those intimate with the couple would know that "Pussy" was Gertrude Stein's pet name for Alice Toklas.

"That was the way it finished for me, stupidly enough, although I still did the small jobs, made the necessary appearances, brought people that were asked for and waited dismissal with most of the other men friends when that epoch came and the new friends moved in." He saw that new and worthless pictures began appearing on the walls among the great ones, the implication being that the new friends, compared to the old, were worthless too. "She quarreled with nearly all of us that were fond of her except Juan Gris and she couldn't quarrel with him because he was dead."[8]

Hemingway's first biographer, Carlos Baker, observed that in the Paris sketches, most of the portraits of people are "limned in acid."[9] This certainly is the case with his depiction of Ford and Fitzgerald. Yet considering the promises Hemingway once made about getting even with Stein when he got around to writing his memoirs, his depiction of her seems just. The three sketches dealing with Stein portray her as often overbearing and dogmatic yet betray no signs of deep or lingering resentment.

As his final encounter with Max Eastman already showed, Hemingway's temperament had mellowed with the years. The anger he once directed at individuals had largely vanished. Perhaps he had grown more lenient as he acquired greater understanding of himself and others. Perhaps he had grown less pugnacious due to age and mounting infirmities. Whatever the cause, this mellowing process, this change in attitude, was further demonstrated in a piece written in 1959 but not published until 1981. Focusing primarily on the art of the short story, Hemingway spoke in passing about how writers should treat each other. He said that writers had no business "fingering" another writer while he was alive, that is, publicly castigate him and call him to account. "I know you shouldn't do it," he wrote,

> because I did it once to Sherwood Anderson. I did it because I was righteous, which is the worst thing you can be, and I thought he was going to pot the way he was writing and that I thought I could kid him out of it by showing him how awful it was. So I wrote *The Torrents of Spring*. It was cruel to do, and it didn't do any good, and he just wrote worse and worse. What the hell business of mine was it if he wanted to write badly? None. But then I was righteous and more loyal to writing than to my friend. I would have shot anybody then, not kill them, just shoot them a little, if I thought it would straighten them up and make them write right.

Hemingway now realized it was pointless to try and reform other writers. They carried in them the seeds of their own destruction and there was nothing anyone could do about it. The best thing to do with writers was get along with them when you see them. Better yet, don't see them.

"I'm sorry I threw at Anderson. It was cruel and I was a son of a bitch to do it. The only thing I can say is that I was as cruel to myself then. But that is no excuse. He was a friend of mine, but that was no excuse for doing it to him."[10]

After Gertrude Stein's death, everything for Alice seemed empty and blurred. "Basket and I stay on here alone," she wrote in a letter. With Gertrude gone, "there can never be any happiness again. There are a few things for me to still do for Gertrude." The most important thing was trying to get Stein's unedited manuscripts published.[11] Gertrude Stein had bequeathed her papers and manuscripts to the library at Yale University. She told Alice she wanted Carl Van Vechten to edit them. Stein willed her portrait by Picasso to the Metropolitan Museum of Art in New York, and she left the rest of her estate, including the remaining pictures, to Alice, after whose death everything was to pass on to Gertrude's nephew Allan Stein and his heirs. Gertrude further authorized that Alice, during her lifetime, was to receive an allowance for living expenses, and that paintings or personal property from Stein's estate were to be sold for that purpose if necessary.

Alice very much wanted to keep the paintings together. She hoped they would eventually go to the Yale University Art Gallery or to some other museum as the Gertrude Stein Collection. Toward that end, she spent much of the next decade living in relative poverty amidst a fortune in art. Paris winters could be brutal, especially for one of her years. With fuel and electricity so expensive, she heated only one room where she and Basket spent most of their time huddled near the radiator. "We ate Madame Cézanne," said Alice, recalling that difficult period during the last war when Gertrude Stein had to sell one of her paintings, "but I don't want — figuratively — to burn a Picasso."[12] Even so, she had to sell a portfolio of Picasso drawings in order to get by.

Allan Stein soon became a problem. He refused to cooperate with Alice or agree to any of her plans regarding the pictures. He demanded to have a say in whatever happened to them, even during Alice's lifetime, and Alice feared that after her death the paintings would be sold piecemeal and "dispersed over the landscape."[13] She was therefore somewhat relieved when Allan Stein suddenly died in January of 1951. It now looked as if she would be able to sell the pictures *en bloc* to a museum as she wished.

Far more distressing than Allan Stein's passing was the death of Basket, due to old age, the following year. "His going has stunned me," she wrote, "— for some time I have realized how much I depended on him and so it is the beginning of living for the rest of my days without anyone who is dependent upon me for anything."[14]

Her greatest satisfaction came when Yale University Press announced that it would publish in nine or ten volumes Gertrude Stein's previously unpublished works. Alice knew how much this would have pleased Gert-

13. Broken Beyond Repair

rude. Getting all her works published is what Alice had been hoping and working for. She had been tireless in promoting Gertrude's cause and in furthering her reputation. She made herself available to anyone who had questions about Stein and who possessed a genuine appreciation for her work. One day a man from the Associated Press dropped in and Alice soon got into "a frightful row with him about Picasso's painting and Hemingway's new book [*Across the River and Into the Trees*] (as if they could be mentioned in one sentence) — he the A.P. man said he thought Picasso was painting carelessly and Hem was writing carelessly!" Alice could tell that he had no idea what he was talking about "because the man didn't know a Picasso from a Gris and thought a Picasso was a Braque." She also had to straighten him out about Hemingway. "I liked defending Hemingway," she said afterward, "— it was the first opportunity I've ever been offered — it will no doubt remain a unique experience."[15]

In the late fifties, due to the dangers and uncertainties brought on by political turmoil in Cuba, the Hemingways spent much of their time in Ketchum, Idaho, not far from Sun Valley, where Ernest and Martha had enjoyed pleasant vacations in the early forties. At first he and Mary rented a place, but later Ernest bought a house that stood isolated on a knoll overlooking the Big Wood River. He usually wrote in the mornings. In the afternoons he often went duck or pheasant shooting with friends in the nearby hills.

By 1959 he was drinking heavily, and Mary noted that "something was changing in him," something that went beyond normal aging.[16] In addition to hypertension and recurring problems with his liver and kidneys, he became more indecisive, fearful, and unsure of himself. It was as if the topmost layer of his personality, the protective covering he had spent a lifetime creating, had begun peeling away to expose what lay carefully hidden beneath. He started to experience nightmares, depression, and excessive fatigue. He lost weight, dropping to 155 pounds. He also began to develop paranoid fears of poverty and persecution.

In November of 1960, two English professors from Montana State University, Seymour Betsky and Leslie Fiedler, drove down to Ketchum to talk with Hemingway. They wanted him to speak on campus as part of a visiting lecturers' series that in the past had hosted W. H. Auden and William Faulkner. Entering the house through the back porch and kitchen, they found everything to be commonplace — "the nondescript furniture of a furnished house, a random selection of meaningless books on the half-empty shelves." A *Readers Digest* and *TV Guide* lay open on tables. The only extraordinary object in the house was Hemingway himself. According to Betsky, the discrepancy between the image they had in their minds and the man they met "was astonishing. We were shocked by his appearance. Hemingway was tall and thin. The only resemblance to the man we had imagined was in the fullness of the face. And even the face was pale and red-veined, not ruddy or weather-beaten. We were particularly struck by the thinness of his arms and legs." Even his barrel chest seemed to have shrunk. "He walked with the tentativeness of a man well over sixty-one. The dominant sense we had was of fragility." The two were also surprised at Hemingway's inarticulateness. He spoke slowly, haltingly, only a few words at a time, seldom in sentences.[17]

"Fragile," Leslie Fiedler recalled thinking, "breakable and broken — one time too often broken, broken beyond repair. And I remembered the wicked sentence reported by Gertrude Stein, 'Ernest is very fragile, whenever he does anything sporting something breaks, his arm, his leg, or his head.'"[18] The professors did not ask Hemingway to speak at the university, and all seemed relieved when, after an hour and a half, the visit ended.

In consultation with their family doctor, Mary decided to have Ernest admitted to the Mayo Clinic in Rochester, Minnesota. This ostensibly was for treating his high blood pressure, but it was more for psychiatric evaluation and therapy. At the Mayo Clinic, Hemingway was subjected to a battery of medical examinations, psychological therapy, and, for his depression and increasing delusions, a series of electric shock treatments. Released after fifty-three days, he returned to Ketchum arguably worse off than when he left. The therapy did little to ease his fears of poverty and persecution, while the electric shock treatments erased portions of his memory and diminished his ability to create. Not being able to write only deepened his depression.

At eleven one morning Mary came downstairs to find Ernest, dressed in pajamas and robe, standing at a window holding a shotgun. Two shells stood close by on the window sill. Mary spoke to Ernest in a soothing voice, reminding him of the good times they had enjoyed in the past and formulating plans for the future. Hemingway remained silent. Mary knew that the doctor would be coming at noon to take Ernest's blood pressure,

13. Broken Beyond Repair

and she kept up a steady monologue until he arrived. Hemingway was placed under heavy sedation at the local hospital and arrangements were made to have him readmitted to the Mayo Clinic.

On the day he was scheduled to leave for Rochester by private plane, he asked to be driven by the house to retrieve something he wanted to take along. Once at the house, he said he would get what he needed and be right back, but a male friend accompanying him said that he had orders not to let Ernest out of his sight. Hemingway then suddenly dashed for the house. Once inside, he seized a shotgun, forced in two shells, and was just getting the barrel under his chin when the male friend, in quick pursuit, was able to grab him. After a brief but violent struggle, the friend, with the help of his wife, managed to break open the gun, pry out the shells, and thereby defuse the situation.

On April 26 Hemingway was again admitted to the Mayo Clinic where he underwent further electric shock treatments. A. E. Hotchner visited him in early June. Hotchner, among other things, had adapted some of Hemingway's works for television and had been a close friend for fourteen years. He asked Hemingway directly, "Papa, why do you want to kill yourself?"

After a brief pause, Hemingway replied, "What do you think happens to a man going on sixty-two when he realizes that he can never write the books and stories he promised himself? Or do any of the other things he promised himself in the good days?"

Hotchner reminded him that he had written a beautiful book about Paris.

"The best of that I wrote before. And now I can't finish it."

But perhaps it *was* finished and...

"Hotch," Hemingway cut in, "if I can't exist on my own terms, then existence is impossible. Do you understand? That is how I've lived, and that is how I *must* live — or not live."[19]

On June 26 Hemingway was discharged, his doctors finding him sufficiently recovered to return home. Mary thought otherwise, but she was powerless to do anything. She and Ernest drove back to Ketchum in a rented car, arriving there the last day of June. Two days later, at 7:30 in the morning, Mary awoke to what sounded like two drawers slamming. "I went downstairs," she said later, "saw a crumpled heap of bathrobe and blood, the shotgun lying in the disintegrated flesh, in the front vestibule of the sitting room." Hemingway had found the key to the basement where the guns were locked away. He had entered, taken a double-barreled shotgun, loaded it, carried it up to the sitting room, put the shotgun to his forehead, and tripped both triggers.[20]

Hemingway's death occasioned an avalanche of reminiscences, reassessments, and speculations. A key issue was what the manner of Hemingway's death revealed about his work and the nature of his entire life. Was his suicide an irrational act for which he was not responsible, or was it the ultimate expression of the cowardice Gertrude Stein had charged him with years before? Some concluded what Stein had recognized decades earlier, that Hemingway had been a sensitive and extremely vulnerable man who went to extraordinary lengths to hide his vulnerability from himself and others. First wife Hadley maintained that a lot of Ernest's toughness had been real, "but a lot was put on to cover his sensitivity. Ernest was one of the most sensitive people I have ever heard of, and easily hurt. Most people thought he was too sure of himself, but I believe he had a great inferiority complex which he didn't show."[21]

Arnold Gingrich agreed: "I think you had here a terribly shy person, dreadfully insecure, who in one instance reflects it by being withdrawn, and in another turns around and is very boisterous. Both are manifestations of the same thing: a dreadful insecurity."[22]

Norman Mailer may have summed it up best:

> It is not likely that Hemingway was a brave man who sought danger for the sake of the sensations it provided him. What is more likely the truth of his own odyssey is that he struggled with his cowardice and against a secret lust to suicide all his life, that his inner landscape was a nightmare, and he spent his nights wrestling with the gods. It may even be that the final judgment on his work may come to the notion that what he failed to do was tragic, but what he accomplished was heroic, for it is possible he carried a weight of anxiety within him from day to day which would have suffocated any man smaller than himself.[23]

On the morning of July 5, 1961, following an outdoor memorial service attended by wife Mary; brother Leicester; sons Jack, Patrick, and Gregory; and various friends, Hemingway was buried in the cemetery at Ketchum, Idaho. The shotgun he had used to kill himself was later cut into pieces by the sheriff and another man and buried at an undisclosed location.[24]

Epilogue

Alice Toklas, upon learning of Hemingway's suicide, said only, "What an inheritance to pass on to his children!"[1] She was now in her mid-eighties, still carrying on alone in the rue Christine apartment, surrounded by the magnificent pictures. Alice had still not been able to do anything with the collection because Allan Stein's widow, Roubina, was now making trouble. She was threatening to appoint a legal guardian for the paintings and to loan them to a museum until Alice's death. Alice could not afford to have the pictures adequately insured, and Roubina feared for their safety. Alice found the entire situation a nuisance but felt that her lawyer would eventually put things to rights.

As a girl, Alice had been baptized in the Catholic Church. Given the notion that "when a Jew dies he's dead," she decided to rejoin the Church, finding comfort in the thought that one day she might be reunited with Gertrude. After attending confession and being given Holy Communion, Alice announced, "I am a good Jesuit."[2]

Due to arthritis, a bout with pneumonia, and a broken hip sustained in a fall, Alice arranged to stay for a time at the Monastery of the Precious Blood, a convent in Rome belonging to a Canadian order of cloistered nuns. She moved there in August of 1960 and was comfortable and happy. "Life is extremely simple but it suits me," she said.[3] Just before she returned to Paris the following summer, Roubina Stein, growing increasingly worried that the paintings might be stolen and that they were not properly insured, got a court order declaring them "endangered." Without Alice's knowledge or consent, she had authorities enter the apartment, remove the pictures, and place them in a bank vault. Years later she and her three grown children sold the collection to a New York consortium for a reported six million dollars, after which the paintings were dispersed over the landscape. Alice remained stoic about the loss. "The pictures are gone permanently," she told a correspondent. "My dim sight could not see them now. Happily a vivid memory does."[4]

When Ernest Hemingway's *A Moveable Feast: Sketches of the Author's Life in Paris in the Twenties* appeared posthumously in 1964, various friends of Alice agreed that it should be kept from her and that Hemingway's name not be mentioned in her presence. She told an acquaintance, however, Lawrence Stewart, that a young man who came every evening to read to her had mentioned Hemingway's book and said he would try to get a copy. "Don't bother," she told him. "I never liked Hemingway." Stewart, who had not seen the book himself, suggested to Alice that it might interest her, since early reviews indicated that much of it concerned her and Gertrude. "I can't believe that," she said, "— he certainly won't be kind to us.... When I first saw Hemingway he was beautiful. He never looked so well again." Another friend, Donald Sutherland, later speculated that Alice would likely have been amused by what Hemingway wrote rather than offended. He also believed that Alice probably got hold of the book anyway although she never mentioned it to him.[5]

By the spring of 1967, penniless and unable to walk or to speak, but with her mind as clear as ever, Alice waited patiently for the end. "Last week," a friend wrote, "the Spanish maid asked her if she wanted something to eat. She shook her head, no. She asked her if she wanted something to drink. She shook her head, no. She asked her if she wanted to die. She shook her head, yes."[6]

Alice Toklas expired quietly on March 7, 1967, less than two months short of her ninetieth birthday. She was buried in Père Lachaise Cemetery next to Gertrude Stein.

Chapter Notes

Preface

1. Scott Donaldson, *Hemingway vs. Fitzgerald: The Rise and Fall of a Literary Friendship* (Woodstock: Overlook Press, 1999). The other book is Matthew J. Bruccoli, *Fitzgerald and Hemingway: A Dangerous Friendship* (New York: Carroll & Graf, 1994).
2. Mabel Dodge Luhan, *European Experiences* (New York: Harcourt, 1935), 332–3.
3. Virgil Thomson, "Remembering Gertrude (1982)," in *Virgil Thomson: A Reader: Selected Writings 1924–1984*, ed. Richard Kostelanetz (New York: Routledge, 2002), 207.
4. Ernest Hemingway to Ezra Pound, c. 27 November 1925, Yale Collection of American Literature, Beinecke Rare Book and Manuscript Library, Yale University.
5. EH to Mrs. Paul Pfeiffer, 26 January 1936, in *Ernest Hemingway: Selected Letters 1917–1961*, ed. Carlos Baker (New York: Scribner's, 1981), 436.
6. EH to Archibald MacLeish, 4 April 1943, in *Selected Letters*, 544.
7. "Arthur A Grammar," in *How to Write* (New York: Dover, 1975), 39.
8. "Portraits and Repetition," in *Lectures in America* (New York: Random House, 1935), 184.
9. Gertrude Stein, "How Writing Is Written" in *Oxford Anthology of American Literature*, ed. William Rose Benét and Norman Holmes Pearson (New York: Oxford University Press, 1938), 2:1450.
10. Robert McAlmon, *The Nightinghouls of Paris*, ed. Sanford J. Smoller (Urbana and Chicago: University of Illinois Press, 2007), 29.
11. Ibid., 160.

Chapter 1

1. Samuel Putnam, *Paris Was Our Mistress: Memoirs of a Lost and Found Generation* (New York: Viking Press, 1947), 136.
2. Ibid., 136–9.
3. GS, *Everybody's Autobiography* (New York: Random House, 1937), 70.
4. Ibid., 77.
5. Mabel Dodge Luhan, *European Experiences* (New York: Harcourt, 1935), 328.
6. *Everybody's Autobiography*, 68.
7. Kay Boyle and Robert McAlmon, *Being Geniuses Together: A Binocular View of Paris in the '20s* (New York: Doubleday, 1968), 257.
8. Carl Van Vechten, "How to Read Gertrude Stein," *Trend* (August 1914): 553.
9. Richard S. Kennedy, *Dreams in the Mirror: A Biography of E. E. Cummings* (New York: Liveright, 1980), 84.
10. Thornton Wilder, introduction to *Four in America*, by GS (New York: Yale University Press, 1947), vii.
11. "Portraits and Repetition," in *Lectures in America* (New York: Random House, 1935), 165.
12. Robert Bartlett Haas, *A Primer for the Gradual Understanding of Gertrude Stein* (Los Angeles: Black Sparrow Press, 1973), 55.
13. GS, "How Writing Is Written" in *Oxford Anthology of American Literature*, ed. William Rose Benét and Norman Holmes Pearson (New York: Oxford University Press, 1938), 2:1448–9.
14. GS, *Three Lives* (Norfolk, Conn.: New Directions, 1909), 137.
15. *Oxford Anthology of American Literature*, 2:1450.
16. *Lectures in America*, 176.
17. Ibid., 171.

18. Ibid., 176.
19. Ibid., 171.
20. See Wilder's introduction to *Four in America*, v–vi.
21. GS, *Portraits and Prayers* (New York: Random House, 1934), 17.
22. "A Transatlantic Interview 1946"; Haas, *Gradual Understanding of Gertrude Stein*, 15.
23. GS, *Tender Buttons* (1914; repr., New York: Gordon Press, 1972), 12.
24. Wambly Bald, *On the Left Bank: 1929–1933*, ed. Benjamin Franklin V. (Athens: Ohio State University Press, 1987), 14.
25. *Everybody's Autobiography*, 123.
26. *transition: an international quarterly for creative experiment* 14 (fall 1928): 13.
27. "Henry James," in *Four in America*, 127–8.
28. *Gradual Understanding of Gertrude Stein*, 30.
29. Ibid., 35.
30. Linda Simon, ed., *Gertrude Stein Remembered* (Lincoln: University of Nebraska Press, 1995), 36.
31. William Carlos Williams, *The Autobiography of William Carlos Williams* (New York: Random House, 1951), 241.
32. *Being Geniuses Together*, 257.
33. Sherwood Anderson, *A Story Teller's Story* (New York: Grove Press, 1951), 359 and 362.
34. Sherwood Anderson, *France and Sherwood Anderson: Paris Notebook, 1921*, ed. Michael Fanning (Baton Rouge: Louisiana State University Press, 1976), 52.
35. Sherwood Anderson, *Letters of Sherwood Anderson*, ed. Howard Mumford Jones (Boston: Little, Brown, 1953), 300.

Chapter 2

1. Robert E. Knoll, ed., *McAlmon and the Lost Generation: A Self-Portrait* (Lincoln: University of Nebraska Press, 1962), 227.
2. Charles A. Fenton, *The Apprenticeship of Ernest Hemingway* (New York: Farrar, Straus & Young, 1954), 72.
3. EH to Charles Scribner, 15 March 1953, Hemingway Collection.
4. Grace Hall Hemingway to her husband Clarence, 27 July 1920, quoted by Max Westbrook, "Grace under Pressure: Hemingway and the Summer of 1920," in *Ernest Hemingway: The Writer in Context*, ed. James Nagel (Madison: University of Wisconsin Press, 1984), 82.
5. 24 July 1920, Hemingway Collection.
6. *Apprenticeship of Ernest Hemingway*, 84.

7. Ray Lewis White, ed., *Sherwood Anderson/Gertrude Stein: Correspondence and Personal Essays* (Chapel Hill: University of North Carolina Press, 1972), 11.
8. EH, *A Moveable Feast: Sketches of the Author's Life in Paris in the Twenties* (New York: Scribner's, 1964), 35.
9. Ibid., 110.
10. Sherwood Anderson, *France and Sherwood Anderson: Paris Notebook, 1921*, ed. Michael Fanning (Baton Rouge: Louisiana State University Press, 1976), 51.
11. GS to "My Dear Mrs. Hemingway," undated, Hemingway Collection.
12. Michael Reynolds, *Hemingway: The Paris Years* (Oxford: Blackwell, 1989), 34.
13. *A Moveable Feast*, 13–14.
14. GS, *Autobiography of Alice B. Toklas* (New York: The Literary Guild, 1933), 261.
15. Harold Acton, *Memoirs of an Aesthete* (London: Methuen, 1948), 161.
16. *A Moveable Feast*, 14.
17. *Autobiography of Alice B. Toklas*, 261–2.
18. *A Moveable Feast*, 15. The French *accrocher* means, among other things, "to hang up; to hook; to catch on a nail."
19. Ibid., 13–16.
20. GS, "How Writing Is Written" in *Oxford Anthology of American Literature*, ed. William Rose Benét and Norman Holmes Pearson (New York: Oxford University Press, 1938), 2:1450.
21. GS, *What Are Masterpieces* (Los Angeles: Conference Press, 1940), 89–90.
22. Florian Vetsch, *Desultory Correspondence: An Interview with Paul Bowles on Gertrude Stein* (Zurich: Memory/Cage Editions, 1997), 40.
23. *A Moveable Feast*, 17.
24. *Autobiography of Alice B. Toklas*, 138.
25. Ibid., 262; Samuel M. Steward, *Dear Sammy: Letters from Gertrude Stein and Alice B. Toklas* (Boston: Houghton Mifflin, 1977), 228.
26. *A Moveable Feast*, 18–21; *Ernest Hemingway: Selected Letters 1917–1961*, ed. Carlos Baker (New York: Scribner's, 1981), 795.
27. *A Moveable Feast*, 26.
28. Ibid., 268.
29. *Autobiography of Alice B. Toklas*, 268.
30. EH to Bernard Berenson, 13 April 1953, Hemingway Collection.
31. EH to SA, 9 March 1922, in *Selected Letters*, 62.
32. Kay Boyle and Robert McAlmon, *Being Geniuses Together: A Binocular View of Paris in the '20s* (New York: Doubleday, 1968), 180.
33. *Being Geniuses Together*, 180.

Chapter 3

1. Ray Lewis White, ed., *Sherwood Anderson/Gertrude Stein: Correspondence and Personal Essays* (Chapel Hill: University of North Carolina Press, 1972), 18. Apparently at Stein's urging, Hemingway wrote a review of *Geography and Plays*, which appeared in the European edition of the *Chicago Tribune* for March 5, 1923. In the review, Hemingway stated, "Gertrude Stein is probably the most first rate intelligence employed in writing today. If you are tired of Mr. D. H. Lawrence who writes extremely well with the intelligence of a head waiter or Mr. [H. G.] Wells who is believed to be intelligent because of a capacity for sustained marathon thinking ... you ought to read Gertrude Stein." He further encouraged the reader to read Stein's *Three Lives:* "The Melanctha story in Three Lives is one of the three best short stories in English." Later in the year, as a return favor, Stein penned a review of Hemingway's *Three Stories & Ten Poems* that appeared in the European edition of the *Chicago Tribune* for November 27, 1923. Stein wrote, "Three stories and ten poems is very pleasantly said. So far so good, further than that, and as far as that, I may say of Ernest Hemingway that as he sticks to poetry and intelligence it is both poetry and intelligent.... I should say that Hemingway should stick to poetry and intelligence and eschew the hotter emotions and the more turgid vision. Intelligence and a great deal of it is a good thing to use when you have it, it's all for the best." (Scott Donaldson, "Gertrude Stein Reviews Hemingway's *Three Stories & Ten Poems,*" *American Literature* 53, no. 1 [March 1981]: 114–5; Michael S. Reynolds, "Hemingway's Stein: Another Misplaced Review," *American Literature* 55, no. 3 [October 1983]: 431–4.)
2. *Ernest Hemingway: Selected Letters 1917–1961,* ed. Carlos Baker (New York: Scribner's, 1981), 62.
3. John Peale Bishop, "Homage to Hemingway," *New Republic,* November 11, 1936.
4. Morley Callaghan, *That Summer in Paris: Memories of Tangled Friendships with Hemingway, Fitzgerald, and Some Others* (New York: Coward-McCann, 1963), 254.
5. Max Eastman, *Great Companions: Critical Memoirs of Some Famous Friends* (New York: Farrar, Straus, and Cudahy, 1959), 45.
6. Bryher, *The Heart to Artemis: A Writer's Memoirs* (New York: Harcourt, Brace & World, 1963), 2.
7. GS, "How Writing Is Written" in *Oxford Anthology of American Literature,* ed. William Rose Benét and Norman Holmes Pearson (New York: Oxford University Press, 1938), 2:1447.
8. GS, *Autobiography of Alice B. Toklas* (New York: The Literary Guild, 1933), 271.
9. EH, *A Moveable Feast: Sketches of the Author's Life in Paris in the Twenties* (New York: Scribner's, 1964), 13.
10. Bravig Imbs, *Confessions of Another Young Man* (New York: Henkle-Yesdale House, 1936), 121.
11. Donald Clifford Gallup, ed., *The Flowers of Friendship: Letters Written to Gertrude Stein* (New York: Knopf, 1953), 44.
12. *Flowers of Friendship,* 5.
13. GS, *Operas and Plays* (Barrytown, NY: Station Hill Press, 1987), 107–8. "Objects Lie On a Table" later contains the following lines: "Do we suppose that a rose is a rose. Do we suppose that all she knows is that a rose is a rose is a rose is a rose" (*Operas and Plays,* 110). Stein first used the phrase "rose is a rose is a rose is a rose" in "Sacred Emily" (1913), a poem about Madame Matisse, the painter's wife.
14. *Selected Letters,* 781.
15. *Autobiography of Alice B. Toklas,* 262 and Denis Brian, ed., *The True Gen: An Intimate Portrait of Ernest Hemingway by Those Who Knew Him* (New York: Grove Press, 1988), 44.
16. Kay Boyle and Robert McAlmon, *Being Geniuses Together: A Binocular View of Paris in the '20s* (New York: Doubleday, 1968),178–9; *That Summer in Paris,* 84.
17. *Being Geniuses Together,* 351–2.
18. John Dos Passos, *The Best Times: An Informal Memoir* (New York: The New American Library, 1966), 142, 219.
19. Margaret Anderson, *My Thirty Years' War* (New York: Covici, Friede Publishers, 1930), 258–60.
20. Sylvia Beach, *Shakespeare and Company* (New York: Harcourt, Brace and Co., 1930), 78. John Peale Bishop, writing in 1936, stated that Hemingway in the 1920s "was among the tenderest of mortals." Yet, having been wounded in the war, "Hemingway was a very apprehensive young man. Indeed, his imagination could hardly be said to exist apart from his apprehension. I should not call this fear. And yet he could hardly hear of something untoward happening to another that he did not instantly, and without thought, attach this event to himself, or to the woman he loved." Bishop suggested that the tender, sensitive Hemingway was early corrupted by the legend he began creating of the manly, lowbrow, hardboiled type: "He appears to have turned

into a composite of all those photographs he has been sending out for years: sunburned from snows, on skis; in fishing get-up, burned dark from the hot Caribbean; the handsome, stalwart hunter crouched over the carcass of some dead beast. Such a man could not have written Hemingway's early books" ("Homage to Hemingway," *The New Republic* [11 Nov. 1936], 39–42).

21. GS to SA, February 1924, in *Anderson/Stein: Correspondence*, 36.

22. GS, *Portraits and Prayers* (New York: Random House, 1934), 193. Kirk Curnutt suggests that Stein intended to mock Hemingway's preoccupation with war and brutality. Curnutt writes, "Her Hemingway poem seems an effort to steer the young writer away from 'savagedom' toward less-pessimistic subjects" (*Ernest Hemingway and the Expatriate Modernist Movement* [Detroit: Gale Group, 2001], 33). Wendy Steiner sees the portrait as depicting competition between Hemingway and Stein. "This competition is really the central point of the portrait," Steiner contends. "The title, 'He and They, Hemingway,' implies, partly through its sound organization, that Hemingway sees himself in opposition to others, either to the other young men [of Stein's acquaintance], to Stein and other teachers [like Anderson], or to 'society'" (*Exact Resemblance to Exact Resemblance* [New Haven: Yale University Press, 1978], 113.) On the contrary, this writer sees nothing provocative or unfriendly in the piece. Stein and Hemingway were on exceptionally good terms at the time. Ulla E. Dydo seems nearer the mark in characterizing the poem as "a send-off piece, a farewell-and-return salute.... Its tone is light and affectionate but also guarded, for Stein had reservations not about Hemingway's gift but about how he used it" (*Gertrude Stein: The Language That Rises 1923–1934* [Evanston: Northern University Press, 2003], 71).

23. *Selected Letters*, 94 and 101.

24. *Anderson/Stein: Correspondence*, 36.

25. Ford Madox Ford, *It Was the Nightingale* (Philadelphia: Lippincott, 1933), 295–6 and 333.

26. *Selected Letters*, 116.

27. Ibid., 111.

28. In a letter to W. G. Rogers in 1948, Hemingway said of Stein: "I always wanted to fuck her and she knew it and it was a good healthy feeling and made more sense than some of the talk. I think Alice was sort of jealous..." (*Selected Letters*, 650).

29. To help augment the seasoned, hardbitten image he wished to project, Hemingway at this time often embellished, and sometimes totally invented, past occurrences. He told Sylvia Beach that he had spent two years in a military hospital getting back the use of his legs. He said he had gone through a rough childhood, having quit school to support his family, and had earned his first money in a boxing match (*Shakespeare and Company*, 78). He later told Gertrude Stein that he once killed a man in the States. None of these things was true.

30. GS, *Autobiography of Alice B. Toklas* (New York: The Literary Guild, 1933), 266.

31. Donald Clifford Gallup, "The Making of *The Making of Americans*," appendix to *Fernhurst, Q.E.D., and Other Early Writings*, by GS (New York: Liveright, 1971), 190.

32. J. Gerald Kennedy and Kirk Curnutt argue that Hemingway consciously appropriated the Stein sentence as a slap at *Geography and Plays*, and that this marked Hemingway's "earliest, most tentative break with Stein." See "In the Temps de Gertrude," in *Hemingway and Fitzgerald: French Connections* (New York: St. Martin's Press, 1999), 124–5.

33. *Autobiography of Alice B. Toklas*, 263.

34. *A Moveable Feast*, 30.

35. "The Art of the Short Story," *The Paris Review* (1981): 88.

36. *Selected Letters*, 122.

Chapter 4

1. McAlmon to Bill Bird, 3 July 1954 and 26 October 1954, Yale Collection of American Literature, Beinecke Rare Book and Manuscript Library. Kay Boyle and Robert McAlmon, *Being Geniuses Together: A Binocular View of Paris in the '20s* (New York: Doubleday, 1968), 275–7. Bird recalled Hemingway hitting himself with the rock and saying repeatedly, "Shall I kill myself? Shall I?" Bird to McAlmon, 16 September 1954, Yale Collection of American Literature, Beinecke Rare Book and Manuscript Library.

2. *Being Geniuses Together*, 230.

3. Donald Clifford Gallup, ed., *The Flowers of Friendship: Letters Written to Gertrude Stein* (New York: Knopf, 1953), 141.

4. *Being Geniuses Together*, 255.

5. Ibid., 229.

6. EH to Ezra Pound, c. 1929, Hemingway Collection.

7. EH to Ernest Walsh, mid–January 1925, Hemingway Collection.

8. Carlos Baker, *Hemingway: A Life Story* (New York: Scribner's, 1969), 158.

9. *Ernest Hemingway: Selected Letters 1917–1961*, ed. Carlos Baker (New York: Scribner's, 1981), 161.

10. John Kuehl and Jackson Bryer, eds., *Dear Scott/Dear Max: The Fitzgerald-Perkins Correspondence* (New York: Scribner's 1971), 78.
11. January 1927, Hemingway Collection.
12. *Selected Letters*, 242. See also Carlos Baker, *Hemingway: The Writer as Artist* (Princeton: Princeton University Press, 1972), 27.
13. EH, *A Moveable Feast: Sketches of the Author's Life in Paris in the Twenties* (New York: Scribner's, 1964), 29. Stein later claimed that it was a hotel keeper in the town of Belley who made the remark. The hotel keeper said that all men go through a civilizing process between the ages of eighteen and twenty-five. If they don't go through the process within that time period, they never become civilized. "And the men who went to the war at eighteen missed the period of civilizing, and they could never be civilized. They were a lost generation" (GS, *Everybody's Autobiography* [New York: Random House, 1937], 52).
14. *A Moveable Feast*, 30.
15. Reviews from *Fernhurst, Q.E.D., and Other Early Writings*, by GS (New York: Liveright, 1971), 211–2.
16. *A Moveable Feast*, 17–18.
17. Alice B. Toklas, *What Is Remembered* (San Francisco: North Point Press, 1985), 114.
18. Quoted in James R. Mellow, *Hemingway: A Life Without Consequences* (New York: Houghton Mifflin, 1992), 316.
19. *Selected Letters*, 673.
20. EH to Ezra Pound, c. 27 November 1925, Yale Collection of American Literature, Beinecke Rare Book and Manuscript Library, Yale University.
21. Michael Reynolds, *Hemingway: The Paris Years* (Oxford: Blackwell, 1989), 328–9.
22. EH, *The Torrents of Spring* (1926; repr., New York: Scribner's, 1972), 74–75.
23. *Selected Letters*, 185.
24. SA to GS, 25 April 1926, in Ray Lewis White, *Sherwood Anderson/Gertrude Stein: Correspondence and Personal Essays* (Chapel Hill: University of North Carolina Press, 1972), 52.
25. Sherwood Anderson, *Sherwood Anderson's Memoirs: A Critical Edition*, ed. Ray Lewis White (Chapel Hill: University of North Carolina Press, 1969), 463–4.
26. 21 May 1926, Hemingway Collection.
27. *Sherwood Anderson's Memoirs*, 462.
28. June 1926, Hemingway Collection.
29. *Selected Letters*, 210.
30. Ben Hecht, *Letters from Bohemia* (Garden City: Doubleday & Co., 1964), 98.
31. *A Moveable Feast*, 28.
32. Alix Du Poy Daniel, "The Stimulating Life with Gertrude & Co.," *Lost Generation Journal* 6 (Summer 1979): 17.
33. Quoted in Alfred G. Aronowitz and Peter Hamill, *Ernest Hemingway: The Life and Death of a Man* (New York: Lancer Books, 1961), 75–76.
34. Alice told Donald Sutherland in 1966 that she had forced Gertrude to get rid of Hemingway. Sutherland realized that "what Alice thought she was preventing was no casual affair but a marriage, which she felt would be a short one" (*Prairie Schooner* [winter 1971–72]: 297–8).

Chapter 5

1. Samuel Sillen, "Obituary of Europe and Gertrude Stein," review of *Everybody's Autobiography*, by GS, *New Masses*, December 7, 1937; Clifton Fadiman, *Party of One: The Selected Writings of Clifton Fadiman* (Cleveland: World Publishing Company, ca. 1955), 90. Stein played no direct role in the Dada movement, but see James R. Mellow, "Gertrude Stein Among the Dadaists," *Arts Magazine*, May 1977.
2. The brothers might have been surprised and embarrassed, but Edith Sitwell had received from Stein a copy of the portrait nearly a year earlier and replied with praise for the piece. Sitwell may have been surprised and embarrassed, however, by Stein reading the portrait in public to a group not entirely sympathetic to Stein's modernist approach.
3. Harold Acton, *Memoirs of an Aesthete* (London: Methuen, 1948), 161–3. Recordings of Stein reading from her works are commercially available and attest to her fine voice. Alice Toklas described it as "deep, full, velvety like a great contralto's" (*What Is Remembered* [San Francisco: North Point Press, 1985], 23). Toklas also noted, as did others, "her fine large laughs" (39). Bravig Imbs wrote, "She had the easiest, most engaging and infectious laugh I have ever heard. Always starting abruptly at a high pitch and cascading down and down into rolls and rolls of unctuous merriment, her hearty laugh would fill the room and then, as it gradually dwindled into chuckles and appreciative murmurs, the silence that followed seemed golden with sunlight. Her laugh was boisterous but I have never known it to offend even the most delicately attuned, for it was so straight from the heart, so human, so rich in sound" (*Confessions of Another Young Man* [New York: Henkle-Yesdale House, 1936], 118–9).
4. Items 524 and 622a, Hemingway Collection.

5. "My Own Life," *New Yorker,* February 12, 1927.
6. EH, *Ernest Hemingway: Selected Letters 1917–1961,* ed. Carlos Baker (New York: Scribner's, 1981), 249.
7. Quoted in Jeffrey Meyers, *Hemingway: A Biography* (New York: Harper & Row, 1985), 179.
8. *Selected Letters,* 232.
9. GS, *Autobiography of Alice B. Toklas* (New York: The Literary Guild, 1933), 304.
10. Sherwood Anderson, *Sherwood Anderson's Memoirs: A Critical Edition,* ed. Ray Lewis White (Chapel Hill: University of North Carolina Press, 1969), 464.
11. *Selected Letters,* 241.
12. *Sherwood Anderson's Memoirs,* 465.
13. Morill Cody, *The Women of Montparnasse* (New York: Cornwall Books, 1984), 82.
14. "Donald Ogden Stewart: An Interview," *Fitzgerald/Hemingway Annual 1973* (1973): 85.
15. *Memoirs of an Aesthete,* 175.
16. Kay Boyle and Robert McAlmon, *Being Geniuses Together: A Binocular View of Paris in the '20s* (New York: Doubleday, 1968), 343; *Autobiography of Alice B. Toklas,* 266.

Chapter 6

1. GS, *Everybody's Autobiography* (New York: Random House, 1937), 119.
2. Bravig Imbs, *Confessions of Another Young Man* (New York: Henkle-Yesdale House, 1936), 296–9. Imbs noted that there were degrees of intimacy in the Stein household. First, you usually had to get by Alice. Then you were invited to lunch. "The supreme degree, of course, was a quarrel" (119).
3. *Confessions of Another Young Man,* 113.
4. Virgil Thomson, *Virgil Thomson* (New York: Knopf, 1966), 90.
5. Ibid., 90.
6. Ibid., 89–92.
7. Ibid., 105.
8. GS, *Lectures in America* (New York: Random House, 1935), 131.
9. *Virgil Thomson,* 105.
10. Ezra Pound to EH, 3 November 1926, Hemingway Collection.
11. Ezra Pound to EH, 22 November 1926, Hemingway Collection.
12. Virgil Thomson to EH, 22 March 1927, Hemingway Collection.
13. Item 758, Hemingway Collection.
14. 24 January 1927, Hemingway Collection.
15. *Ernest Hemingway: Selected Letters 1917–1961,* ed. Carlos Baker (New York: Scribner's, 1981), 273–4.
16. *A Moveable Feast: Sketches of the Author's Life in Paris in the Twenties* (New York: Scribner's, 1964), 119.
17. Ulla E. Dydo with William Rice, *Gertrude Stein: The Language That Rises 1923–1934* (Evanston: Northern University Press, 2003), 368.
18. "The Gradual Making of The Making of Americans," in *Lectures in America* (New York: Random House, 1935), 135.
19. *Everybody's Autobiography,* 92.
20. GS, *Autobiography of Alice B. Toklas* (New York: The Literary Guild, 1933), 270. In April 1960, Alice Toklas recounted the same story more emphatically. "And one day I said to Gertrude Stein, If you come back from your walk in the Luxembourg with the dog—exercising the dog—with Hemingway on your arm, I go out! I won't stay here with him! And by Jove she came in with him one day" (Lawrence D. Stewart, "Hemingway and the Autobiographies of Alice B. Toklas," *Fitzgerald/Hemingway Annual 1970* (1970): 121.
21. *Autobiography of Alice B. Toklas,* 271. Zelda Fitzgerald, Scott's wife, also thought Hemingway a fake. When asked by Gerald Murphy what she had against Ernest, she answered "He's bogus." Zelda one time told Hemingway to his face, "Ernest, nobody is as male as all that." She told Scott, who was awed by Hemingway's talent and personality, "He's phony as a rubber check and you know it." Honoria Murphy Donnelly with Richard N. Billings, *Sara & Gerald: Villa America and After* [New York: Times Books, 1982], 21; Sara Mayfield, *Exiles from Paradise: Zelda and Scott Fitzgerald* [New York: Delacorte Press, 1971], 112–3.)
22. Allen Tate, *Memoirs and Opinions 1926–1974* (Chicago: The Swallow Press), 63–64. Tate, in an earlier extemporaneous talk, gave a slightly different version of this day's events. See "Random Thoughts on the 1920's," *The Minnesota Review* 1, no. 1 (October 1960): 46–56.
23. Fitzgerald here echoes the first line of Robert Browning's poem "Memorabilia":
"Ah, did you once see Shelley plain,
And did he stop and speak to you
And did you speak to him again?
How strange it seems and new!"
24. Ulla E. Dydo, an expert in Gertrude Stein's obscure methods and techniques, says that in the first two parts of "Evidence," Stein is "writing a malicious, personal attack on Hemingway." For Dydo's analysis of this piece, see *Gertrude Stein: The Language That Rises,* 379–86. The complete text of "Evidence" appears in *A Stein Reader,* ed. Ulla E.

Dydo (Evanston: Northern University Press, 1996), 541–6.
25. Lawrence D. Stewart, "Hemingway and the Autobiographies of Alice B. Toklas," *Fitzgerald/Hemingway Annual 1970* (1970): 118–9. See also Alice B. Toklas, *What is Remembered* (San Francisco: North Point Press, 1985), 116–7.
26. *Selected Letters*, 309–11.
27. EH to Max Perkins, 17 November 1929, Hemingway Collection.
28. See Matthew J. Bruccoli, ed., *The Only Thing That Counts: The Ernest Hemingway-Max Perkins Correspondence* (New York: Scribner, 1996), 132–3 and 348–9.
29. *Autobiography of Alice B. Toklas*, 270–1.

Chapter 7

1. *Everybody's Autobiography* (New York: Random House, 1937), 45 and 48.
2. Edward Burns, ed., *The Letters of Gertrude Stein and Carl Van Vechten* (New York: Columbia University Press, 1986), 235.
3. Ulla E. Dydo with William Rice, *Gertrude Stein: The Language That Rises 1923–1934* (Evanston: Northern University Press, 2003), 413.
4. *Atlantic Monthly*, August 1933, 208.
5. *Ernest Hemingway: Selected Letters 1917–1961*, ed. Carlos Baker (New York: Scribner's, 1981), 156 and 236.
6. Michael Reynolds, *Hemingway: The Final Years* (New York: W. W. Norton, 1999), 86.
7. R. L. Duffus, "Hemingway Now Writes of Bull-Fighting as a Sport," *New York Times Book Review*, September 25, 1932.
8. Robert M. Coates, "Bullfights," *New Yorker*, October 1, 1932.
9. "Bulls and Bottles," *Nation*, November 9, 1932.
10. "Bull in the Afternoon," *New Republic*, June 7, 1933.
11. Matthew J. Bruccoli, ed., *The Only Thing That Counts: The Ernest Hemingway-Max Perkins Correspondence* (New York: Scribner, 1996), 190.
12. Ibid., 191.
13. *New Yorker*, 4 March 1933, 33.
14. *Selected Letters*, 751 and 761.
15. Ibid., 387–8.
16. Michael Reynolds, *Hemingway: The 1930s* (New York: W. W. Norton, 1997), 123.
17. *Selected Letters*, 384.
18. *Atlantic Monthly*, May 1933, 516 and 523.
19. Ibid., July 1933, 65.
20. Ibid., July 1933, 69.
21. Ibid., August 1933, 198.
22. Ibid., August 1933, 198–9.
23. Ibid., August 1933, 200–208.
24. *The Only Thing That Counts*, 193.
25. 22 July 1933, Yale Collection of American Literature, Beinecke Rare Book and Manuscript Library, Yale University.
26. *Hemingway: The 1930s*, 147.
27. Ray Lewis White, ed., *Sherwood Anderson/Gertrude Stein: Correspondence and Personal Essays* (Chapel Hill: University of North Carolina Press, 1972), 76.
28. *Hemingway: The 1930s*, 147.
29. William Troy, "A Note on Gertrude Stein," *Nation*, September 6, 1933.
30. "Integer Vitae," *New Statesman and Nation*, October 14, 1933.
31. GS, *Autobiography of Alice B. Toklas* (New York: The Literary Guild, 1933), 265.

Chapter 8

1. Edward Burns, ed., *The Letters of Gertrude Stein and Carl Van Vechten* (New York: Columbia University Press, 1986), 274.
2. "Testimony Against Gertrude Stein," *Transition: An International Workshop for Vertigralist Transmutation*, ed. Eugene Jolas, July 1935.
3. *Letters of Stein and Van Vechten*, 404; GS, *Everybody's Autobiography* (New York: Random House, 1937), 32.
4. Leo Stein, *Journey Into the Self: Being the Letters, Papers & Journals of Leo Stein*, ed. Edmund Fuller (New York: Crown Publishers, 1950, 134.
5. Ibid., 142.
6. *Everybody's Autobiography*, 47.
7. Ibid., 44–45.
8. Ibid., 47.
9. Ibid., 50.
10. Ibid., 21–22.
11. Ibid., 84.
12. "Portraits and Repetition," in *Lectures in America* (New York: Random House, 1935), 170.
13. GS, "Lecture 3," in *Narration: Four Lectures by Gertrude Stein* (Chicago: University of Chicago Press, 1930), 34.
14. *Principles of Psychology* (New York: Holt, 1890), 2:110.
15. GS, *Picasso* (New York: Dover, 1984), 27; *Everybody's Autobiography*, 68.
16. *Everybody's Autobiography*, 91.
17. Ibid., 128 and 111.
18. Ibid., 65.
19. Ibid., 92.
20. GS, "And now," *Vanity Fair*, September 1934, 35.

21. *Everybody's Autobiography*, 85.
22. See Ulla E. Dydo with William Rice, *Gertrude Stein: The Language That Rises 1923–1934* (Evanston: Northern University Press, 2003), 311.
23. Quoted in Anthony Tommasini, *Virgil Thomson: Composer on the Aisle* (New York: W. W. Norton, 1997), 214.
24. Virgil Thomson, *Virgil Thomson* (New York: Knopf, 1966), 196. See also Stein's account, "Left to Right," *Story* 3, no. 16, November 1933. In Stein's account, Arthur William is Hugnet and Generale Erving is Thomson.
25. "Left to Right," *Story*.
26. For an excellent account of how *Four Saints* came to be produced, see Steven Watson, *Prepare for Saints: Gertrude Stein, Virgil Thomson, and the Mainstreaming of American Modernism* (Berkeley: University of California Press, 2000).
27. *Virgil Thomson*, 136.
28. Ibid., 243.
29. The story behind Stein's decision to finally lecture in America is more complex than Stein made public or that is appropriate to go into here. For more details, see Dydo, *Gertrude Stein: The Language That Rises*.
30. "The Friend of Spain: A Spanish Letter," *Esquire*, January 1934, 138.
31. Matthew J. Bruccoli, ed., *The Only Thing That Counts: The Ernest Hemingway–Max Perkins Correspondence* (New York: Scribner, 1996), 198.
32. Matthew J. Bruccoli, ed., *Hemingway and the Mechanism of Fame* (Columbia: University of South Carolina Press, 2006), 24. See also James Thurber, *The Years with Ross* (Boston: Little, Brown, 1959), 157–8.
33. *Hemingway and the Mechanism of Fame*, 28–29.
34. Item 265a, Hemingway Collection.
35. Morill Cody, *The Women of Montparnasse* (New York: Cornwall Books, 1984), 84.
36. *The Only Thing That Counts*, 206.
37. *Esquire*, April 1934, 19.
38. *Ernest Hemingway: Selected Letters 1917–1961*, ed. Carlos Baker (New York: Scribner's, 1981), 402–3.
39. Michael Reynolds, *Hemingway: The 1930s* (New York: W. W. Norton, 1997), 167.
40. Kay Boyle and Robert McAlmon, *Being Geniuses Together: A Binocular View of Paris in the '20s* (New York: Doubleday, 1968), 352.
41. *Being Geniuses Together*, 180.

Chapter 9

1. "Gertrude Stein, Home, Upholds Her Simplicity," *New York Herald Tribune*, October 25, 1934, sec. 1.
2. Fanny Butcher, "Book Presents Gertrude Stein as She Really Is," review of *The Making of Americans*, by GS, *Chicago Tribune*, February 10, 1934.
3. Reed Hynds, "Gertrude Stein in 'Portraits and Prayers,'" review of *Portraits and Prayers*, by GS, *St. Louis Star-Times*, November 16, 1934.
4. "Palilalia and Gertrude Stein," *Journal of the American Medical Association* 103, no. 2 (1 December 1934): 1711–2.
5. Peggy Bacon, "Facts about Faces: Gertrude Stein," *New Republic*, March 13, 1935.
6. "Gertrude Stein Home After Thirty-One Years," *Literary Digest*, November 3, 1934.
7. Evelyn Seeley, "Alice Toklas Hides in Shadow of Stein," *New York World-Telegram*, October 25, 1934.
8. Tim Page and Vanessa Weeks Page, eds., *Selected Letters of Virgil Thomson* (New York: Summit Books, 1988), 117.
9. "Gertrude Stein: A Radio Interview," *Paris Review*, 116 (fall 1990): 85–97.
10. *Everybody's Autobiography* (New York: Random House, 1937), 193; GS, *Picasso* (New York: Dover, 1984), 50.
11. *Everybody's Autobiography*, 194.
12. "Gertrude Stein, Harold Gilbert Talk." http://www.lkwdpl.org/lfiles/gilbert/stein.htm. For a more scholarly interpretation, see Ulla E. Dydo with William Rice, *Gertrude Stein: The Language That Rises 1923–1934* (Evanston: Northern University Press, 2003), 196–7.
13. Quoted in W. G. Rogers, *When This You See Remember Me: Gertrude Stein in Person* (New York: Rinehart, 1948), 140–1.
14. *Everybody's Autobiography*, 188.
15. Ellen F. Bloom, "Three Steins: A Very Personal Recital," *Texas Quarterly* 19 (Summer 1970): 15–22.
16. *Everybody's Autobiography*, 5.
17. Ibid., 282–3.
18. John Hyde Preston, "A Conversation," *Atlantic Monthly*, August 1935.
19. Arnold Gingrich to EH, 8 November 1934, Hemingway Collection.
20. *Ernest Hemingway: Selected Letters 1917–1961*, ed. Carlos Baker (New York: Scribner's, 1981), 410–1.
21. *Scribner's Magazine*, June 1935.
22. Matthew J. Bruccoli, ed., *The Only Thing That Counts: The Ernest Hemingway–*

Max Perkins Correspondence (New York: Scribner, 1996), 225.
23. Ibid., 228.
24. EH, *Green Hills of Africa* (New York: Scribner's, 1935), 65–66.
25. *Saturday Review of Literature,* October 26, 1935.
26. *Letters of Sherwood Anderson,* ed. Howard Mumford Jones (Boston: Little, Brown, 1953), 345.
27. Edmund Wilson, *The Shores of Light: A Literary Chronicle of the Twenties and Thirties* (New York: Farrar, Straus and Young, 1952), 619–20.
28. *The Only Thing That Counts,* 229.
29. *Selected Letters,* 414.
30. Ibid., 415.
31. "Charles and Lorine Thompson: A Key West Friendship," in James Plath and Frank Simons, eds., *Remembering Ernest Hemingway* (Key West: Ketch & Yawl Press, 1999),17–18; *Selected Letters,* 438–9.
32. *Selected Letters,* 439.
33. *Picasso,* 45–46.
34. Samuel M. Steward, *Dear Sammy: Letters from Gertrude Stein and Alice B. Toklas* (Boston: Houghton Mifflin, 1977), 26.
35. *Everybody's Autobiography,* 307.
36. GS, *The Geographical History of America or The Relation of Human Nature to the Human Mind* (1936; repr, Baltimore: Johns Hopkins University Press, 1995), 62.

Chapter 10

1. EH, *By-Line: Ernest Hemingway,* ed. William White (New York: Scribner's, 1967), 228.
2. Ibid., 209.
3. Ibid., 228.
4. F. Scott Fitzgerald, *The Crack-Up,* ed. Edmund Wilson (New York: New Directions, 1945), 69–70.
5. *Esquire,* August 1936.
6. John Kuehl and Jackson Bryer, *Dear Scott/Dear Max: The Fitzgerald-Perkins Correspondence* (New York: Scribner's, 1971), 231. Ezra Pound about this time also expressed annoyance with the changes he had witnessed in Hemingway, but Pound attributed the changes to Ernest having left Europe to live in the States. "Every artist," Pound told a friend in conversation, "be he a capitalist or a fucking half-arsed Marxist, he's sure to go to pot in the wonderful U.S.A. They grow corrupted, every one of them, and they end by turning into harlots or castrati or alcoholics. Take Hemingway! Good God! What can you do with a man like that? Swollen muscles, swollen head, swollen ego and he's done for!" (Frederic Prokosch, *Voices: A Memoir* [New York: Farrar, Straus, Giroux, 1983], 101.)
7. Items 204 and 212, Hemingway Collection.
8. "Scott, Ernest and Whoever," *Esquire,* December 1966.
9. Matthew J. Bruccoli, ed., *The Only Thing That Counts: The Ernest Hemingway-Max Perkins Correspondence* (New York: Scribner, 1996), 266.
10. Max Eastman, *Great Companions: Critical Memoirs of Some Famous Friends* (New York: Farrar, Straus, and Cudahy), 58–64.
11. Samuel M. Steward, *Dear Sammy: Letters from Gertrude Stein and Alice B. Toklas* (Boston: Houghton Mifflin, 1977), 55.
12. Denis Brian, ed., *The True Gen: An Intimate Portrait of Ernest Hemingway by Those Who Knew Him* (New York: Grove Press, 1988), 69.
13. *Everybody's Autobiography* (New York: Random House, 1937), 318.
14. Quoted in Richard Bridgman, *Gertrude Stein in Pieces* (New York: Oxford University Press, 1970), 364.
15. Janet Flanner, *Paris Was Yesterday: 1925–1939,* ed. Irving Drutman (New York: Viking Press, 1972), 187.
16. Edward Burns, ed., *The Letters of Gertrude Stein and Carl Van Vechten* (New York: Columbia University Press, 1986), 2:616.
17. *Letters of Stein and Van Vechten,* 2:616–7.
18. Ibid., 2:618.
19. *The Only Thing That Counts,* 274.
20. Eric Sevareid, *Not So Wild a Dream* (New York: Knopf, 1946), 89–90.
21. Cecil Beaton, *Self Portrait with Friends: The Selected Diaries of Cecil Beaton, 1946–1974,* ed. Richard Buckle (London: Weidenfeld and Nicolson, 1979), 72.
22. GS, "The Winner Loses: A Picture of Occupied France," *Atlantic Monthly,* November 1940.
23. "The Winner Loses."
24. *The Only Thing That Counts,* 277.
25. Ibid., 285.
26. EH, *For Whom the Bell Tolls* (New York: Scribner's, 1940), 30.
27. Ibid., 289.

Chapter 11

1. GS, *Wars I Have Seen* (London: Batsford, 1945), 6.
2. GS, "The Winner Loses: A Picture of Occupied France," *Atlantic Monthly,* November 1940.

3. W. G. Rogers, *When This You See Remember Me: Gertrude Stein in Person* (New York: Rinehart, 1948), 246 and 198.
4. Ibid., 246.
5. *Wars I Have Seen*, 81.
6. Ibid., 31–32.
7. Ibid., 32.
8. Alice B. Toklas, *The Alice B. Toklas Cookbook* (London: Michael Joseph, 1954), 212; Eric Sevareid, *Not So Wild a Dream* (New York: Knopf, 1946), 459.
9. *Wars I Have Seen*, 77.
10. Robert E. Sherwood, review of *For Whom the Bell Tolls*, "The Atlantic Bookshelf," *Atlantic Monthly*, November 1940.
11. Matthew J. Bruccoli, ed., *The Only Thing That Counts: The Ernest Hemingway–Max Perkins Correspondence* (New York: Scribner, 1996), 275.
12. *Ernest Hemingway: Selected Letters 1917–1961*, ed. Carlos Baker (New York: Scribner's, 1981), 521.
13. *The Only Thing That Counts*, 309.
14. Tillie Arnold, who knew Ernest and Martha well in Idaho, stated that when the couple later divorced, "they agreed ... that she wouldn't write anything that would mention his name at all, so she didn't" ("Tillie Arnold: Sun Valley Years," in James Plath and Frank Simons, eds., *Remembering Ernest Hemingway* [Key West: Ketch & Yawl Press, 1999], 148).
15. *Selected Letters*, 536.
16. Bernice Kert, *The Hemingway Women* (New York: W. W. Norton, 1983), 391–2.
17. *The Hemingway Women*, 392; EH to Martha Gellhorn, 31 January 1944, Hemingway Collection.
18. MG to Hortense Flexner, ?17 May 1944, in *Letters of Martha Gellhorn*, ed. Caroline Moorehead (London: Chatto & Windus, 2006), 163.
19. *The Hemingway Women*, 398.
20. *Selected Letters*, 571; EH to Bernard Berenson, 27 May 1953, Hemingway Collection.
21. *Alice B. Toklas Cookbook*, 216.
22. Ibid., 217.
23. *Wars I Have Seen*, 156.
24. *Alice B. Toklas Cookbook*, 218.
25. "Voyage to Victory," *Collier's*, July 22, 1944; *By-Line: Ernest Hemingway*, 340–55. Hemingway did not go ashore at Normandy, but Martha Gellhorn did. She hid in the bathroom of a hospital ship and went ashore on the morning of D-Day plus one, June 7. After returning to England, she was arrested for having entered a war zone without the proper credentials. Ordered to the American nurses' training camp outside London, she climbed over the wire fence, hitched a ride to a nearby military air base, and caught an unauthorized flight to Naples, Italy.
26. Sylvia Beach, *Shakespeare and Company* (New York: Harcourt, Brace and Co., 1930), 219–20.
27. EH, *Across the River and Into the Trees* (New York: Scribner's, 1950), 133–4.
28. *Wars I Have Seen*, 156.
29. Ibid., 141.
30. *Alice B. Toklas Cookbook*, 218.
31. *Wars I Have Seen*, 161.
32. *Not So Wild a Dream*, 458.
33. Ibid., 460–1.
34. Ibid., 458–9.
35. See Donald Clifford Gallup, ed., *The Flowers of Friendship: Letters Written to Gertrude Stein* (New York: Knopf, 1953), 370–1 and "We Are Back in Paris," in *Wars I Have Seen*, 172–4.
36. *Wars I Have Seen*, 174.
37. Quoted in Carlos Baker, *Hemingway: A Life Story* (New York: Scribner's, 1969), 427.
38. *Shakespeare and Company*, 33.
39. EH to W. G. Rogers, 29 July 1948, in *Selected Letters*, 650.

Chapter 12

1. Alice B. Toklas, *What Is Remembered* (San Francisco: North Point Press), 170.
2. GS, "The New Hope in Our 'Sad Young Men,'" *New York Times Magazine*, June 3, 1945.
3. W. G. Rogers, *When This You See Remember Me: Gertrude Stein in Person* (New York: Rinehart, 1948), 226–7.
4. Bennet Cerf to GS, 27 March 1945, in *The Flowers of Friendship: Letters Written to Gertrude Stein*, ed. Donald Clifford Gallup, (New York: Knopf, 1953), 376.
5. Virgil Thomson, *Virgil Thomson*, (New York: Knopf, 1966), 366.
6. GS, *Last Operas and Plays*, ed. Carl Van Vechten (New York: Rinehart, 1949), 87–88.
7. Stein marked the event by writing "She Bowed to Her Brother," published in *Portraits and Prayers* (New York: Random House, 1934), 236–40.
8. *Virgil Thomson*, 180.
9. VT to GS, 15 April 1946, in *The Flowers of Friendship*, 397–8.
10. Laura Riding Jackson, "The Word-Play of Gertrude Stein," *Critical Essays on Gertrude Stein*, ed. Michael J. Hoffman (Boston: G. K. Hall, 1986), 256; Ellen F. Bloom, "Three Steins," *The Texas Quarterly* (Summer 1970): 22.
11. Mary's Journal, 13 October 1945, quoted

in Michael Reynolds, *Hemingway: The Final Years* (New York: W. W. Norton, 1999), 133.
 12. EH to Carol Hemingway Gardner, 1945, quoted in Norberto Fuentes, *Hemingway in Cuba* (Secaucus, NJ: Lyle Stuart, 1984), 387–8.
 13. MG to EH, 13 August 1945, Hemingway Collection.
 14. EH to MG, 5 August 1946, Hemingway Collection.
 15. *What Is Remembered*, 171.
 16. Ibid., 170–2.
 17. *Virgil Thomson*, 373.
 18. *What Is Remembered*, 172.
 19. Ibid.
 20. Ibid., 173.
 21. Ibid. "About Baby's last words," Toklas wrote to Carl Van Vechten in 1953. "She said upon waking from a sleep — What is the question. And I didn't answer thinking she was not completely awakened. Then she said again — What is the question and before I could speak she went on — If there is no question then there is no answer. And she turned and went to sleep again. Were they not a summing up of her life and perhaps a vision of the future — often they mean that to me and then they are a comfort" (*Staying on Alone: Letters of Alice B. Toklas*, ed. Edward Burns [New York: Liveright, 1973], 276).
 22. "Letter from Paris," *New Yorker*, August 10, 1946.
 23. Kirk Curnutt, *Critical Response to Gertrude Stein* (Westport, Conn.: Greenwood Press, 2000), 289.
 24. Max Eastman, *Great Companions: Critical Memoirs of Some Famous Friends* (New York: Farrar, Straus, and Cudahy, 1959), 75–76.
 25. *Ernest Hemingway: Selected Letters 1917–1961*, ed. Carlos Baker (New York: Scribner's, 1981), 649–50.
 26. EH to Bernard Berenson, 4 May 1953, Hemingway Collection and *Selected Letters*, 736.
 27. EH to Bernard Berenson, 4 May 1953, Hemingway Collection.
 28. *Selected Letters*, 781 and 736.
 29. Ibid., 736. See p. 781 where EH, in a letter to Donald C. Gallup, refers to Alice as "that Toklas ____."
 30. Denis Brian, *The True Gen: An Intimate Portrait of Ernest Hemingway by Those Who Knew Him* (New York: Grove Press, 1988), 68.
 31. *Staying On Alone*, 38.
 32. Jack Hemingway, *Misadventures of a Fly Fisherman: My Life with and Without Papa* (Dallas: Taylor 1986), 247–8. When interviewing Paul Bowles in 1995, Florian Vetsch remarked that in photographs of Gertrude Stein and Alice Toklas together, Alice was always in the background, "like the servant of genius." Vetsch asked if Toklas was not a little shy, and Bowles replied, "Oh no. Well, she remained in the background for Gertrude, as a favor, you might say. Because she knew that Gertrude liked it that way. She was the important one. Toklas provided the background. But then, as soon as Gertrude Stein died, Toklas became very talkative. She changed completely" (Florian Vetsch, *Desultory Correspondence: An Interview with Paul Bowles on Gertrude Stein* [Zurich: Memory/Cage Editions, 1997], 17).
 33. MG to William Walton, 3 February 1950, in *Letters of Martha Gellhorn*, ed. Caroline Moorehead (London: Chatto & Windus, 2006), 204.
 34. Maxwell Geismar, "To Have and to Have and to Have," *Saturday Review of Books*, September 9, 1950.
 35. Alfred Kazin, "The Indignant Flesh," *New Yorker*, September 9, 1950.
 36. "The Author's Name Is Hemingway," *New York Times Book Review*, September 10, 1950.
 37. Harvey Breit, "Talk with Mr. Hemingway," *New York Times Book Review*, September 17, 1950.
 38. Matthew J. Bruccoli, ed., *The Only Thing That Counts: The Ernest Hemingway-Max Perkins Correspondence* (New York: Scribner, 1996), 335.
 39. Robert E. Fleming, "Hemingway's Last Word on Stein: A Joke in the Manuscript of Islands," *The Hemingway Review* 9, no. 2 (Spring 1990): 174–5.
 40. EH, *The Old Man and the Sea* (New York: Scribner's, 1952), 90.
 41. Ibid., 109–10.
 42. Carlos Baker, *Hemingway: A Life Story* (New York: Scribner's, 1969), 504–5.
 43. *Shenandoah* 3, no. 3 (Autumn 1952): 55.
 44. In his Nobel Prize acceptance speech, Hemingway alluded to the correlation between the old fisherman and the artist, the writer especially, and even more particularly, Hemingway himself. He wrote, "It is because we have had such great writers in the past that a writer is driven far out past where he can go, out to where no one can help him" (quoted in *Hemingway: A Life Story*, 529).
 45. 5 October 1951, in *Selected Letters*, 738.

Chapter 13

1. McAlmon to Bill Bird, 3 July, 1954, Yale Collection of American Literature, Beinecke Rare Book and Manuscript Library.
2. McAlmon to Bob Wetterau, 25 February 1952, unpublished letter in private collection.
3. McAlmon to Bill Bird, 26 October 1954, Yale Collection of American Literature, Beinecke Rare Book and Manuscript Library. McAlmon died of pneumonia at age sixty in Desert Hot Springs on February 2, 1956.
4. http://nobelprize.org/nobel_prizes/literature/laureates/1954/index.html
5. Mary Welsh Hemingway, *How It Was* (New York: Knopf, 1976), 373.
6. Ibid., 390.
7. EH to Harvey Breit, 16 June 1957, Hemingway Collection.
8. In his several renditions of this story, Hemingway never specified what words Toklas used. This writer asked A. E. Hotchner if Hemingway ever revealed to him precisely what terrible things Toklas said to Stein. Hotchner stated he had not. "Maybe it had something to do with Ernest," he speculated.
9. Carlos Baker, *Hemingway: A Life Story* (New York: Scribner's, 1969), 540.
10. "The Art of the Short Story," *Paris Review,* 79 (1981): 100–101.
11. Alice B. Toklas, *Staying on Alone: Letters of Alice B. Toklas*, ed. Edward Burns (New York: Liveright, 1973), 12.
12. Ibid., 41.
13. Ibid., 227.
14. Ibid., 268.
15. Ibid., 209.
16. *How It Was,* 471.
17. Seymour Betsky, "A Last Visit," *Saturday Review,* July 29, 1961.
18. Leslie Fiedler, "An Almost Imaginary Interview: Hemingway in Ketchum," *Partisan Review* 29 (Summer 1962): 400.
19. A. E. Hotchner, *Papa Hemingway: A Personal Memoir* (New York: Random House, 1966), 297.
20. *How It Was,* 502.
21. Denis Brian, ed. *The True Gen: An Intimate Portrait of Ernest Hemingway by Those Who Knew Him* (New York: Grove Press, 1988), 52.
22. *The True Gen,* 59.
23. Norman Mailer, "Punching Papa," review of *That Summer in Paris* by Morely Callaghan, *New York Review of Books,* August 1963.
24. James Plath and Frank Simons, eds., *Remembering Ernest Hemingway* (Key West: Ketch & Yawl Press, 1999), 140.

Epilogue

1. Sutherland, "Alice and Gertrude and Others," *Prairie Schooner* (Winter 1971–72): 296–7.
2. Alice B. Toklas, *Staying on Alone: Letters of Alice B. Toklas*, ed. Edward Burns (New York: Liveright, 1973), 129.
3. Ibid., 386.
4. Ibid., 403.
5. Lawrence D. Stewart, "Hemingway and the Autobiographies of Alice B. Toklas," *Fitzgerald/Hemingway Annual 1970,* 119–20; Sutherland, "Alice and Gertrude and Others," *Prairie Schooner* (Winter 1971–72): 296.
6. Joseph Barry, "Alice B. Toklas," *The Village Voice,* March 16, 1967.

Select Bibliography

Acton, Harold. *Memoirs of an Aesthete.* London: Methuen, 1948.
Anderson, Margaret. *My Thirty Years' War.* New York: Covici, Friede, 1930.
Anderson, Sherwood. *France and Sherwood Anderson: Paris Notebook, 1921.* Edited by Michael Fanning. Baton Rouge: Louisiana State University Press, 1976.
———. *Letters of Sherwood Anderson.* Edited by Howard Mumford Jones. Boston: Little, Brown, 1953.
———. *Sherwood Anderson's Memoirs: A Critical Edition.* Edited by Ray Lewis White. Chapel Hill: University of North Carolina Press, 1969.
———. *A Story Teller's Story.* New York: Grove Press, 1951.
Arnold, Tillie, with William L. Smallwood. *The Idaho Hemingway.* Buhl, Idaho: Beacon Books, 1999.
Aronowitz, Alfred G., and Peter Hamill. *Ernest Hemingway: The Life and Death of a Man.* New York: Lancer Books, 1961.
Bacon, Peggy. "Facts about Faces: Gertrude Stein." *New Republic,* March 13, 1935.
Baker, Carlos. *Ernest Hemingway: A Life Story.* New York: Scribner's, 1969.
———. *Hemingway: The Writer as Artist.* Princeton: Princeton University Press, 1972.
Bald, Wambly. *On the Left Bank: 1929–1933.* Edited by Benjamin Franklin V. Athens: Ohio State University Press, 1987.
Barry, Joseph. "Alice B. Toklas." *Village Voice,* March 16, 1967.
Beach, Sylvia. *Shakespeare and Company.* New York: Harcourt, Brace, 1930.
Beaton, Cecil. *Self Portrait with Friends: The Selected Diaries of Cecil Beaton, 1946–1974.* Edited by Richard Buckle. London: Weidenfeld and Nicolson, 1979.
Betsky, Seymour. "A Last Visit." *Saturday Review,* July 29, 1961.
Bishop, John Peale. "Homage to Hemingway." *New Republic,* November 11, 1936.
Bloom, Ellen F. "Three Steins: A Very Personal Recital." *Texas Quarterly* (Summer 1970): 15–22.
Bowles, Paul. *Without Stopping: An Autobiography.* New York: Putnam's Sons, 1972.
Boyle, Kay, and Robert McAlmon. *Being Geniuses Together: A Binocular View of Paris in the '20s.* New York: Doubleday, 1968.
Braque, Georges, Eugene Jolas, Maria Jolas, Henri Matisse, André Salmon, and Tristan Tzara. "Testimony Against Gertrude Stein." *Transition: An International Workshop for Vertigralist Transmutation* 23 (July 1935): 2–15.
Breit, Harvey. "Talk with Mr. Hemingway." *New York Times Book Review,* September 17, 1950.

Brian, Denis, ed. *The True Gen: An Intimate Portrait of Ernest Hemingway by Those Who Knew Him*. New York: Grove Press, 1988.
Bridgman, Richard. *Gertrude Stein in Pieces*. New York: Oxford University Press, 1970.
Brinnin, John Malcolm. *The Third Rose: Gertrude Stein and Her World*. Boston: Little, Brown, 1959.
Bruccoli, Matthew J. "Donald Ogden Stewart: An Interview." *Fitzgerald/Hemingway Annual 1973* (1973): 83–89.
_____. *Fitzgerald and Hemingway: A Dangerous Friendship*. New York: Carroll & Graf, 1994.
_____, ed. *Hemingway and the Mechanism of Fame*. Columbia: University of South Carolina Press, 2006.
_____. "Interview with Allen Tate." *Fitzgerald/Hemingway Annual 1974* (1974): 101–113.
_____, ed. *The Only Thing That Counts: The Ernest Hemingway–Max Perkins Correspondence*. New York: Scribner, 1996.
Bruccoli, Matthew J., with Judith S. Baughman, eds. *The Sons of Maxwell Perkins: Letters of F. Scott Fitzgerald, Ernest Hemingway, Thomas Wolfe, and Their Editor*. Columbia: University of South Carolina Press, 2004.
Bryher [Winifred Ellerman]. *The Heart to Artemis: A Writer's Memoirs*. New York: Harcourt, Brace & World, 1962.
Burns, Edward, ed. *The Letters of Gertrude Stein and Carl Van Vechten*. New York: Columbia University Press, 1986.
Butcher, Fanny. "Book Presents Gertrude Stein as She Really Is." Review of *The Making of Americans*, by GS. *Chicago Tribune*, February 10, 1934.
Callaghan, Morley. *That Summer in Paris: Memories of Tangled Friendships with Hemingway, Fitzgerald, and Some Others*. New York: Coward-McCann, 1963.
Carpenter, Humphrey. *Geniuses Together: American Writers in Paris in the 1920s*. Boston: Houghton Mifflin, 1988.
Church, Ralph. "Sherwood Comes to Town." *Fitzgerald/Hemingway Annual 1972* (1972): 149–56.
Coates, Robert M. "Bullfighters." Review of *Death in the Afternoon*, by EH. *New Yorker*, October 1, 1932.
Cody, Morrill. *The Women of Montparnasse*. New York: Cornwall Books, 1984.
Curnutt, Kirk, ed. *The Critical Response to Gertrude Stein*. Westport, Conn.: Greenwood Press, 2000.
_____. *Literary Topics: Ernest Hemingway and the Expatriate Modernist Movement*. Farmington Hills, MI: Gale Group, 2000.
DeFazio III, Albert J., ed. *Dear Papa, Dear Hotch: The Correspondence of Ernest Hemingway and A. E. Hotchner*. Columbia: University of Missouri Press, 2005.
DeVoto, Bernard. "Hemingway in the Valley." Review of *Green Hills of Africa*, by EH. *Saturday Review of Books*, October 26, 1935.
Dodge, Mabel. *See* Luhan, Mabel Dodge.
Donaldson, Scott. "Gertrude Stein Reviews Hemingway's *Three Stories & Ten Poems*. *American Literature* 53 no. 1 (March 1981): 114–15.
_____. *Hemingway vs. Fitzgerald: The Rise and Fall of a Literary Friendship*. Woodstock, NY: Overlook Press, 1999.
Donnelly, Honoria Murphy, with Richard N. Billings. *Sara & Gerald: Villa American and After*. New York: Times Books, 1982.
Dos Passos, John. *The Best Times: An Informal Memoir*. New York: The New American Library, 1966.
Duffus, R. L. "Hemingway Now Writes of Bull-Fighting as a Sport." Review of *Death in the Afternoon*, by EH. *New York Times Book Review*, September 25, 1932.

Dydo, Ulla E., with William Rice. *Gertrude Stein: The Language That Rises 1923–1934*. Evanston: Northern University Press, 2003.
_____. *A Stein Reader*. Evanston: Northern University Press, 1996.
Eastman, Max. "Bull in the Afternoon." Review of *Death in the Afternoon*, by EH. *New Republic*, June 7, 1933.
_____. *Great Companions: Critical Memoirs of Some Famous Friends*. New York: Farrar, Straus, and Cudahy, 1959.
Fadiman, Clifton. *Party of One: The Selected Writings of Clifton Fadiman*. Cleveland: World Publishing Company, ca. 1955.
Faulkner, William. Untitled review of *The Old Man and the Sea*, by EH. *Shenandoah* 3 no. 3 (Autumn 1952): 55.
Fenton, Charles A. *The Apprenticeship of Ernest Hemingway*. New York: Farrar, Straus & Young, 1954.
Fiedler, Leslie. "An Almost Imaginary Interview: Hemingway in Ketchum." *Partisan Review* 29 (Summer 1962): 395–405.
Fitzgerald, F. Scott. *The Crack-Up*. Edited by Edmund Wilson. New York: New Directions, 1945.
Flanner, Janet (Genêt). "Letter from Paris." *New Yorker*, August 10, 1946.
_____. *Paris Was Yesterday: 1925–1939*. Edited by Irving Drutman. New York: Viking Press, 1972.
Fleming, Robert E. "Hemingway's Last Word on Stein: A Joke in the Manuscript of *Islands*." *Hemingway Review* 9 no. 2 (Spring 1990): 174–75.
Ford, Ford Madox. *It Was the Nightingale*. Philadelphia: Lippincott, 1933.
Fuentes, Norberto. *Hemingway in Cuba*. Secaucus, NJ: Lyle Stuart, 1984.
Gallup, Donald Clifford, ed. *The Flowers of Friendship: Letters Written to Gertrude Stein*. New York: Knopf, 1953.
Geismar, Maxwell. "To Have and to Have and to Have." Review of *To Have and Have Not*, by EH. *Saturday Review of Books*, September 9, 1950.
Gellhorn, Martha. *The Letters of Martha Gellhorn*. Selected and edited by Caroline Moorehead. London: Chatto & Windus, 2006.
_____. *Travels with Myself and Another*. New York: Dodd, Mead, 1978.
"Gertrude Stein: A Radio Interview." *Paris Review* 116 (Fall 1990): 85–97.
"Gertrude Stein Home After Thirty-One Years." *Literary Digest* 118 (November 13, 1935): 34.
"Gertrude Stein, Home, Upholds Her Simplicity." *New York Herald Tribune*, October 25, 1934.
Gingrich, Arnold. "Scott, Ernest and Whoever." *Esquire*, December 1966.
Gold, Michael. "Gertrude Stein: A Literary Idiot." In *Change the World!*, 23–26. New York: International, ca. 1937.
Hass, Robert Bartlett. "Gertrude Stein Talking—A Transatlantic Interview." *Uclan Review* (Summer 1962): 3–11, (Spring 1963): 40–48, (Winter 1964): 44–48.
_____. *A Primer for the Gradual Understanding of Gertrude Stein*. Los Angeles: Black Sparrow Press, 1973.
Hecht, Ben. *Letters from Bohemia*. Garden City: Doubleday, 1964.
Hemingway, Ernest. *Across the River and Into the Trees*. New York: Scribner's, 1950.
_____. "The Art of the Short Story." *Paris Review* 79 (1981): 85–102.
_____. *By-Line: Ernest Hemingway*. Edited by William White. New York: Scribner's, 1967.
_____. *Ernest Hemingway: Selected Letters 1917–1961*. Edited by Carlos Baker. New York: Scribner's, 1981.

———. *For Whom the Bell Tolls.* New York: Scribner's, 1940.
———. "The Friend of Spain: A Spanish Letter." *Esquire,* January 1934.
———. *The Garden of Eden.* New York: Scribner's, 1986.
———. *Green Hills of Africa.* New York: Scribner's, 1935.
———. "Marlin off the Morro: A Cuban Letter." *Esquire,* Autumn 1933.
———. *A Moveable Feast: Sketches of the Author's Life in Paris in the Twenties.* New York: Scribner's, 1964.
———. "My Own Life." *New Yorker,* February 12, 1927.
———. *The Old Man and the Sea.* New York: Scribner's, 1952.
———. "A Paris Letter." *Esquire,* February 1934.
———. *The Torrents of Spring.* 1926. Reprint, New York: Scribner's, 1972.
Hemingway, Gregory H., M.D. *Papa: A Personal Memoir.* Boston: Houghton Mifflin, 1976.
Hemingway, Jack. *Misadventures of a Fly Fisherman: My Life with and Without Papa.* Dallas: Taylor, 1986.
Hemingway, Mary Welsh. *How It Was.* New York: Knopf, 1976.
Hemingway, Valerie. *Running with the Bulls: My Years with the Hemingways.* New York: Ballantine Books, 2004.
Hicks, Granville. "Bulls and Bottles." Review of *Death in the Afternoon,* by EH. *Nation,* November 9, 1932.
Hotchner, A. E. *Papa Hemingway: A Personal Memoir.* New York: Random House, 1966.
Hynds, Reed. "Gertrude Stein in 'Portraits and Prayers.'" Review of *Portraits and Prayers,* by GS. *St. Louis Star-Times,* November 16, 1934.
Imbs, Bravig. *Confessions of Another Young Man.* New York: Henkle-Yesdale House, 1936.
James, William. *Principles of Psychology.* New York: Holt, 1890.
Kazin, Alfred. "The Indignant Flesh." Review of *Across the River and Into the Trees,* by EH. *New Yorker,* September 9, 1950.
Kennedy, J. Gerald, and Kirk Curnutt. *Hemingway and Fitzgerald: French Connections.* New York: St. Martin's Press, 1999.
Kennedy, Richard S. *Dreams in the Mirror: A Biography of E. E. Cummings.* New York: Liveright, 1980.
Kert, Bernice. *The Hemingway Women.* New York: W. W. Norton, 1983.
Knoll, Robert E., ed. *McAlmon and the Lost Generation: A Self-Portrait.* Lincoln: University of Nebraska Press, 1962.
———. *Robert McAlmon, Expatriate Publisher and Writer.* Lincoln: University of Nebraska Press, 1957.
Kuehl, John, and Jackson Bryer, eds. *Dear Scott/Dear Max: The Fitzgerald-Perkins Correspondence.* New York: Scribner's, 1971.
Loeb, Harold. *The Way It Was.* New York: Criterion Books, 1959.
Luhan, Mabel Dodge. *European Experiences.* New York: Harcourt, 1935.
———. *Movers and Shakers.* New York: Harcourt, Brace, 1936.
McAlmon, Robert. *The Nightinghouls of Paris.* Edited by Sanford J. Smoller. Urbana and Chicago: University of Illinois Press, 2007.
Madeline, Laurence, ed. Translated by Lorna Scott Fox. *Pablo Picasso Gertrude Stein Correspondence.* London: Seagull Books, 2008.
Mailer, Norman. "Punching Papa." Review of *That Summer in Paris,* by Morely Callaghan. *New York Review of Books,* August 1963.
Malcolm, Janet. *Two Lives: Gertrude and Alice.* New Haven: Yale University Press, 2007.
Mayfield, Sara. *Exiles from Paradise: Zelda and Scott Fitzgerald.* New York: Delacorte Press, 1971.

Mellow, James R. *Charmed Circle: Gertrude Stein & Company.* New York: Praeger, 1974.
_____. "Gertrude Stein Among the Dadaists." *Arts Magazine,* May 1977.
_____. *Hemingway: A Life Without Consequences.* New York: Houghton Mifflin, 1992.
_____. *Invented Lives: F. Scott & Zelda Fitzgerald.* Boston: Houghton Mifflin, 1984.
Meyer, Steven. *Irresistible Dictation: Gertrude Stein and the Correlations of Writing and Science.* Stanford: Stanford University Press, 2001.
Meyers, Jeffrey. *Hemingway: A Biography.* New York: Harper & Row, 1985.
Morris, Lawrence S. "Frolicking on Olympus." Review of *The Torrents of Spring,* by EH. *New Republic,* September 15, 1926.
Nagel, James, ed. *Ernest Hemingway: The Writer in Context.* Madison: University of Wisconsin Press, 1984.
Nuffer, David. *The Best Friend I Ever Had: Revelations about Ernest Hemingway from those who knew him.* N.p.: Xlibris, 2008.
O'Hara, John. "The Author's Name Is Hemingway." Review of *Across the River and Into the Trees,* by EH. *New York Times Book Review,* September 10, 1950.
Page, Tim, and Vanessa Weeks Page, eds. *Selected Letters of Virgil Thomson.* New York: Summit Books, 1988.
"Palilalia and Gertrude Stein." *Journal of the American Medical Association* 103 no. 22 (December 1934): 1711–12.
Plath, James, and Frank Simons, eds. *Remembering Ernest Hemingway.* Key West: Ketch & Yawl Press, 1999.
Poli, Bernard J. *Ford Madox Ford and the Transatlantic Review.* Syracuse: Syracuse University Press, 1967.
Preston, John Hyde. "A Conversation." *Atlantic Monthly,* August 1935.
Prokosch, Frederic. *Voices: A Memoir.* New York: Farrar, Straus, Giroux, 1983.
Putnam, Samuel. *Paris Was Our Mistress: Memoirs of a Lost and Found Generation.* New York: Viking Press, 1947.
Reynolds, Michael. *Hemingway: The Final Years.* New York: W. W. Norton, 1999.
_____. *Hemingway: The 1930s.* New York: W. W. Norton, 1997.
_____. *Hemingway: The Paris Years.* Oxford: Blackwell, 1989.
_____. "Hemingway's Stein: Another Misplaced Review." *American Literature* 55 n. 3 (October 1983): 431–34.
Rogers, W. G. *Stein Is Gertrude Stein: Her Life and Work.* New York: Crowell, 1973.
_____. *When This You See Remember Me: Gertrude Stein in Person.* New York: Rinehart, 1948.
Rollyson, Carl. *Nothing Ever Happens to the Brave: The Story of Martha Gellhorn.* New York: St. Martin's Press, 1990.
Seeley, Evelyn. "Alice Toklas Hides in Shadow of Stein." *New York World-Telegram,* October 25, 1934.
Sevareid, Eric. *Not So Wild a Dream.* New York: Knopf, 1946.
Sherwood, Robert E. "The Atlantic Bookshelf." Review of *For Whom the Bell Tolls,* by EH. *Atlantic Monthly,* November 1940.
Simon, Linda. *The Biography of Alice B. Toklas.* Lincoln: University of Nebraska Press, 1977.
_____, ed. *Gertrude Stein Remembered.* Lincoln: University of Nebraska Press, 1995.
Smoller, Sanford J. *Adrift Among Geniuses: Robert McAlmon, Writer and Publisher of the Twenties.* University Park: Pennsylvania State University Press, 1975.
Souhami, Diana. *Gertrude & Alice.* London: Phoenix Press, 1991.
Squires, Radcliffe. *Allen Tate: A Literary Biography.* New York: Pegasus, 1971.
Stein, Gertrude. "And Now." *Vanity Fair,* September 1934.

———. *The Autobiography of Alice B. Toklas.* New York: The Literary Guild, 1933.
———. *Composition as Explanation.* London: Hogarth Press, 1926.
———. *Everybody's Autobiography.* New York: Random House, 1937.
———. *Fernhurst, Q.E.D., and Other Early Writings.* New York: Liveright, 1971.
———. *Four in America.* New Haven: Yale University Press, 1947.
———. *Four Saints in Three Acts: An Opera to be Sung.* New York: Random House: 1934.
———. *The Geographical History of America or The Relation of Human Nature to the Human Mind.* 1936. Reprint Baltimore: Johns Hopkins University Press, 1995.
———. *How to Write.* New York: Dover, 1975.
———. "How Writing Is Written." In *The Oxford Anthology of American Literature,* chosen and edited by William Rose Benét and Norman Holmes Pearson, 1446–51. New York: Oxford University Press, 1938.
———. *Last Operas and Plays.* Edited by Carl Van Vechten. New York: Rinehart, 1949.
———. *Lectures in America.* New York: Random House, 1935.
———. "Left to Right." *Story* 3 no. 16 (November 1933): 17–20.
———. *Narration: Four Lectures by Gertrude Stein.* Chicago: University of Chicago Press, 1930.
———. "The New Hope in Our 'Sad Young Men.'" *New York Times Magazine,* June 3, 1945.
———. "Off We All Went to See Germany." *Life,* August 6, 1945.
———. *Operas and Plays.* Barrytown, NY: Station Hill Press, 1987.
———. *Picasso.* New York: Dover, 1984.
———. *Portraits and Prayers.* New York: Random House, 1934.
———. *Tender Buttons.* 1914. Reprint New York: Gordon Press, 1972.
———. *Three Lives.* Norfolk, Conn.: New Directions, 1909.
———. *Wars I Have Seen.* London: Batsford, 1945.
———. *What Are Masterpieces.* Los Angeles: Conference Press, 1940.
———. "The Winner Loses: A Picture of Occupied France." *Atlantic Monthly,* November 1940.
Stein, Leo. *Journey Into the Self: Being the Letters, Papers & Journals of Leo Stein.* Edited by Edmund Fuller. New York: Crown, 1950.
Steiner, Wendy. *Exact Resemblance to Exact Resemblance: The Literary Portraiture of Gertrude Stein.* New Haven: Yale University Press, 1978.
Steward, Samuel M. *Dear Sammy: Letters from Gertrude Stein and Alice B. Toklas.* Boston: Houghton Mifflin, 1977.
Stewart, Donald Ogden. "Recollections of Fitzgerald and Hemingway." *Fitzgerald/Hemingway Annual 1971* (1971): 177–88.
Stewart, Lawrence D. "Hemingway and the Autobiographies of Alice B. Toklas." *Fitzgerald/Hemingway Annual 1970* (1970): 117–22.
Sutherland, Donald. "Alice and Gertrude and Others." *Prairie Schooner* (Winter 1971–72): 284–99.
Tate, Allen. *Memoirs and Opinions 1926–1974.* Chicago: The Swallow Press, 1975.
———. "Random Thoughts on the 1920's." *Minnesota Review* 1 no. 1 (October 1960): 46–56.
Thomson, Virgil. *Virgil Thomson.* New York: Knopf, 1966.
———. *Virgil Thomson: A Reader: Selected Writings 1924–1984.* Edited by Richard Kostelanetz. New York: Routledge, 2002.
Thurber, James. *The Years with Ross.* Boston: Little, Brown, 1959.
Toklas, Alice B. *The Alice B. Toklas Cookbook.* London: Michael Joseph, 1954.

---. *Staying on Alone: Letters of Alice B. Toklas.* Edited by Edward Burns. New York: Liveright, 1973.
---. *What Is Remembered.* San Francisco: North Point Press, 1985.
Tommasini, Anthony. *Virgil Thomson: Composer on the Aisle.* New York: W. W. Norton, 1997.
Van Vechten, Carl. "How to Read Gertrude Stein." *Trend,* August 1914.
Vetsch, Florian. *Desultory Correspondence: An Interview with Paul Bowles on Gertrude Stein.* Zurich: Memory/Cage Editions, 1997.
Wagner-Martin, Linda. *"Favored Strangers": Gertrude Stein and Her Family.* New Brunswick, NJ: Rutgers University Press, 1995.
Watson, Steven. *Prepare for Saints: Gertrude Stein, Virgil Thomson, and the Mainstreaming of American Modernism.* Berkeley: University of California Press, 2000.
White, Ray Lewis. "Hemingway's Private Explanation of *The Torrents of Spring.*" *Modern Fiction Studies* 13 no. 2 (Summer 1967): 261–63.
---, ed. *Sherwood Anderson/Gertrude Stein: Correspondence and Personal Essays.* Chapel Hill: University of North Carolina Press, 1972.
Williams, William Carlos. *The Autobiography of William Carlos Williams.* New York: Random House, 1951.
Wilson, Edmund. *The Shores of Light: A Literary Chronicle of the Twenties and Thirties.* New York: Farrar, Straus and Young, 1952.

Index

Numbers in ***bold italics*** indicate pages with photographs.

"Accents in Alsace" (Stein) 44
Across the River and Into the Trees (Hemingway) 167, 170–72, 181
Acton, Harold 62, 64, 70
"a.d. in Africa: A Tanganyika Letter" (Hemingway) 113
Adventures of Huckleberry Finn (Twain) 50
Aldrich, Mildred 76
"An American and France" (Stein) 129, 146
American Mercury 74
Anderson, Sherwood ***57***; and *The Autobiography of Alice B. Toklas* 94–95; and *Dark Laughter* 55, 57; death 146, 149; EH breaks with 68–70; and EH in Paris 68–69; EH influenced by 5, 23, 26, 33, 44, 61; EH regrets attack on 4, 179; and Ezra Pound, 23; and *Green Hills of Africa* 126–27; to GS 23, 24, 97; and GS discuss EH 68, 94–95; and GS in New Orleans 119; and GS in Paris 68; GS praises 30, 32, 120; GS to 32, 40, 41; GS's influence on 18–19; and "I Want to Know Why" 68; and "I'm a Fool" 68; and *Many Marriages* 55, 58; and *Sherwood Anderson's Memoirs* 68; and *A Story Teller's Story* 55, 57; and Sylvia Beach 18; and *The Torrents of Spring* 55–60; and *Windy McPherson's Son* 18; and *Winesburg, Ohio* 18
Anthony, Susan B. 161–62
Apparel Arts 92
"Arthur A Grammar" (Stein) 5
Atlantic Monthly: and EH 22, 27, 74, 177; and GS 27, 88, 93, 97, 108, 145
Auden, W. H. 181
"The Autobiography of Alice B. Hemingway" (Hemingway) 109, 169
The Autobiography of Alice B. Toklas (Stein) 5, 91, 102–3, 115, 130; *Atlantic Monthly* serializes 88, 93–94; EH in 91–92; 94–95; 120–21; EH reacts to 92, 95–97, 108–9, 127, 168; and Maxwell Perkins 125; public reactions to 99–100; reviews of 97; Sherwood Anderson reacts to 97

Baker, Carlos 179
Bald, Wambly 9–12
Balzac, Honoré de 166
Basket I (the dog) 79, 137, 140
Basket II (the dog) 140, 146, 179, 180
Beach, Sylvia 18, 24, 40, 154, 158
Before the Flowers of Friendship Faded Friendship Faded (Stein) 105, 123
Bell, Clive 94
Belley, France 71, 87, 155
Berners, Lord Gerald 129, 137
The Best Stories of 1923 37
Betsky, Seymour 181–82
"Big Two-Hearted River" (Hemingway) 45–46, 56
Bilignin, France 78, 87–88, 106–7, 129, 147
Bimini 127–28
Bird, Sally 48
Bird, William 38–39, 40, 42, 47, 50, 67
Bishop, John Peale 80
Boni and Liveright 45, 50–51, 54, 57
Bradley, William Aspenwall 102, 103, 106–7
Braque, Georges 10, 99, 117, 181
Brewsie and Willie (Stein) 161, 166
Brillat-Savarin, Jean 87, 166
Brinnin, John Malcolm 177
Bromfield, Louis 161
Bruccoli, Matthew J.
"Bull in the Afternoon" (Eastman) 90–91, 135
Bumby *see* Hemingway, John Hadley Necanor

Callaghan, Morley 4, 32
Cambridge University 62, 129
Camus, Albert 175

Index

Cather, Willa 55
Cerf, Bennett 115, 161
Cervantes, Miguel de 55
Cézanne, Paul 10, 141, 146, 180; and EH 28, 33, 35, 46; and GS 16, 28, 34
Chaplin, Charlie 119-20
Charters, Jimmy 111-12, 114
China 148-49
Cody, Morrill 110, 111-12, 114
Collier's 127, 142, 149-50, 153, 161
Composition as Explanation (Stein) 62-64
Contact (magazine) 49
Contact Editions 37, 38, 48, 49, 53
Cooper, Gary 89
Co-Operative Commonwealth (Chicago) 23
"The Crack-Up" (Fitzgerald) 132
Crane, Hart 133
Crosby, Harry 133
Cubism 10, 14, 16, 91, 99
Culoz, France 147, 152, 155, 156
Cummings, E.E. 13, 16, 126

Dark Laughter (Anderson) 55, 57
Daumier, Honoré 166
Davidson, Jo 102
Death in the Afternoon (Hemingway) 88-89, 90-91, 107, 123, 127
Defoe, Daniel 95
Delacroix, Eugène 166
DeVoto, Bernard 126
"Discovering Picasso and Matisse" (Stein) 93
Distinguished Air: Grim Fairy Tales (McAlmon) 50
Dodge, Mable *see* Luhan, Mable Dodge
Donaldson, Scott
Doolittle, Hilda 49
Doran, George 50
Dorman-Smith, Chink 44, 47
Dos Passos, John 4, 39-40, 47, 70, 133
Doughty, Charles M. 88

Eastman, Eliena 168
Eastman, Max 4; and *Death in the Afternoon* 90-91, 92; and EH in Havana 167-68, 179; EH on 91, 149; and EH scuffle 135-36, 167; on EH 32-33, 178-79
Einstein, Albert 101
Eisenhower, Gen. Dwight D. 154
Eliot, T.S. 49, 94
Emerson, Ralph Waldo 80
Enfances (Hugnet) 104-5
"Ernest Hemingway and the Post-War Decade" (Stein) 94
Esquire: Arnold Gingrich launches 92; EH in 93, 107, 110-11, 123-24, 131, 132; F. Scott Fitzgerald in 132; and *To Have and Have Not* 133

European Experiences (Luhan)
Everybody's Autobiography (Stein) 130
"Evidence" (Stein) 181, 192n24

A Farewell to Arms (film) 89
A Farewell to Arms (Hemingway) 78-79, 81, 89, 120, 127, 171
"The Farm" (Miró) 108-9
Faulkner, William 169, 174, 181
Faÿ, Bernard 80
Fiedler, Leslie 181-82
Fielding, Henry 55
"Fifty Grand" (Hemingway) 74
Finnegans Wake (Joyce) 43
Firbank, Ronald 29
Fitzgerald, F. Scott 1-2, 4, 70, 76, *83*, 169; and "The Crack-Up" 132; death 146, 149; and EH 51, 56, 59, 67, 81-82, 149; and GS 29, 30, 80-81, 119, 120, 146, 192n23; and Maxwell Perkins 51, 132-33; mentioned in "The Snows of Kilimanjaro" 132; mentioned in *To Have and Have Not* 133; and *A Moveable Feast* 177, 179; Robert McAlmon on 82, 175; and Sherwood Anderson 59; and *Tender Is the Night* 149
Fitzgerald, Zelda 119, 192n21
Flanner, Janet 91-92
For Whom the Bell Tolls (Hemingway) 139, 143-44, 148
Ford, Ford Madox: and EH 4, 41-43, 53-54, 177, 179; and GS 42-43, 53-54, 80, 95; and *transatlantic review* 41-43, 48
Four Saints in Three Acts (Stein and Thomson) 72-74, 120, 115; in Chicago 116-18, 124; in Hartford 103-4, 106, 114; in New York 106, 114
Franklin, Benjamin 147
"The Friend of Spain: A Spanish Letter" (Hemingway) 107
Frost, Robert 120

The Garden of Eden (Hemingway) 167
Gauguin, Paul 10
Gellhorn, Martha *see* Hemingway, Martha Gellhorn
The Geographical History of America, or The Relation of Human Nature to the Human Mind (Stein) 129
Geography and Plays (Stein) 44, 62, 72, 189n1
Gershwin, George 106
"Get a Seeing-Eyed Dog" (Hemingway) 177
Gingrich, Arnold: and EH 92-93, 96-97, 113, 123-24, 127-28, 184; and GS 123-24; and *To Have and Have Not* 134; *see also Esquire*
Goering, Hermann 148
Grant, Ulysses S. 68
Green Hills of Africa (Hemingway) 124-27

Gris, Juan 75, 178, 181
Guthrie, Pat 51

Hammet, Dashiell 119
Harcourt and Brace 88
Harper's Magazine 74
Harris, Frank 65, 90
Hayes, Helen 89
"He and They, Hemingway" (Stein) 40–41, 190n22
Hemingway, Carol (sister of EH) 163
Hemingway, Clarence E. (father of EH) 22, 78, 89
Hemingway, Ernest: **25**, **158**, **171**; and Adrienne Monnier 33, 154; afraid of GS 70, 158; in Africa 110, 112–14, 176–77; ailments of 39–40, 177, 181; and Allen Tate 80–81; ambitious women frighten 89, 110, 151–52; to Anderson 32, 57; Anderson and GS discuss 68, 94–95; Anderson breaks with 68–70; and Anderson in Paris 68–69; Anderson's influence on 5, 23, 26, 33, 44, 61; and Arnold Gingrich 92–93, 96–97, 113, 123–24, 127–28, 184; attack on Anderson regretted by 4, 179; Bill Bird on 38–39; and bullfighting 28, 31, 38–39, 40, 47, 88–89, 121; in Canada 40–41; Cézanne and 28, 33, 35, 46; and Chard Powers Smith 51–52; cowardice attributed to 5, 97–98, 184; critics compare, to Anderson 56; critics compare, to GS 56; in Cuba 4, 139, 142–43, 149–50, 160, 163, 168; *Death in the Afternoon* inscribed to GS 123; Eastman and *Death in the Afternoon* 90–91, 92; and Eastman in Havana 167–68, 179; Eastman scuffles with 135–36, 167; Ezra Pound and 4, 24, 30–31, 41–42, 74, 195n6; and F. Scott Fitzgerald 4, 51, 56, 59, 70, 81–82, 149; and father's suicide 78, 89; and fight with Joseph Knapp 127–28; and fight with Wallace Stevens 128–29; and Ford Madox Ford 4, 41–43, 53–54, 177, 179; fragility of 95, 96, 182; *Geography and Plays* reviewed by 189n1; grace under pressure of 134, 149, 154, 157–58; GS accuses, of cowardice 97–98, 184; on GS and effects of menopause 65, 77, 84, 92, 93, 96, 108, 112, 124, 168; GS called "bitch" by 96, 123, 124, 125; GS critiques works of 26–27, 32; GS described by 25; GS ejects, from apartment 60; GS envies success of 161; GS has "a weakness" for 2, 5, 6, 43–44, 79, 95; GS intimidates 143, 158–59; GS parodied by 56, 64–65, 143–44, 190n32; GS reconciles with 76–77, 138; GS says, no good since 1925 120–21; GS thinks, a homosexual 84, 92, 121, 137; GS thinks, "yellow" 5, 6, 108, 121; GS will not review *In Our Time* 54; GS's final meeting with 158–59; GS's influence on 26–27, 28–30, 33–34, 44, 46, 100, 171 172–73, 178; Hadley marriage to 23, 61, 67, 75, 139; and Harold Loeb 51, 67; and Harry Crosby 133; and Hart Crane 133; and "He and They, Hemingway" 40–41; and Henry James 55, 66, 90; and Hürtgen Forest 157, 160, 171; injuries of 39–40, 95, 176; insecurity of 23, 184; James Joyce on 40, 66, 108–9; and James Thurber 108; and John Dos Passos 4, 39–40, 47, 70, 133; "the lost generation" and 52–53; and *The Making of Americans* 42–44, 45, 53–54, 95, 100; and Martha begin affair 138–40; Martha marriage to 142–43, 148–51, 160, 163–64; Martha on "insane reviling" by 150; and Max Eastman 4, 32–33, 149, 178–79; marriage to Mary 167, 176–77, 181, 182–84; and Mary meet 163; to Maxwell Perkins 51, 65, 76, 88, 91, 108, 113, 125–26, 127, 142–43; and McAlmon in Spain 38–39, 47–48; McAlmon knocked down by 114; McAlmon's writing praised by 50; mentions Fitzgerald in "The Snows of Kilimanjaro" 132; mentions Fitzgerald in *To Have and Have Not* 133; mood swings of 20, 39–40, 69, 135–36; and Morrill Cody 110–12, 114; and mother 21, 22, 89, 152; and Normandy invasion 153; in Pamplona, Spain 40, 47–48, 51, 75–76; Paris liberation and 154–55; parodies Anderson in *The Torrents of Spring* 55–60; Pauline marriage to 75, 77–78, 89, 138–39; phoniness attributed to 79, 91, 98, 127, 129, 175, 192n21; phoniness denied by 176; and Picasso 75; and plane crashes 175–76; to Pound 42, 54, 55; Pound and "self-hardening process" of 39; Pound critiques works of 32, 40, 75; Pound's influence on 172; quarrels with friends 4, 69–70; reacts to *The Autobiography of Alice B. Toklas* 92, 95–97, 108–9, 127, 168; Robert McAlmon on 6, 20, 31, 82–83, 175; says GS lazy 5, 53, 65, 77, 109, 169; sensitivity of 5, 6, 20, 28, 39, 40, 98, 121, 138, 184, 189n20; sexually attracted to GS 43, 190n28; and shadowboxing 20, 23, 31, 41–42; and shadow-bullfighting 114; "smells of the museums" 70; on suicide 67; suicide of 182–84, 185; and Sylvia Beach 24, 154, 158; *Three Lives* reviewed by 189n1; on Toklas 168–69; Toklas defends 181; Toklas dislikes 43, 79, 109, 169, 186, 192n20; Toklas jealous of 43, 79, 168, 169; and *transatlantic review* 41–43; and Virgil Thomson 74; vulnerability of 5, 40, 70, 98, 184; works of: "a. d. in Africa: A Tanganyika Letter" 113;

Index

Across the River and Into the Trees 167, 170–72, 181; "The Autobiography of Alice B. Hemingway" 109, 169; "Big Two-Hearted River" 45–46, 56; *Death in the Afternoon* 88–89, 90–91, 107, 123, 127; *A Farewell to Arms* 78–79, 81, 120, 127, 171; "Fifty Grand" 74; *For Whom the Bell Tolls* 139, 143–44, 148; "The Friend of Spain: A Spanish Letter" 107; *The Garden of Eden* 167; "Get a Seeing-Eyed Dog" 177; *Green Hills of Africa* 124–27; "How I Broke with John Wilkes Booth" 65–66; "How I Broke with My Children" 66; *in our time* (1924) 40, 41, 45; *In Our Time* (1925) 54, 127, 167; "Indian Camp" 43; *Islands in the Stream* 167, 172–73; "A Man of the World" 177; "Marlin Off the Morro: A Cuban Letter" 107; *Men Without Women* 75; "Mr. and Mrs. Elliot" 44, 51–52; *A Moveable Feast* 186; "My Old Man" 33, 37, 40; "My Own Life" 65–67; *The Old Man and the Sea* 167, 172–74, 175; "Out of Season" 40; "A Paris Letter" 110–11; "The Snows of Kilimanjaro" 131–32; "A Soldier's Home" 21, 44; "A Strange Enough Ending" 178; *The Sun Also Rises* 52–53, 67, 69, 75, 126, 127; "The Three Day Blow" 177; *Three Stories & Ten Poems* 37, 40, 45; *To Have and Have Not* 133–34, 170; *The Torrents of Spring* 55–61, 68, 74, 95; "The True Story of My Break with Gertrude Stein" 66; "The Undefeated" 57; "Up in Michigan" 26–27, 40; *Winner Take Nothing* 108
Hemingway, Grace Hall (mother of EH) 21, 22, 89, 152
Hemingway, Gregory (son of EH) 89, 184
Hemingway, Hadley Richardson (first wife of EH) 20, 40, 149, 177, 184; and GS 23–26, 60–61, 177; and marriage to EH 23, 61, 67, 75, 139; McAlmon on 83; pregnancies of 37–38, 41, 48
Hemingway, John Hadley Necanor "Bumby" (son of EH) 41, 44–45, 66, 170, 184
Hemingway, Leicester (brother of EH) 184
Hemingway, Martha Gellhorn (third wife of EH) 138–40, 142–43, 148; on *Across the River and Into the Trees* 170; and EH in China 148–49; and German U-boats in the Caribbean 149; and GS 152; and marriage to EH 148–51, 160, 163–64, 170; and war in Europe 150–51, 156, 196n25
Hemingway, Mary Welsh (fourth wife of EH) 163, 167, *171*, 176–77, 181, 182–84
Hemingway, Patrick (son of EH) 77–78, 149, 151, 184
Hemingway, Pauline Pfeiffer (second wife of EH) 61, 67; and GS 76; and marriage to EH 75, 138–39; McAlmon on 82–83; pregnancies of 77–78, 89
Hemingway, Ursula (sister of EH) 128
Hemingway vs. Fitzgerald: The Rise and Fall of a Literary Friendship (Donaldson) 2
Hergesheimer, Joseph 55
Hicks, Granville 90
Hitler, Adolf 131, 138, 140, 146, 156
The Hogarth Press 64
Hoover, Herbert 80
Hotchner, A.E. 183, 198n8
Houseman, John 105–6
"How I Broke With John Wilkes Booth" (Hemingway) 65–66
"How I Broke With My Children" (Hemingway) 66
Huebsch, B.W. 50
Hugnet, Georges 3, 104–5, 123
Hürtgen Forest 157, 160, 171
Huxley, Aldous 30
Huysmans, Joris Karl 56

"I Want to Know Why" (Anderson) 68
Ida A Novel (Stein) 146, 161
"I'm a Fool" (Anderson) 68
Imbs, Bravig 71
Impressionism 10, 14
in our time (Hemingway 1924) 40, 41, 45
In Our Time (Hemingway 1925) 54, 127, 167
"Indian Camp" (Hemingway) 43
Islands in the Stream (Hemingway) 167, 172–73

James, Henry: and EH 55, 66, 90; and GS 11, 12, 14, 49, 80
James, William 14, 101
Jolas, Eugene 99
Joseph Andrews (Fielding) 55
Journal of the American Medical Association 116
Joyce, James 2, 4, 40, 43, 66, 108–9, 175

Kazin, Alfred 170
Ketchum, Idaho 181, 182, 184
Key West, Florida 77–78, 84, 89, 107, 133–34
Knapp, Joseph 127–28

Larus the Celestial Visitor 74
Lawrence, D.H. 30
Leclerc, Gen. Phillipe 154
Lewis, Sinclair 55
Life 174
Life on the Mississippi (Twain) 98
Lincoln, Abraham 65–66, 68
Liveright, Horace 50–51, 56–57
Loeb, Harold 4, 51–52, 67
Lowell, Amy 9, 49

Index

Loy, Mina 49
Luhan, Mable Dodge 3

MacLeish, Archibald 4
Mailer, Norman 184
The Making of Americans (Stein) 5, 14, 29, 62, 63, 102; and EH 42–44, 45, 53–54, 95, 100; and Ford Madox Ford 42–43, 95; and Robert McAlmon 48–49, 53
"A Man of the World" (Hemingway) 177
Manet, Édouard 33
Many Marriages (Anderson) 55, 58
"Marlin Off the Morro: A Cuban Letter" (Hemingway) 107
Masson, André 117
Matisse, Henri 10, 93, 99
Maupassant, Guy de 54
Mayo Clinic 182, 183
McAlmon, Robert 4, *39*, 49–50, 76, 82–83, 84; and Contact Editions 38; and *Contact* magazine 49; death of 198n3; and *Distinguished Air: Grim Fairy Tales* 50; on EH 6, 20, 31, 82–83, 175; and EH in Spain 38–39, 47–48; EH knocks down 114; EH praises writing of 50; and Ezra Pound 175; and GS 48–49; on Hadley 83; James Joyce on 40; and *The Making of Americans* 48–49, 53; and Maxwell Perkins 82–83; on Pauline 82–83; and *Three Stories & Ten Poems* 37, 40; and *Village: As It Happened Through a Fifteen Year Period* 50; and William Carlos Williams 49
Men Without Women (Hemingway) 75
Menjou, Adolphe 89
Milne, A.A. 90
Miró, Joan 108–9
"Mr. and Mrs. Elliot" (Hemingway) 44, 51–52
Modern Library 56, 115
Monet, Claude 33
Monnier, Adrienne 33, 154
Monroe, Harriet 49
Moore, Marianne 49
The Mother of Us All (Stein) 161–62, 163
A Moveable Feast: Sketches of the Author's Life in Paris in the Twenties (Hemingway) 186
Mrs. Reynolds (Stein) 146
Mussolini, Benito 131, 140
My Life and Hard Times (Thurber) 108
My Life and Loves (Harris) 65
"My Old Man" (Hemingway) 33, 37, 40
"My Own Life" (Hemingway) 65–67

Nation 97
New Republic 53, 116
New Statesman and Nation 97
New York Times 171

New York Times Magazine 160
New Yorker 65, 67, 75, 91, 108, 167, 170
Nobel Prize for Literature 174, 175, 177
Normandy invasion 153
North American News Alliance 135, 138

"Objects Lie On a Table" (Stein) 37
O'Hara, John 171
The Old Man and the Sea (Hemingway) 167, 172–74, 175
"Out of Season" (Hemingway) 40
Oxford University 62, 129

Pamplona, Spain 40, 47, 51, 75–76, 78
Paper Chase (film) 106
Paris France (Stein) 129, 146, 161
Paris Herald 80
"A Paris Letter" (Hemingway) 110–11
Paris Tribune 97
Perkins, Maxwell 96, 172; death of 170; EH and Max Eastman scuffle in office of 135–36; 167; EH to 51, 65, 76, 88, 91, 108, 113, 125–26, 127, 142–43; and F. Scott Fitzgerald 51, 132–33, 149; and *A Farewell to Arms* 78; and *Green Hills of Africa* 125, 127; and GS 125; and *The Torrents of Spring* 57
Pfeiffer, Gus 113
Pfeiffer, Pauline *see* Hemingway, Pauline Pfeiffer
Picasso, Pablo: and *The Autobiography of Alice B. Toklas* 91, 93; and EH 75; and GS 10, 11, 16, 99, 137, 165; and GS on genius 70, 101–2; paintings of 3, 24, 79, 117, 157, 180, 181
Picasso's *Gertrude Stein* 10, *11*, 76, 141, 180
"A Piece of Coffee" (Stein) 16
Pilar (yacht)
PM 149
Poe, Edgar Allan 12, 14
Poetry Magazine 49
"Portrait of Henri Matisse" (Stein) 18, 36
"Portrait of Mable Dodge" (Stein) 3
"Portrait of Picasso" (Stein) 16, 18, 36
Post-Impressionism 10, 35
Pound, Ezra *33*, 49, 76; and EH 4, 24, 30–31, 41–42, 74, 195n6; EH influenced by 172; EH to 42, 54, 55; on EH's "self-hardening process" 39; EH's works critiqued by 32, 40, 75; and Ford Madox Ford 41–42; and GS 21, 74, 94; and Nobel Prize 175; and Robert McAlmon 175; and Sherwood Anderson 23, 74
The Principles of Psychology (James) 101
Proust, Marcel 5
Pulitzer Prize 174
Putnam, Samuel 9–12

Quinn, John 41, 48

Random House 115, 129
"Remembering Gertrude" (Thomson)
Renoir, Pierre Auguste 10
Richardson, Hadley *see* Hemingway, Hadley Richardson
Robinson Crusoe (Defoe) 95
Rogers, W.G.
Roosevelt, Franklin D. 140

Saturday Review of Books 126
Schnabel, Artur 140
Scribner, Charles 174
Scribner's (publisher) 56–57, 125, 174
Scribner's Magazine 124, 125
Sevareid, Eric 140, 156
Shakespeare, William 49, 55
Shakespeare and Company (bookstore) 18, 24, 64, 78, 154
Sherwood Anderson's Memoirs 68
Sitwell, Edith 62, 64, 149, 191n2
Sitwell, Osbert 62, 64, 149
Sitwell, Sacheverell 62, 64, 149
"Sitwell Edith Sitwell" (Stein) 64, 191n2
Smith, Bill 51
Smith, Chard Powers 51–52
Smith, Olive 51
"The Snows of Kilimanjaro" (Hemingway) 131–32
"A Soldier's Home" (Hemingway) 21, 44
Spanish Civil War 130, 131, 133, 135, 138, 139
Star (Kansas City) 22
Star Weekly (Toronto) 22–23, 24, 38, 40, 41
Stein, Allan 165–66, 180
Stein, Gertrude *11, 73*; in America 102, 106–7, 115–20; and American GI's 160, 161, 165; and Anderson in New Orleans 119; Anderson influenced by 18, 119; Anderson praised by 30, 32, 120; Anderson to 23, 24, 94; to Anderson 32, 40, 41; appearance of 10, 116; and Basket 79, 137, 140; and Belley, France 71, 87, 155; and Bennett Cerf 115; and Bilignin, France 78, 87–88, 106–7, 147; and Bumby 169–70; and Carl Van Vechten 99, 115, 117, 138, 106, 167, 180; and Charlie Chaplin 119–20; and continuous present 14, 15, 27, 63; and Culoz, France 147, 152, 155, 156; and Dashiell Hammett 119; and *Death in the Afternoon* 89, 123; and effects of menopause 65, 77, 84, 92, 93, 96, 108, 112, 124, 168; EH afraid of 70, 158; EH compared by critics to 56; EH described by 25; EH describes 25; EH ejected from apartment of 60, 137; EH influenced by 26–27, 28–30, 33–34, 44, 46, 100, 171, 172–73; EH meets 25; EH no longer needs 61; EH parodies 56, 64–65, 143–44, 190n32; EH reconciles with 76–77,

138, 157; EH says, a "bitch" 96, 123, 124, 125; EH sexually attracted to 43, 190n28; EH thinks, lazy 5, 53, 65, 77, 109, 169; EH thought a homosexual by 84, 92, 121, 137; EH thought conventional by 5, 70, 79, 101, 121, 137; EH's last meeting with 157; EH's success envied by 61, 161; EH's works critiqued by 26–27, 32; in England 62–64, 129, 137; and Eric Sevareid 140, 156; and Ezra Pound 2, 94; and F. Scott Fitzgerald 80–82, 119, 120, 146, 192n23; and *A Farewell to Arms* 78, 81; final illness of 164–66; and *For Whom the Bell Tolls* 143; and Ford Madox Ford 42–43, 53–54, 80, 95; genius of 10–13, 18, 19, 37, 43, 70, 101–2, 103, 129; and Georges Braque 10; and Georges Hugnet 3, 104–5, 123; godmother to Bumby 44; and Henri Matisse 10, 93, 99, 137; and Henry James 11, 12, 14, 49, 30; and homosexuality 29, 84, 92, 108, 136–37, 169; and *In Our Time* 54; and James Joyce 2; and Leo Stein 3, 12, 99–100, 162; and lesbianism 29, 77, 168, 136–37; and Lord Gerald Berners 129, 137; "the lost generation" and 52–53, 191n13; and Louis Bromfield 161; and Mabel Dodge 3; and *A Moveable Feast* 178, 186; obituaries on 166–67; and Pablo Picasso 10, 11, 16, 99, 137, 165; and Paul Cézanne 16, 28, 34, 146; and quarrels with young friends 87, 103, 108, 178, 192n2; and repetition 5, 13, 15–16, 26, 29, 35, 36–37, 44, 53, 63, 116, 173; and Robert McAlmon 48–49; Roman emperor resemblance of 9, 76–77, 120, 164–65; and "a rose is a rose is a rose" 15, 62, *122*, 123, 189n13; and Samuel Steward 136–37; says EH "smells of the museums" 70; and Sherwood Anderson discuss EH 68, 94–95; and *Three Stories and Ten Poem* 189n1; Toklas cuts hair of 68, 76–77; and *The Torrents of Spring* 56, 60; and T.S. Eliot 94; and Virgil Thomson 72–74, 105, 116, 161–62, 163; and her "weakness for Hemingway" 2, 5, 6, 43–44, 79, 95; and William Carlos Williams 13, 18; and William James 14, 101; works of: "Accents in Alsace" 44; "An American and France" 129, 146; "Arthur A Grammar" 5; *The Autobiography of Alice B. Toklas* (see separate listing); *Before The Flowers of Friendship Faded Friendship Faded* 105, 123; *Brewsie and Willie* 161, 166; *Composition as Explanation* 62–64; "Discovering Picasso and Matisse" 93; "Ernest Hemingway and the Post-War Decade" 94; *Everybody's Autobiography* 130; "Evidence" 81; *Four Saints in Three Acts* 72–74, 103–4, 114, 115, 116, 117–18, 124, 161; *The Geographical History*

of America, or The Relation of Human Nature to the Human Mind 129; *Geography and Plays* 44, 62, 72; "He and They, Hemingway" 40–41; *Ida A Novel* 146 161; *The Making of Americans* (*see separate listing*); *The Mother of Us All* 161–62, 163; *Mrs. Reynolds* 146; "Objects Lie On a Table" 37; *Paris France* 129, 146, 161; "A Piece of Coffee" 16; "Portrait of Henri Matisse" 18, 36; "Portrait of Mable Dodge" 3; "Portrait of Picasso" 16, 18, 36; "Sitwell Edith Sitwell" 64; "Susie Asado" 72; *Tender Buttons* 13, 16–17, 18, 72, 126; *They Must. Be Wedded. to Their Wife* 129; *Three Lives* 11, 15, 36, 63, 115; "The War and Gertrude Stein" 93; *Wars I Have Seen* 160–61; "A Wedding Bouquet" 137; "What Are Master-Pieces and Why Are There So Few of Them" 129; "When We Were Very Young" 93; "The Winner Loses: A Picture of Occupied France" 145, 161; *The World Is Round* 145–46; writer's block and 103, 129
Stein, Leo 3, 9–10 12, 99–100, 162
Stein, Roubina 185–86
Steinbeck, John 169
Stevens, Wallace 128–29
Steward, Samuel 136–37
Stewart, Donald Ogden 4, 47, 51, 69–70
Stewart, Lawrence 186
A Story Teller's Story (Anderson) 55, 57
"A Strange Enough Ending" (Hemingway) 178
The Sun Also Rises (Hemingway) 52–53, 67, 69, 75, 126, 127
Sun Valley, Idaho 142, 148, 181
"Susie Asado" (Stein) 72
Sutherland, Donald 186

Tate, Allen 80–81
Tender Buttons (Stein) 13, 16–17, 18, 72, 126
Tender Is the Night (Fitzgerald) 149
That Summer in Paris (Callaghan) 32
They Must. Be Wedded. to Their Wife (Stein) 129
This Must Be the Place: Memoirs of Montparnasse (Charters) 111–12
This Quarter 57
Thomas, Dylan 177
Thompson, Charles 177
Thomson, Virgil *73*; and EH 74; and *Four Saints in Three Acts* 72–74, 104–6, 117, 118; and Georges Hugnet 104–5; and GS 71–74, 105, 116, 161–63, 165; and *The Mother of Us All* 161–62, 163; and *Tender Buttons* 72; and Toklas 3, 71–72, 104
"The Three Day Blow" (Hemingway) 177

Three Lives (Stein) 11, 15, 36, 63, 115, 189n1
Three Mountains Press 40, 42, 50
Three Stories & Ten Poems (Hemingway) 37, 40, 45, 189n1
Thurber, James 108
Time 100, 163
To Have and Have Not (Hemingway) 133–34, 170
Toklas, Alice B. *117*; and Allan Stein 180; appearance of 26, 116; and Basket 137, 140, 179, 180; and Carl Van Vechten 166, 169; and Catholic Church 185; death of 186; EH defended by 181; EH disliked by 43, 79, 109, 169, 186, 192n20; and *A Farewell to Arms* 81; and Georges Hugnet 3; godmother to Bumby 44–45, 169–70; GS wills estate to 180; GS's hair cut by 68; and GS's posthumous papers 180–81; jealousy of 43, 69, 79, 168, 169, 190n28, 191n34; and Leo Stein 3; and Mabel Dodge 3; and *A Moveable Feast* 178, 186; quarrels and separations instigated by 2, 3, 67, 71, 77, 104, 168; and Roubina Stein 185–86; and Sherwood Anderson 19; and *What Is Remembered* 81
Tolstoy, Leo 55
The Torrents of Spring (Hemingway) 55–61, 68, 74, 95
Toscanini, Arturo 106
Toulouse-Lautrec, Henri de 10
transatlantic review 41–43, 48
Transition 99
Travels in Arabia Deserta (Doughty) 88
Travels with Myself and Another (Gellhorn) 149
"The True Story of My Break With Gertrude Stein" (Hemingway) 66
Turgenev, Ivan 54
Twain, Mark (Samuel Langhorne Clemens) 50, 98, 119
Twysden, Lady Duff 51
Tzara, Tristan 99

Ulysses (Joyce) 5, 108–9
"The Undefeated" (Hemingway) 57
"Up in Michigan" (Hemingway) 26–27, 40

Vanity Fair 74
Van Vechten, Carl: and *The Autobiography of Alice B. Toklas* 99, and GS 99, 106, 115, 117, 138, 180; on GS's work 167; and Toklas 166, 169
Village: As It Happened Through a Fifteen Year Period (McAlmon) 50
Vogue 61, 92

Wadsworth Atheneum 104
Walsh, Ernest 4, 50

Index

"The War and Gertrude Stein" (Stein) 93
Wars I Have Seen (Stein) 160–61
Washington, George 73, 161
"A Wedding Bouquet" (Stein and Berners) 137
Welles, Orson 106
Welsh, Mary *see* Hemingway, Mary Welsh
Wesleyan University 118
"What Are Master-Pieces and Why Are There So Few of Them" (Stein) 129
What Is Remembered (Toklas) 81
"When We Were Very Young" (Stein) 93
Whitehead, Alfred North 11
Whitman, Walt 12, 14

Wilde, Oscar 166
Williams, William Carlos 13, 18, 49
Wilson, Edmund 53, 127
Windy McPherson's Son (Anderson) 18
Winesburg, Ohio (Anderson) 18
"The Winner Loses: A Picture of Occupied France" (Stein) 145, 161
Winner Take Nothing (Hemingway) 108
Woolf, Leonard 64
Woolf, Virginia 64
The World Is Round (Stein) 145–46

Yeats, William Butler 49